Shaw's Daughters

THEATER: Theory/Text/Performance

Enoch Brater, Series Editor
University of Michigan

Editorial Board

This series focuses on playwrights and other theater practitioners who have made their impact on the twentieth-century stage. Books in the series emphasize the work of a single author, a group of playwrights, or a movement that places dramatists in new aesthetic or historical contexts.

Around the Absurd: Essays on Modern and Postmodern Drama
   edited by Enoch Brater and Ruby Cohn

Tom Stoppard and the Craft of Comedy: Medium and Genre at Play
   by Katherine E. Kelly

Performing Drama/Dramatizing Performance: Alternative Theater and the Dramatic Text
   by Michael Vanden Heuvel

Tragicomedy and Contemporary Culture: Play and Performance from Beckett to Shepard
   by John Orr

The Plot of the Future: Utopia and Dystopia in Modern Drama
   by Dragan Klaić

Shaw's Daughters: Dramatic and Narrative Constructions of Gender
   by J. Ellen Gainor

Shaw's Daughters

Dramatic and Narrative Constructions of Gender

J. Ellen Gainor

Ann Arbor

THE UNIVERSITY OF MICHIGAN PRESS

Copyright © by the University of Michigan 1991
All rights reserved
Published in the United States of America by
The University of Michigan Press
Manufactured in the United States of America

1994   1993   1992   1991   4   3   2   1

A CIP catalogue record for this book is available from the British Library.

Library of Congress Cataloging-in-Publication Data

Gainor, J. Ellen.
   Shaw's daughters : dramatic and narrative constructions of gender
/ J. Ellen Gainor.
      p.   cm. — (Theater — theory/text/performance)
   Includes bibliographical references and index.
   ISBN 0-472-10219-2 (cloth : alk.)
   1. Shaw, Bernard, 1856–1950—Characters—Women. 2. Feminism and
literature—Great Britain. 3. Women and literature—Great Britain.
4. Sex role in literature.   I. Title.   II. Series.
PR5368.W6G3   1991
822'.912—dc20   91-31421
                                                                        CIP

But the Woman as Man made her scarcely suits our modern notions,
With her nicely guarded instincts and her primitive emotions;
We have dropped the weaker vessel and the tame domestic pet,
And our taste finds something wanting in that saint-like statuette.

So our literary gentlemen have touched it up afresh,
And have changed the plaster image to a Demon of the Flesh,
Half Mother Fiend, half Maenad: lest the generations fail,
"Armed and engined," fanged and poisoned, for the hunting of the male.

With the morals of the hen-coop, with the Jungle's code of law,
As described by Rudyard Kipling after (some way after) Shaw.
'Tis no doubt a graceful fancy; but the woman Time has made
Doesn't recognize the likeness so ingeniously portrayed.
                              —Sidney Low, "The Species of the Female"

Preface

"Is there really anything left to be said about Shaw?" This question—which I have heard frequently— has haunted me throughout the research and writing of this book. At this moment, almost forty years after Shaw's death, and more than a century since his writing first appeared in print, it is indeed difficult to say completely original things about an author who has tantalized so many commentators. Yet as literary critics periodically discover, new critical methodologies spur new ways of thinking about texts. Recent advances in gender studies and in the application of the new historicism to drama have prompted me to situate Shaw's work in new structural and contextual positions.

Just seven years after Shaw's death, Howard Mumford Jones announced that Shaw "belongs to that eminent and prolific era, the Victorian Age" (165). J. L. Wisenthal has more recently observed that Shaw is "an essentially Victorian writer . . . and his attitudes towards history are part of the Victorian intellectual world" (vii). But while Jones compares Shaw's work to the major literary and philosophical movements of the nineteenth century, and Wisenthal seeks to place his drama "in a Victorian intellectual context," to investigate Shaw's sense of history (vii), I hope to explore Shaw's position in a society fascinated by issues of sexuality and gender identity, at a moment when intellectual and scientific discoveries profoundly affected views about human relations. I, too, believe Shaw's intellectual development in the late nineteenth century shaped his entire career, and I hope to demonstrate that his stance on these issues remained consistent throughout—in many ways making him still a Victorian in the mid–twentieth century.

Many individuals have given generously of their time and energy to help me in the completion of this book. I particularly wish to thank Stanley Kauffmann, Michael Goldman, and Sandra Gilbert for their invaluable suggestions on drafts of the manuscript; Dennis Kennedy, Michael Cadden, and Cary Mazer for their support and encouragement of this project; Dan Laurence, who provided numerous pieces of important information; James Tyler of the Burgunder Shaw Collection and the interlibrary loan division of Cornell University's Olin Library, as well as Mary Ann Jensen, John Logan, Mary George, Joe Consoli, and the interlibrary loan division of Princeton University's Firestone Library, for their research assistance; Steven Frank, for his help acquiring the cover illustration; my editor, LeAnn Fields, and the staff of the University of Michigan Press, who guided me through the publication process; my parents, Mary and Charles Gainor, for their unflagging belief in my work; and David, whose love makes this and all things possible.

Acknowledgments

The author gratefully acknowledges The Society of Authors on behalf of the Bernard Shaw Estate for permission to quote from his works; The Raymond Mander & Joe Mitchenson Theatre Collection for permission to reproduce the illustration of Madame Vestris and photographs of *Candida*, Miss Sybil Arundale, Miss Lillah McCarthy, Miss Sybil Thorndike, and Miss Gertrude Elliott and Mr. Forbes Robertson; The Billy Rose Theatre Collection of the New York Public Library for the Performing Arts for permission to reproduce the Vandamm photograph of Miss Clare Eames and Mr. Tom Powers; the General Research Division, New York Public Library, Astor, Lenox and Tilden Foundations, for permission to reprint the cover illustration by Alfred Leeze from *Time and Tide*, March 14, 1930; and The British Film Institute for providing the photograph of Miss Wendy Hiller and Miss Wilfrid Lawson, and Janus Films for permission to reproduce same.

The author also acknowledges the *New England Theatre Journal*, which published an earlier version of material contained in part 1, and *Themes in Drama*, which published an earlier version of the material contained in part 3.

Contents

Introduction: Feminist Criticism and the Work of Shaw

                      In the 1960s, the women's movement prompted scholarly interest in the attitudes of male authors toward their female characters and the representation of women in literature. Early feminist critics often sorted through texts by men to see which presented women in a positive light or characterized them in a realistic fashion. Sue-Ellen Case has recently summarized this form of criticism of the drama:

> Works on images of women still predominate in the feminist criticism of classical texts. Numerous revisions of Aeschylus and Shakespeare are currently being published. There are two basic types of image: positive roles, which depict women as independent, intelligent and even heroic; and a surplus of misogynistic roles commonly identified as the Bitch, the Witch, the Vamp and the Virgin/Goddess. (6)

Like early feminist critics of Shakespeare in particular, several female scholars tried to establish Shaw in a positive, progressive light by grouping female character types and proposing that Shaw's depiction of women reveals a sympathetic understanding of the real woman of his time, not the literary fiction perpetuated by the myth of the Victorian womanly ideal. Such critics as Barbara Bellow Watson, Rodelle Weintraub, Sonja Lorichs, and Margot Peters made distinctive contributions to the first full-scale efforts to analyze Shaw's relation to women, both in his personal life and in his plays. Watson's *A Shavian Guide to the Intelligent Woman* (1964), the first book to consider exclusively Shaw's female characters, covers his entire career and made a marked impact on subsequent Shavian scholarship; many works including my own use Watson as a touchstone. Lorichs's *The Unwomanly Woman in Bernard Shaw's Drama and Her Social and Political Background* (1973), Weintraub's essay collection *Fabian Feminist* (1977), and Margot Peters's critical biography, *Bernard Shaw and the Actresses* (1980) all contribute important information on specific historical, cultural, and personal influences underlying Shaw's work. Yet the title of Weintraub's collection also shows the effort to position Shaw as one of "the good guys" in the categorization of male authors that accompanied early feminist criticism (although not all the contributors agree).

Many of these authors are still actively engaged in Shaw scholarship in general, and some still focus on Shaw and women in particular. Yet the style and content of their more recent writings indicate that feminist criticism of Shaw has not progressed significantly over the past twenty years, as this example from the opening of a 1987 essay by Weintraub shows:

Unlike most playwrights since Shakespeare, "St. Bernard," patron saint of the women's movement, as Bernard Shaw jestingly referred to himself, wrote plays for strong, vital women. Often the play's central figure, his woman does not easily fall into the bitch goddess, virgin mother, whore, ingenue, nor castrating neurotic formula. . . . When asked how he came to write roles for *real* women, he responded that he had never imagined women as different from himself. He frequently based his characterizations, however, not merely on himself but on persons he knew and episodes from their lives. Until now critics have, for the most part, overlooked a very significant model for his female character development, one who contributed much of the inspiration for the strong, independent women portrayed in his later plays as well as for his royal wives—his wife. ("Irish Lady" 77)

For the current generation of feminist critics, of which I consider myself a member, there is a desire to move beyond this "representations of women" approach and engage with subtler textual issues of language and structure. Many feminist critics no longer feel it is appropriate to study works by male authors, but some, such as Adrienne Munich, maintain that "a male writer is a fact of *women's* history" and therefore merits our continued attention (250). Munich observes the "male dominance over language" (238) and refers to French feminists' theories of the "male gender" of language. "Discourse—linear, logical and theoretical—is masculine. When women speak, therefore, they cannot help but enter male-dominated discourse; speaking women are silent as women" (239). Surely these remarks have particular resonance for the drama, where playwrights such as Shakespeare and Shaw have had such profound literary and social impact in part through their creation of women's speech. As one early critic succinctly put it, "Bernard Shaw, more than any other one person, has created the manners of our age" (Barnard 272).

Questions of language, structure, and context lie at the heart of my interest in Shaw. In tackling another "round" of feminist criticism of his plays (I trust he would appreciate the pugilistic metaphor), I seek to understand not only what made the above-mentioned Shavian scholars draw their conclusions, but also why my approach may point toward another view. I have isolated three groupings of characters, three subgenres of plays, that seem integrally connected with the broad notion of Shavian feminism set forth by these earlier critics. By examining structural patterns of plot and dialogue surrounding the female characters highlighted by Watson and others, I seek to expose subtler elements of Shavian dramaturgy, which, in turn, may shed new light on the feminism and/or feminist criticism of Shaw.

One of the achievements of early feminist analyses of Shaw is the removal of his work from a critical vacuum. Lorichs, for example, put Shaw into a historical context that her predecessors had often ignored by focusing only on the works themselves or employing only the tools of biographical criticism to fill out their readings. I hope to further this contextualization of Shaw by showing his conformation to certain cultural forces of his era that recent feminist and gender studies have shown to be significant.[1] By positioning Shaw more firmly among his contemporaries, and by showing his adherence to Victorian concepts throughout his career, I question the view of him as remarkably progressive that some scholars propound.

My examination of Shaw falls into three parts: his depiction of the late-Victorian figure of the New Woman, his use of androgynous traits to inform characterizations, and his predilection for the father/daughter relation in the shaping of his dramas. Each of these parts questions in its own way Shaw's constructions of gender. Accepting the theory that gender is socially formulated—that the terms "feminine" and "masculine" do not have fixed meanings, but connotations specific to a time and place—I investigate Shaw's assumptions about gender and the way these assumptions control character, action, and dialogue. Given Shaw's self-proclaimed position as a didactic playwright, I find particularly important the dramas and narratives that focus on processes of education and maturation—plays where learning about the self and society, and the way to present the self in society, underlie the distinctions of plot and character. The texts reveal ongoing tension between the playwright's fascination for certain types of female characters and the cultural context they inhabit. Each group of characters reveals different strains in this nexus, as Shaw grapples not only with biographical influences, but also with his personal philosophy—which was often at odds with the rapidly changing social milieus that inform his dramatic worlds.

After the publication of *The Quintessence of Ibsenism* (1891), Shaw established himself as the champion of the domestic woman rather than the professional woman, who he thought could take care of herself without his help. The following 1895 letter to an "unidentified young American woman" shows Shaw's concern with the plight of the "Womanly Woman," whom he seems to conflate with the domestic woman, and suggests why this character figures so prominently in his plays. The letter is worth quoting at length for both its didactic tone and its indication of female contemporaries' responses to Shaw's work.

> I am much obliged to you for the kind expressions in your letter about the "Quintessence of Ibsenism." It is always inter-

esting to have a woman's opinion of anything written about women, *when she can be persuaded to express it sincerely.* It may perhaps interest you to know that one of my latest works is a play asserting the full strength of the domestic position for women [*Candida*]. You call yourself an undomestic woman; but I suggest to you that *a lack of aptitude for household management is too negative a qualification to take an effective stand upon.* A positive aptitude for something else is better; but such a positive aptitude gets recognized nowadays; for instance, women of ability in the professions, or in politics or business, (or even fashion and pleasure) do not find it impossible, or even unreasonably difficult, *to delegate their domestic duties and pursue their careers. The really hard position for the moment is that of the domestic woman.* . . .

I therefore am strongly of opinion that the undomestic woman, when she has once secured her position by escaping from domestic servitude as men escape from unskilled labor; that is, by mastering a trade or profession, can maintain her own individuality to the full extent of her own strength . . . with less difficulty than the domestic woman.

So it is not for your own hand that you will have to fight so much as for that of the domestic woman from whose ill paid, ill organized, ill recognized, and consequently ill executed industry, you, as an undomestic woman, will presumably emancipate yourself.

I say this because without it my little book might possibly lead you to overlook it. Someday, if I ever have time, I will try to make a second edition of the Quintessence cover more of the "Womanly Woman" case than it does at present. (*Collected Letters* 1:474–75; my emphasis)

I find this letter revealing both for the instructional tone Shaw takes toward his correspondent and for his insistence on her adopting his cause, the domestic woman. His comments clearly show a binary kind of thinking: women are either domestic or professional. This opposition dominates his characterizations of women; only Mrs Clandon in *You Never Can Tell* inhabits both these worlds relatively successfully, and as the author of domestic treatises, her profession conforms to acceptable Victorian conventions for women. As Carol Dyhouse has observed, "Only a few feminists openly broached the question of careers for married women in the late-nineteenth century" (145). She quotes from the writing of Elizabeth Garrett Anderson, one of the few women who "managed to combine motherhood with strong professional commitment" (145): "The woman question will never be solved in any complete way so long as marriage is thought to be incompatible with freedom and an independent career" (Dyhouse 145). Thus Shaw's maintenance of either/or options for women, despite his laudable drive for remuneration for married domestic service, positions him in the mainstream of thinking about women's careers for his era.

Part of Shaw's thinking about such issues may have come from his close association with Beatrice Webb, who with her husband Sidney and Shaw formed the backbone of the Fabian society. According to Elaine Showalter,

> Beatrice Webb saw motherhood as a biological trap that drained women's political and intellectual energies. In 1887 she wrote in her diary that "it will be needful for women with strong natures to remain celibate; so that the special force of womanhood—motherly feeling—may be forced into public work." (*Literature* 189)

But by 1894, Beatrice Webb's views had changed (although she retained the biologically essentialist notion of women's professional and public abilities stemming from their reproductive capacities):

> First and foremost I should wish a woman I loved to be a mother. . . . It pains me to see a fine, intelligent girl, directly she marries, putting aside intellectual things as no longer pertinent to her daily life. And yet the other alternative, so often nowadays chosen by intellectual women, of deliberately forgoing motherhood, seems to me to thwart all the purposes of their nature. . . . If I were again a young woman and had the choice between a brainworking profession or motherhood, I would not hesitate which life to choose. . . .
>
> I do not much believe in the productive power of woman's intellect. . . . Neither do I believe that mere training will give her that fullness of intellectual life which distinguishes the really

able man. The woman's plenitude consists of that wonderful combination of tenderness and judgement which is the genius of motherhood, a plenitude springing from the very sources of her nature, not acquired or attained by outward training. . . .

But what will be the solution of the woman's question? . . . No thoughtful person wishes to see the old regimen of economic and personal dependence preserved from the attacks of the modern woman's movement for complete freedom and emancipation. But most of us distrust the reform as much as we dislike the evil. We do not believe that the cry for equal opportunities . . . will bring woman to her goal. If women are to compete with men, to struggle to become wealth producers and energetic citizens . . . then I believe they will harden and narrow themselves, degrade the standard of life of the men they try to supplant. . . . And above all, to succeed in the struggle, they must forgo motherhood, even if, in training themselves for the prize fight, they do not incapacitate themselves for childbearing. And what shall we gain? . . . Surely we need some human beings who will watch and pray, who will observe and inspire, and above all, who will guard and love all who are weak, unfit or distressed? Is there not a special service of woman, as there is a special service of man? . . . Should not women, too, be enrolled as servants of the community, creators of something more precious than commodities, creators of the nation's children? And as man with his unremitting activity and physical restlessness seems fitted to labour, direct and organize, so woman, with her long periods of passive existence and her constantly recurring physical incapacity, seems ordained to watch over the young and guard over the rising generation and preserve for the community the peaceful and joyful home.

All this points to the endowment of motherhood and raising the "generation and rearing" of children into an art through the elaboration of science. Sometimes I imagine how the men and women of a hundred years hence will wonder at our spending all our energy and thought on the social organization of adult men and women, and omitting altogether the vastly more important question of the breeding of the generation that is to succeed them. (*Diary* 2:52–54)

I quote from Webb at length because this entry coincides so clearly with much of Shaw's thinking about the eugenic need for women to return to their childbearing function and his depiction of the feminine gender "not [as] acquired or attained by outward training" as many feel today, but as inherent in woman. Michael Holroyd shows how this essentialism comes through in Shavian philosophy:

> It was Shaw's apparent assumption that the social purpose of women was the breeding of children. . . . Elsewhere he insisted that "motherhood is not every woman's vocation." . . .
> Certain consequences followed from the fact only women became pregnant. . . . The advantage to women came in the form of greater natural wisdom about sex. They could hardly help themselves. Shaw maintained that the instinct of women acted as a sophisticated compass in steering our course for the future. . . .
> The ingenious exercise of protecting women against their protectors appealed to Shaw. . . . He believed that society changed only when women wanted it to—though the reconnaissance work towards such change was often made by men. Men tended to be idealists; women were more practical: a combination of idealism and practicality made for reality. To substitute this reality for the artificial segregation of society was the aim of Shaw's political work. ("George Bernard Shaw" 18–22)

Thus although some women are not disposed toward motherhood as a career, nevertheless their inherent maternal capacities would benefit society. Furthermore, this change would come about even if women stayed, essentially, behind men, influencing them to bring about the development they desired. This coupling of male and female qualities to bring forth "reality" prompted Shaw to support women's suffrage under the auspices of the "Coupled Vote": one that would be valid only if composed of a man-woman pair. Holroyd comments, "Only on this bicycle-made-for-two, ensuring that all elected bodies were bisexual, could we peddle [sic] our way to a state of real democracy" ("George Bernard Shaw" 29).

The 1895 letter quoted above is also significant for Shaw's sense that women's commentary on writing about them "is always interesting." He suggests that honest appraisal of such work is rare, yet although much of the early criticism of Shaw was indeed written by men, there is a small body of intelligent commentary by Shaw's female contemporaries. Few lengthy studies of Shaw by women appeared during his lifetime, as most commentary took the form of reviews of publications or productions, but three analyses of broader scope were written between 1906 and 1930. None of the more recent scholarship draws on this contemporaneous material, with the exception of Watson's work, which briefly identifies only deprecating views of Shaw. Watson claims these fall into two categories, "the lady's and the sensualist's" and maintains, "The lady's point of view is well represented by Constance Barnicoate's [*sic*] article" from 1906 (*Shavian Guide* 18). There are many other examples, however, both laudatory (Lillah McCarthy's, for example) and critical, which merit attention for their evaluation of Shaw at the time he was writing— moments of shared cultural and political consciousness that feminist critics today must reconstruct. These documents present distinctive views of Shaw that demonstrate the marked effect he had on his female readers and audiences. Their omission from more recent studies raises provocative questions about the differing agendas of female critics during Shaw's lifetime and in the first few decades after his death.

Watson subtly criticizes Barnicoat for her "ladylike" position but misses, I feel, the real thrust of her argument. Barnicoat feels Shaw's problem is indeed that he "never draws a genuine lady," as Watson maintains, but Barnicoat clarifies her statement with a definition of "lady" that Watson omits: "a woman who will pass as a woman all round and as a lady, too" (Barnicoat 517). In other words, Barnicoat is criticizing Shaw's inability to draw fully rounded female characters—ones that really represent the women of his day. It is clear from her writing that Barnicoat stands for a more traditional view of woman's behavior and social function than do some other female commentators, but her relative conservatism makes the following statement all the more striking:

If women as a sex are as Mr. Shaw depicts them, taking the majority of his women characters, especially the earlier ones, then it is good-bye "for always and always and always" to any real improvement in our position as a sex. (519)

This comment suggests that Barnicoat looked to Shaw for an image of what women could be, perhaps because she thought his female characterizations would be progressive, or even feminist. That his plays did not correspond to her sense of what types of characters would be fitting as assets to the woman's movement gives early evidence of women questioning the views of Shaw.

Eight years later, in 1914, Emma Goldman, the noted feminist and anarchist, delivered a series of lectures in New York that formed the basis for *The Social Significance of Modern Drama*. Rebecca West credits Goldman with making Shaw's ideas popular in America (Carlson vi), and Goldman's discussion of these ideas exemplifies what this female contemporary thought of his depictions of women. In a word, Goldman didn't. She views Shaw "as propagandist and as artist" (E. Goldman 96), but has nothing to say about Shaw as feminist or as concerned with women's roles or issues. In her study of nineteen playwrights, she identifies a number with feminist concerns, including Shaw's colleague Stanley Houghton *(Hindle Wakes)*, but Shaw is not among them. She praises Shaw only for his socialist dramas, such as *Mrs Warren's Profession* and *Major Barbara*, and despite the female characters at the center of these plays, Goldman discusses only their political, economic, and moral import (E. Goldman 96–107).

In 1930, the first lengthy study of Shaw's women appeared in *Time and Tide*. The author, Lady Rhondda, was the editor of the journal, a noted feminist, and a friend of Shaw's. Her six-part series featured such provocative subtitles as "Artist-Philosophers and Their Dangers," "Why Ann Is a Cad," "The Conduit-Pipe Theory," and "If St. Joan Had Not Been a Saint . . . ?"[2] Not only does Rhondda establish Shaw in his social and historical context, discussing such issues as problems with women's education in conjunction with an analysis of *Man and Superman*, she also independently confirms a number of points Barnicoat made a quarter-century earlier. She senses the incompleteness of Shaw's female characters within a realistic dramatic setting (331), and alludes to the social impact of Shaw as a writer: "The England of to-day is in part a Shaw-made and a Wells-made democracy" (300). She continues:

It must be clear then, that if Mr. Shaw, Mr. Wells and Mr. Bennett want watching in all directions, they want it especially when they come to dealing with that half of the human race to which they themselves do not belong. It is dangerous enough that these people should have the power to suggest to us what we should be and how we should behave, when they are prescribing also for themselves, but that they should be—as they undoubtedly are—in a position to dictate to us the type of person we should be, when they are prescribing for a group to which they never have belonged, and to which they never can belong, is not merely terrifying, it is really ludicrous.

. . . Our male guides are apt to paint portraits of us quite different from those they make of themselves—and to keep women twisting themselves into the most impossible contortions attempting to conform to these masculine-made images.

. . . And, indeed, there can be little doubt that in actual fact Mr. Shaw is the one who really needs watching. Few intelligent people take Wells seriously on women. . . . Real women might very well start making themselves over in the shape of Shaw's women. The world might very well accept, in fact it has to some extent accepted, Shaw's theories about women and about the relations of men and women. That is why Shaw's generalizations on these matters want watching. (301)

Lady Rhondda attacks the assumptions Shaw makes about women's inherent nature, pointing the way to our current belief in gender learning, as opposed to gender inheritance:

Shaw's view of women is always that they are very personal and preoccupied with personal relations: which is true enough on the whole, but is, as he does not seem to realize, the result not so much of nature as of a most deliberate, painstaking and prolonged course of training and suggestion which starts almost before they are out of the cradle. (436)

She believes Shaw's claim to representing shared human attributes is not fully realized within the plays:

The fact is, of course (and it is a pity that Shaw, who, of all men writers has come nearest to glimpsing this obvious truth, should have just missed actually grasping it) that all human beings, male and female, are born with much the same propensities and desires. (395)

Rhondda's insightful observations are too numerous to quote here at greater length, but her study stands out as a forerunner of current feminist criticism, and with the writing of other Shaw contemporaries such as Elizabeth Robins, Beatrice Ethel Kidd, and Eunice Fuller Barnard (whose analyses will be examined in conjunction with discussions of *Great Catherine, Man and Superman,* and *You Never Can Tell,* respectively), these female critics demonstrate significant early twentieth-century feminist concern with Shaw's work.

Rhondda's and others' critiques should rightly be considered the first wave of feminist criticism of Shaw, the next wave of which began in 1959 with Toni Block's short piece, also entitled "Shaw's Women." Block's study reflects the biographical trend in Shavian research that has subsequently dominated the field and moves away from the close engagement with the text and its subtextual impact that Rhondda ably demonstrates. In the following discussion, I hope to confirm the historical legitimacy of this long-ignored early twentieth-century feminist criticism. By expanding the scope of the dialogue these women began, I am seeking to establish more firmly the context from which their views arose and to explore the significant connections between current feminist discourse and the cultural ambience that helped establish it a century ago.

PART ONE

G. B. S.'s NEW WOMEN

1

The New Woman and the Victorian Novel

Bernard Shaw's *Plays Unpleasant* and *Plays Pleasant* were written between 1892 and 1896, at the height of Victorian consciousness of the New Woman. This female icon—in part the creation of journalists, novelists, playwrights, and artists, in part a legitimate representation of the behavior and beliefs of progressive women at the time—figured prominently in heated debates on the "Woman Question" found in such periodicals as the *Saturday Review* and the *Nineteenth Century*[1] and appeared as a central character in the prolific outpouring of "New Woman" novels (both sympathetic and hostile) at the end of the century.[2]

It is difficult to pinpoint the precise characteristics of this individual. According to Patricia Stubbs,

> The vague but popular phrase "the new woman" was coined in the 'nineties in an effort to describe women who had either won or were fighting for, a degree of equality and personal freedom. (54)

Nevertheless it is possible to isolate traits associated with the figure, as they recur in both fictional and journalistic portraits. The New Woman was noted for independence of spirit and action; she refused to conform to the conventional, male-determined code of feminine behavior or to accept an inferior status legally, intellectually, or socially. This personal adventurousness manifested itself externally in such "unwomanly" activities as cigarette smoking and in the rejection of traditional, purely decorative and cumbersome feminine attire in favor of a more practical wardrobe that suited an active lifestyle. The New Woman was notorious for her outspokenness, particularly as it pertained to her sexuality and the freedom she sought in personal relationships. She was also an advocate of women's education and the creation of professional opportunities in fields traditionally barred to women, and she often eschewed maternal and domestic roles—at least as the sole recourse for a woman whose only other legal option was spinsterhood and potential destitution. Lastly, as Gail Cunningham observes in her study of the figure, "A woman was only genuinely New if her conflict with social convention was on *a matter of principle*" (10). Primarily middle-class, New Women took stances "on matters of personal choice" (Cunningham 10), whether they pertained to lifestyles or professional options.

Ellen Jordan traces the use of the term "the New Woman," with its all-important capital letters, to the May 1894 issue of the *North American Review* (Jordan 19–20).[3] Although Jordan acknowledges that the concept originated more than a decade earlier (19), the phrase "the New Woman" is most closely associated with the 1890s, particularly with the "decadence" of the fin de siècle (Dowling 435) as well as with the anticipation of the forthcoming century—the vogue, as Shaw put it in 1898, for designating "everything advanced 'the New' at that time" (*Plays Unpleasant* 11).

Historians of this figure differ on the end of her era, in part because the locution quickly became part of standard usage. During times of transition for gender roles throughout the last century, the expression "the New Woman" has been evoked to describe the latest female behavior and attitudes. Most recently in the United States, for example, the title *New Woman* graces a popular magazine of the 1980s, geared at female readers with full-time careers and families—the image of the emerging generation of women who want "to have it all."[4] Yet although the expression has remained current, its context has changed over time; the clearest example of this may be the attitude toward motherhood and careers. While the 1890s New Woman fought for professional status and rejected maternity, the 1980s saw a transition to women's attempts to balance successful careers with childrearing. Thus when looking at the literature of another era, we must remember both the connotations of the term for the author and the perceptions the audience would bring to the works and keep in mind that a designation of "New Woman" would have had a specific resonance for the late Victorian and Edwardian periods that no longer prevailed after their close.

When thinking about the New Woman and Shaw, it is important to note that Shaw's own use of the term ended in 1903, with the publication of *Man and Superman*. Shaw shifts his focus from the New Woman to the "New Man" early in act 2 of that play, when he has John Tanner describe the character Henry Straker:

> Here have we literary and cultured persons been for years set-
> ting up a cry of the New Woman whenever some unusually old
> fashioned female came along, and never noticing the advent of
> the New Man. Straker's the New Man. (89)

In making this change, Shaw was reflecting the shifts already under-way in the depiction of progressive female characters. Gail Cunning-ham maintains that "the New Woman heroine did not outlast the Victorian age" (152), and the novels of the Edwardian era indeed demonstrate a shift back to greater conventionality and to revised notions of gender behavior. With the end of Edward VII's reign, the advent of the Great War, the subsequent granting of the vote to women, and the rise of the "roaring twenties," women's lives changed markedly, and other phrases, such as "the flapper," more aptly described women who actively challenged certain social con-ventions. Different criteria and different terminology must therefore be employed when analyzing characters from these later periods.

Within Shaw criticism, however, the designation "New Woman" has been used to categorize a range of characters Shaw created from the 1890s through the late 1930s. Arthur H. Nethercot, for example, discusses figures from *The Philanderer* (1898) through *Geneva* (1939) all under that heading (104–15), while Barbara Bellow Watson traces a line of comic New Women from *Man and Superman* to *The Millionairess* (1936) ("The New Woman" 114–28). Archibald Henderson errs in the other direction, deeming Mrs Clandon in *You Never Can Tell* one (*George Bernard Shaw* xiv), whereas Jordan would more properly consider her one of the "parents and midwives" (19) to the true New Woman. While Shaw clearly responded to many of the traits associated with the New Woman and incorporated them into later characterizations, it is important to remember the historical context in which this figure initially developed and to distinguish between that original version and her variants, who exist in a Shavian world quite different from that of the 1890s. The next two chapters will explore Shaw's New Women of that earliest historical moment, when his use of the term and his audience's understanding of it coincided within a complex but shared frame of reference.

The Victorian era has long been viewed as a literary period dominated by the novel, and since the drama was synonymous with popular entertainment at that time, the theater did not receive serious critical study. According to Shaw's biographer Michael Holroyd, "Lucrative literature meant the novel—drama, economics, philosophy were unsaleable" (*Search For Love* 81). R. F. Dietrich, in an analysis of Shaw's novels, remarks, "Victorian drama being the corpse it was, Shaw was typical of the young writer of that day in his almost automatic choice of the novel as his form" (4). Perhaps with a bit more charity toward the genre, Shaw himself said of his early writing, "The novel was not my proper medium. I wrote novels because everybody did so then; and the theatre, my rightful kingdom, was outside literature" (*Collected Letters* 4:675).

Several works on the New Woman in fiction have appeared, but none focuses on the figure in her dramatic context, despite the tremendous impact of Ibsen and his English imitators on her depiction in both the theater and the novel (Cunningham 46). It would also be difficult simultaneously to discuss the character as she appears in both genres, since the influence of the French *pièce bien faite* (or well-made-play) shaped the drama of the 1890s as profoundly as did Ibsen, resulting in a theatrical representation that responded to extant dramatic characters, situations, and structures significantly different from those of the novel. One of the few commentators on the New Woman in drama describes her as having been influenced more by Arthur Wing Pinero, whose play *The Second Mrs. Tanqueray* (1893) owes much to the characters and action of the well-made-play:

> Following the success of *The Second Mrs. Tanqueray* a number of
> *risqué* heroines appeared on the stage in what came to be known

as the "New Woman" plays of the 1890s. All these women live for love and their greatest tragedy is growing old and unattractive. (Holledge 35)

Although I would disagree with the purely sexual and physical orientation of this definition of dramatic New Women,[5] the issue of sexuality in the theater did receive considerable attention because of the highly publicized control of the stage censor, who played no role in the publication of New Woman novels.

The novel, with its essentially unlimited potential to develop plot and character, could, unlike the drama—constrained by performance time and stage space—afford to plumb the psychological and emotional depths of a heroine, as well as depict her in numerous settings and situations. Thus it is not surprising that this genre could explore many more facets of the New Woman, including her life both within and outside her personal relationships. Yet feminist analysts of representative examples have discovered a surprising uniformity among the books. Many of the male-authored New Woman tales conform to structural patterns in the depiction of their heroines: they emphasize these characters' emotional lives over their professional lives, or lives outside the home, and/or they follow a consistent plot line in which the New Woman, independent at the opening of the work, is reinscribed in a conventional emotional or domestic role by its conclusion. Feminist scholars read these structures as indications of the anxiety surrounding the independence and strength of these female figures, and their potential threat to traditionally patriarchal society.[6]

Shaw, who was notoriously unsuccessful at finding publishers for his novels, and whose fiction is still little known, is not discussed by the critics of New Woman novelists such as George Meredith, Thomas Hardy, and George Gissing. But his early writing just preceded the vogue for New Woman fiction,[7] and he conforms to the structures of the genre favored by his male contemporaries and later identified by feminist critics.

Each of Shaw's five novels,[8] written between 1879 and 1883, features at least one independent, progressive female character: Harriet Russell *(Immaturity)* opens her own dressmaking shop to financial success; Susanna Connolly *(The Irrational Knot)*, an actress, chooses to live with the man she loves and bears him a child out of wedlock; Letitia Cairns *(Love Among the Artists)* holds a college degree and supports the suffrage movement; Lydia Carew *(Cashel Byron's Profession)*, the product of her father's advanced belief in education for women, competently manages the estate after his death; and Agatha Wylie *(An Unsocial Socialist)* rejects her girls' boarding school precepts in favor of outspokenness and "unwomanly" behavior.

But Shaw compromises each of these women. Harriet sells her shop to marry and have children; Susanna dies alone and destitute in New York City (surely the punishment for her unconventional lifestyle); Letitia, a spinster, longs hopelessly for love affairs and gossip (her fate for having chosen celibacy earlier); Lydia abandons plans as a writer to marry Cashel and raise a family, while he enjoys no fewer than four additional professions in which he is highly successful; and Agatha subjects herself to the misogyny and selfishness of Sidney Trefusis for "love." Michael Holroyd observes an almost sadistic pleasure in Shaw, "a tingling sense of excitement as the novelist creates his strong-minded women, . . . takes them on and sees them defeated" *(Search for Love* 82). Independent women either ultimately conform to the Victorian patriarchal view of home as the proper feminine sphere, or suffer greatly for straying from its prescribed code of feminine behavior. Shaw's choice of these conclusions allies him with the New Woman novelists, all of whom made similar decisions regarding the fates of their heroines.[9]

The novels also reveal a tension between Shaw's recognition of the conventions of prose realism, important for acceptance and publication at that time, and his own desires to inform his writing with unconventional characters and subjects. Shaw's early contact with socialism, culminating in his joining of the Fabian Society in 1884, certainly affected the composition of at least his last finished novel, *An Unsocial Socialist* (1883). Michael Holroyd has recently observed Shaw's inversion of Victorian novelistic convention *(Search for Love* 82), but the depiction of the women who populate these novels does not keep up with the distinctive unconventionality of the men. The female characters are much more of a piece with those of the New Woman novelists, although the males are notable for their breaks with both Victorian and contemporary literary tradition.

One might expect that Shaw's newly formed political beliefs—an adherence to the Fabian doctrine of working within the established sociopolitical structure to bring about gradual change and the amelioration of social ills—would continue to find voice in his subsequent writing. Shaw's frequent reference to his didactic purpose in play-writing[10] leads one to expect a dramatic environment that would illustrate both the social evils he observed and some movement toward their rectification. His first "unpleasant" plays exemplify the relative emphasis he places on the exposure of social hypocrisy and capitalist exploitation, but not on their remedy. Unlike propagandistic dramaturgy, Shaw's early works do not opt for artificial resolutions or clear lessons in politically correct behavior. What does emerge is Shaw's concern with social problems—slum landlordism, prostitution, and the artificiality of any current cultural craze—rather than the issue of the individual trying to assert him- or herself within society, or within the family as a microcosm of that larger social environment. Ibsen, Shaw's forebear in the problem play genre, gave greater weight to the solitary figure in conflict with reigning ideology or convention: Dr. Thomas Stockmann *(An Enemy of the People)* and Nora Helmer *(A Doll House)* immediately come to mind. Shaw spotlights the fallacies in the social structure itself; his characters all appear in the service of a larger social purpose, even though they are drawn distinctively and with sensitivity to the needs and interests of actors.[11]

Thus it is not surprising that in the transition from novelist to playwright, Shaw does not alter his figuration of the character that had come to be designated the New Woman; in the drama as well as in novels, she takes second billing to her social milieu. Yet at a historical moment when many women were choosing to emphasize their professional identities or personal independence, Shaw prefers to focus on their affectional lives. He not only carries the patterns of his own and the New Woman novels with him to his plays, he also reveals the priority he places on the institution of marriage, with its attendant procreative potential (which benefits society), over the development of the individual. Although not published until 1911, Shaw's preface to his play *Getting Married* is of interest here, as it illustrates his firm belief in the institution—despite the problems he sees with it—as well as his subjective disparagement of any alternative lifestyle.

We may take it then that when a joint domestic establishment, involving questions of children or property, is contemplated, marriage is in effect compulsory upon all *normal* people; and until the law is altered there is nothing *for us* but to make the best of it as it stands. Even when no such establishment is desired, clandestine *irregularities* are negligible as an alternative to marriage. How common they are nobody knows. . . . *But they are neither dignified nor safe and comfortable, which at once rules them out for normal decent people.* Marriage remains practically inevitable; and the sooner we acknowledge this, *the sooner we shall set to work* to make it *decent and reasonable.* (14; my emphasis)

Shaw's movement from novels to plays is of a piece with these sociopolitical concerns, as the comedic dramatic genre he selected (whether darkly "unpleasant" or more lightheartedly "pleasant") by convention incorporates a conclusion with affectional focus—most often marriage. What emerges from an examination of these dramas of transition—the first products of Shaw's evolution from novelist to playwright—is the continuity of theme, action, and character from one genre to the other. Shaw's switch of medium clearly allowed him to exhibit his strengths as a writer: to create distinctive characters quickly through speech and action, and to weave together witty dialogue with the social purpose of his didactic dramaturgy. Yet the compression of the dramatic form—its relative brevity and necessarily rapid development of plot and character—also highlights Shaw's appropriation of novelistic conventions for his plays. In the case of Shaw's treatment of the New Woman, the dramas emphasize in a short space of time the structures that span hundreds of pages in the novels. Thus the troubling figure of the New Woman can be both quickly identified and then defused through the exigencies of generic form, furthering the sense of the suitability of the medium to the playwright's needs. In this condensed medium he could broadcast the conclusion, or resolution, he deemed most suitable: the securing of women within a social structure that insured the continuation of society, which in turn made it available for Fabian influence over the course of time.

Like Shaw's novels, each of the early *Plays Unpleasant* and *Plays Pleasant* features at least one female character easily identifiable for her "modern" or "advanced" views and behavior. In three of the seven plays, this figure appears initially associated more with her professional than with her personal life,[12] but the plot developments invariably involve her more with emotional concerns, and her work becomes increasingly complicated by the issues of her private life. This movement not only conforms to the pressures of the dramatic structure, but also coincides with the pattern of New Women novels, as "a woman who worked was very rarely the centre of interest in a novel. And even where the heroine did work the emphasis was still on her emotional life" (Stubbs 124). Shaw places a working New Woman, Vivie Warren, at the center of only one of his early plays, while in *Candida,* he uses a working woman as a secondary character, a pitifully comic figure marginalized like her real-life counterparts by her economic and spinster status.

The Philanderer and *You Never Can Tell* merit attention for Shaw's employment of New Women in their emotional context. Here, as in the novels, the movement is toward matrimony, and those characters who opt for different life choices tend to recede from the final center of attention. It is also noteworthy that Shaw is drawn toward certain qualities of New Women, especially their sexual aggression and/or expression of emotional interest or desire, and he appropriates these qualities for his characterization of much more conventional women, creating a crossbreed better suited to his own philosophy of the Life Force,[13] but which undermines the integrity of the New Woman by masking a traditional figure with the former's more obvious attributes.

Lastly, these first plays deserve study for their early demonstration of the problem of gender identity to be found throughout Shaw. Having recently completed *The Quintessence of Ibsenism* (1891), with its central essay on the "womanly woman" and her "unwomanly" counterpart, Shaw was clearly sensitive to Victorian social conventions of female appearance and demeanor, as well as current deviations from that norm. Shaw gives clear examples in these first plays of characters' indeterminate sexuality—a demonstration of his engagement with the discourses of gender identity emerging in the late nineteenth century. (The related issue of androgyny will be discussed in part 2.) The New Woman figure, historically identified with gender ambiguity, thus serves as the ideal character for Shaw to begin his own exploration of masculinity and femininity in his society.

2

New Women and Odd Women at Work

Proserpine Garnett, the Reverend James Morell's female secretary in *Candida* (1898), is not a central character in the play, but rather a secondary one who adds to the realistic ambience and serves as a structural and comic foil to Candida, the maternal "perfect" woman idealized by what Shaw called the "Candidamaniacs" (*Collected Letters* 2:415). In a letter to Richard Mansfield, a prominent actor planning a production of the play, Shaw calls Proserpine

> a young woman of the standing of a female clerk, rather a little spitfire, a bit common, but with some comic force and a touch of feeling when needed. She must not be slowtongued: the part requires smart, pert utterance. (*Collected Letters* 1:494)

From this rather straightforward description, one would think Proserpine an interesting but relatively inconsequential character. On the contrary, she is complex and integral to the action, as her exchanges with the curate Lexy Mill foreshadow the final conflict and discussion in the play, and her spat with Candida's father Burgess motivates the revelation of many of the other characters' feelings.

The mythological significance of her name sheds light on her position in the drama. The story of Proserpine (Persephone) features her abduction and rape by Pluto. Her mother, Ceres, upon discovering the loss of her daughter, appealed to Proserpine's father, Jupiter, for the return of her child. Ultimately Jupiter decreed that Proserpine would spend half the year with Pluto as queen of the underworld, half with her mother on earth.

Numerous ironic parallels to the tale emerge in *Candida*. Shaw's Prossy is hardly the beauty Pluto found irresistible; she knows Lexy finds her "dowdy and second rate" (12). And for the mythic flowery fields and descent to the underworld, Shaw substitutes the more lucrative city environs and movement to the quieter, poorer suburbs. Pluto is transformed into the charismatic Christian Socialist Morell, whom Proserpine is drawn to, rather than abducted by. Morell's name, of course, is evocative of the morel mushroom—the fungus black nightshade—associated with underground growth and darkness. His wife's name similarly corresponds to a yeast-like fungus commonly found in nature.[1] Most important, Shaw's Proserpine is no queen, but a willing servant with no mention of a mother to bargain with the gods for her release.

Thus Shaw twists rape and the forced imprisonment of a woman into voluntary self-victimization—not overtly sexual, but certainly with sexual desire lying just beneath the surface of Prossy's speech. And Prossy represents just one of many enthralled by Morell, who remains oblivious to his magnetism until enlightened by Candida, the woman who fills the place to which so many others hopelessly aspire. Thus Morell's "guilt" of "rape" is transformed into Prossy's flattering attraction to him (a variant of the defense that women desire or invite their attackers), and the sexual component of their (mythic) relationship is safely sublimated because of Morell's marriage to Candida and its monogamy. Shaw's matrix of inverted allusions provocatively challenges the issues of responsibility and victimization in the myth and its parallel.[2] Prossy's last name, Garnett, resonates within this context as well, as it refers to the relatively inexpensive red gemstone that becomes a synecdoche for all her second-rate qualities, which are no match for the shining, brilliant (from the Latin "Candidus") Candida.

This mythic, allusive backdrop precludes consideration of Proserpine solely in her professional capacity as Morell's assistant, although it is in this light that we first see her. An older, unmarried woman, she supports herself by doing clerical work and other odd jobs for the household in order to be near the object of her (unacknowledged) affection, the Reverend Morell. By giving Morell a female secretary, Shaw invokes the recent historical movement of women into such professions, which produced one kind of New Woman who could be financially and ideologically independent, who could join the middle class and make choices about where and how to live and under what conditions. By drawing on these advances in women's opportunities for self-support, Shaw suggests to his audience the milieu of the New Woman, although he does not explicitly designate Proserpine as such. Quick and efficient, she "is clattering away busily at her machine" (8) as the play opens. She shares with Vivie Warren a commitment to and pride in work, which she demonstrates by exclaiming to Lexy: "It will do you good to earn your supper before you eat it, for once in a way, as I do" (10).[3]

Yet Prossy's age and single status also identify her as a "female supernumerary," part of the quarter of the British population that was female, over 30, unmarried, and unlikely to be married (Rover 18; Neff 11–12). Drawing on the title of George Gissing's novel, *The Odd Women* (1893), which depicts a secretarial school for women, Elaine Showalter recently categorized an entire group of women with feminist sensibilities at the fin de siècle as "Odd Women," separating them from New Women by their single status (*Sexual Anarchy* 18–37). Other critics see these figures as a subset of the larger and more broadly defined group, the New Woman. Constance Rover notes that, in publications such as *Punch*, this spinsterish New Woman was often the brunt of rather vitriolic humor (45), a pattern Shaw replicates in timely fashion in *Candida*, using Prossy repeatedly as an object of both other characters' and the audience's mirth. Prossy's dialogues with Lexy, Burgess, and Marchbanks, coupled with her hopeless emotional attachment to Morell, reinforce the personal strain connected with the marriage statistics. This strain is introduced early in the play, in the scene with Lexy immediately preceding Burgess's entrance.

The scene is brief but important, for it raises "the Woman Question," which will be pertinent to the final discussion scene with its emphasis on Candida's right to make choices about her life. This reference to the topical debate on women exemplifies Shaw's efforts to make the play contemporary and demonstrates both how inter-

Fig. 1. In this 1909 production still from *Candida*, Proserpine interacts
with her typewriter, while the other characters enjoy human exchange.
Note the similarity in costumes for Prossy and Candida: the singular
distinguishing feature is a flowing scarf for Candida, which connects
her to Marchbanks through his equally generous tie, whereas Prossy
sports a short bow, closer to a man's bow tie.

woven feminist and personal issues are in the drama and how the personal concerns of women overpower the social issues of women in society, which ultimately serve only as backdrops. After Morell's first exit, Proserpine expresses impatience with his adoration of his wife, an adoration clearly shared by Lexy:

Lexy (saddened by her depravity) I had no idea you had any feeling against Mrs Morell.

Proserpine (indignantly) I have no feeling against her. She's very nice, very good-hearted: I'm very fond of her, and can appreciate her real qualities far better than any man can. (He shakes his head sadly. She rises and comes at him with intense pepperiness). You dont believe me? You think I'm jealous? Oh, what a knowledge of the human heart you have, Mr Lexy Mill! How well you know the weaknesses of Woman, dont you? It must be so nice to be a man and have a fine penetrating intellect instead of mere emotions like us, and to know that the reason we dont share your amorous delusions is that we're all jealous of one another! (She abandons him with a toss of her shoulders, and crosses to the fire to warm her hands).

Lexy. Ah, if you women only had the same clue to Man's strength that you have to his weakness, Miss Prossy, there would be no Woman Question.

Proserpine (over her shoulder, as she stoops, holding her hands to the blaze) Where did you hear Morell say that? You didnt invent it yourself: youre not clever enough.

Lexy. Thats quite true. I am not ashamed of owing him that, as I owe him so many other spiritual truths. He said it at the annual conference of the Women's Liberal Federation. Allow me to add that though they didnt appreciate it, I, a mere man, did. (He turns to the bookcase again, hoping that this may leave her crushed).

Proserpine (putting her hair straight at a panel of mirror in the mantelpiece) Well, when you talk to me, give me your own ideas, such as they are, and not his. You never cut a poorer figure than when you are trying to imitate him. (12–13)

Prossy seems to have gotten the best of the argument here, despite her potential discomfiture at Morell's statement, which she opts to ignore. But her triumph over Lexy is rapidly undermined by Burgess's infuriating observation that she appears older than Morell's former secretary. The focus thus shifts away from larger, social issues back to the purely personal, and no further mention is made of the conflict over women's roles in society.

As noted earlier, Proserpine's partial function as a foil for Candida makes this scene with Lexy resonate with others in the drama. The famous discussion scene in act 3 where Candida talks with Morell and Marchbanks about her relations with each, echoes this act 1 conflict, but with a significant difference. The fact that the act 3 discussion scene has ramifications for Candida only within the domestic sphere—that the reality of her position will only be recognized in the sanctity of her home, allowing Morell to retain his appearance of strength and control to the outside world—reinforces the sense of contradiction inherent to Shaw's treatment of women's issues here. Neither kind of woman, "womanly" or "New," has an impact outside the Morell household, despite the specter of the Woman Question in their midst. The struggle over women's independence never extends beyond the confines of the home, and thus Shaw safeguards the larger, extant patriarchal order.

The argument between Prossy and Lexy reveals a great deal about these two characters, and leaves some questions behind. We realize, of course, that Prossy *is* jealous, despite her denial. As a contrast figure to Candida, Proserpine looks poor; she hasn't the beauty, the charm, the home, and particularly the husband that the former has. Acutely aware of the conventional opposition of the sexes: female/emotion, male/intellect, Proserpine neatly exposes Lexy's emotional hypocrisy about Candida. But Shaw's own opposition of the artist-man, mother-woman[4] is not too far removed from Lexy's belief, and one wonders where to draw the line with Shaw between conventional gender definition and his sense of fitting roles for each sex. Proserpine also claims to see Candida's "real qualities far better than any man can," but she does not name them. Instead, we continue to see Candida through the male perspectives of Morell and Marchbanks, which reinforce her standing as a womanly ideal, "THE Mother" as Shaw told Ellen Terry (*Collected Letters* 1:641).

Lexy's quotation of Morell on the Woman Question not only demonstrates the ambiguity of the minister's rhetoric, it also gives a brief flash of feminist insight into the workings of Morell's point of view.

The exact relation between male strength and the Woman Question is not clear, but the reaction of the Women's Liberal Federation is. "They didnt appreciate" the "spiritual truth" of Morell's speech, probably because the implication was that if women understood male strength, they would recognize its superiority, rendering their struggle needless. (An alternate reading, that men are not as strong as society presents them, would no doubt be equally dismissed by the women's group as inaccurate.) Candida exposes Morell's "strength" as weakness in act 3, but the struggle at that point is individual, dealing exclusively with the relations of Candida, Marchbanks, and Morell. The universal quality of the conflict has given way to personal concerns.

The relation of Proserpine's personal to her professional life continues in act 2. In her scene with Marchbanks (which neatly balances the earlier scene with Lexy), Shaw reveals more of her feelings, exposing the emotional motivation behind her attachment to the Reverend. Through Marchbanks, Shaw establishes the prerequisite of emotion for effective work, essentially proving that for Prossy the professional is dependent on the personal.

> Marchbanks. . . . I thought clever people—people who can do business and write letters and that sort of thing—always had to have love affairs to keep them from going mad. (34)

Shortly thereafter, Candida reveals the nature of an illness from which Proserpine suffers—a disease that causes emotional outbursts as well as self-abasement: "Prossy's complaint" (47). The malady, essentially lovesickness for Morell, has been the fate of "all the other secretaries" (47) as well. But according to Shaw, "Candida sacked" the former assistant, the one Burgess had noticed "was younger," whereas Prossy

> is a very highly selected young person indeed, devoted to Morell to the extent of helping in the kitchen, but to him the merest pet rabbit, unable to get the smallest hold on him (*Collected Letters* 2:414–15),

and therefore no threat to Candida.

Prossy's complaint seems an ironic version of the illnesses suffered by New Women in Victorian fiction, who were prone to "nervous disorder, disease, . . . [m]ental breakdown, [and] madness," often as a result of their affectional or life choices (or absence thereof) (Cunningham 49). Despite her professional independence, Prossy suffers from conventional lovesickness, and becomes even more sadly comic to the audience as a result. One could certainly argue that, in addition to his primary motive of contriving a humorous character to contrast with other figures and aid plot development, Shaw also exposes through Prossy the emptiness of some of these new lives for women, with their barely adequate remuneration and minimal personal fulfillment. In our last view of her, she is inebriated and "unable to trust [herself] with anybody" (67), even Lexy, whom she despises. Her fear of loss of sexual control, kept closely in check by a wall of social propriety, reminds the audience of her status as a superfluous woman. Shaw does not tell his readers and actors here, as he does at the conclusion of *The Philanderer*, to view this self-sacrificing woman with sadness. Rather, Proserpine emerges as a comically pathetic individual, more important to the play as a source of humor than as a sympathetic model of a woman of whom there were so many real versions at the time.

Shaw used another type of real woman as the model for Vivie in *Mrs Warren's Profession* (1898): the young, independent, university-educated sort, like Philippa Fawcett, who "placed above the Senior Wrangler at Cambridge in the examination results of 1890" (Rover 13).[5] Vivie Warren is a prototypical "modern young woman" (*Collected Letters* 1:472) who chooses to remain unmarried at the play's conclusion, yet suffers no ill effects for her decision, as did many progressive Victorian fictional heroines, including Shaw's own.[6] Unlike Grace Tranfield, who also rejects marriage at the end of *The Philanderer*,[7] Vivie remains the central focus of the last act, and her decision to apply herself solely to her career seems to be presented in a positive and energetic light by Shaw. She has stated her professional intentions early in act 1, and she follows through with them, appearing completely at ease in her office environment in act 4.

Part of the credit for this distinctive characterization, and indeed for the structure of the entire piece, must go to Shaw's friend and fellow Fabian, Beatrice Webb (M. Peters 118). Shaw would use Webb's early experience of working in a tailor's sweatshop in his late play *The Millionairess* (1936) (Webb *Letters* 3:407), and her concern with women's issues may well have influenced this play also. Shaw claims to have modeled Vivie on Mrs. Webb, deeming the portrait "an absolutely new type in modern fiction" (*Collected Letters* 2:34), and said the play "was written to please Beatrice Webb by introducing to the stage the Vivie Warren type of modern girl and dramatizing a strong social and economic subject" (*Collected Letters* 3:838). Shaw's admiration for Webb's commitment to her work and to the Fabian cause, as well as her lack of "sexual sentimentality" (*Collected Letters* 2:143), may be more responsible for Vivie's personal and professional independence at the end of the play than a desire by Shaw to break a fictional mold, especially since he never chose to repeat this configuration of character and denouement.

Shaw told his then prospective biographer Archibald Henderson in 1904 that *Mrs Warren's Profession* was one of his "economic & political essays—[his] Socialist manifestoes," written along lines similar to his first play, *Widowers' Houses* (*Collected Letters* 2:425). The economic concerns of the two pieces are parallel: both Sartorius and Mrs Warren take advantage of the capitalist structure of society, and both dramas feature young people who are appalled to learn of their association with the profits of the older generation's investments. The implications of poverty and their direct relation to the involvement of women in prostitution probably spurred Shaw's dramatization, rather than concern with women's issues *per se*. Nevertheless, Shaw

> affirm[ed] that Mrs Warren's Profession is a play for women; that it was written for women; that it has been performed and produced mainly through the determination of women . . . that not one of these women had any inducement to support it except their belief in the timeliness and the power of the lesson the play teaches. (*Mrs Warren's Profession: A Play* 200)

This statement from his preface to the play (1902) is corroborated by the testimony of Mary Shaw (no relation), who wrote in 1912 of her experiences originating the role of Mrs Warren in America, and confronting the hostility to the play:

> This play I knew to be what stage people call a "woman's play"—one in which the theme appeals more powerfully to

women than to men. In all the hubbub, not a woman's voice had been heard; it was simply one vast aggregate of men and their opinions. It seemed to me reasonable to attempt to find out what women thought about it. . . .

I wish it recorded here, to the great credit of women throughout the country, that in every community I was cordially welcomed by the best class of organized women. They were most interested and eager to hear my side of the case. In every instance a vote was taken to visit the theater and see the play, and to form an independent judgment of it. . . . I always made it a part of my duty to learn their verdict; and of the many hundreds of women I interviewed, I never talked with one who was shocked by "Mrs. Warren's Profession." On the other hand, it was most unusual to find a man who was not shocked by it. (M. Shaw 692)

Regardless of Shaw's success in reaching a female audience and winning its approbation with the "woman's play," *Mrs Warren's Profession* stands as the only such piece in the canon. It serendipitously united Shaw's overriding economic and political interests with the topical concerns of women, as demonstrated by his comments on the play and its connection to Beatrice Webb. This prioritized hierarchy accounts for the extremely problematic role of women in Shaw's only other "woman's play,"[8] the one-act *Press Cuttings*, ostensibly "a topical sketch compiled from the editorial and correspondence columns of the daily papers during the Women's War of 1909" (223), but really "more concerned with the issue of compulsory military service and the contemporary hysteria over the build-up of armaments in Germany" (Holledge 68) than the fight for women's suffrage.[9]

A distinction should be made here between a "woman's play" such as *Mrs Warren's*, as defined thematically by the actress Mary Shaw, and a feminist drama. The latter would both feature women's issues and present them from a feminist perspective, with perhaps at least one feminist voice to convey the author's political message, as with the plays commissioned and performed by the Actresses' Franchise League, started in 1908 (Holledge 2–3, *passim*). Although Vivie Warren is a New Woman, strictly speaking she is not a feminist, and neither is her mother, although each is concerned with the position of women in society in her own way. Early in act 1, Shaw gives Vivie a line that gestures in a feminist direction, when she responds to Praed's description of people's romantic, novelistic behavior in his youth with the comment, "Yes, I imagine there must have been a frightful waste of time. Especially women's time" (216). But it becomes clear during the course of the play that Vivie is more the voice of Shaw's work ethic, which applies to men and women alike, than a spokesperson for women alone. Her lack of overt feminist concern for her fellow women is highlighted by a passing remark of Frank's in act 3, when he arrives at Vivie's office to induce her to spend the Saturday half-holiday with him: "The staff had not left when I arrived. He's gone to play cricket on Primrose Hill. Why dont you employ a woman, and give your sex a chance?" (268). Vivie does not respond to Frank's jab, perhaps indicating this is not an important issue for her, or perhaps showing she does not want Frank to construe her professional decisions along purely feminist lines. Vivie's and Honoria's operation of their firm along traditional, patriarchal hiring lines, with a young male clerk (as Shaw himself was at an early age), is very much in keeping with the economic thrust of Shaw's play: both Mrs Warren and Vivie conduct their business affairs strictly within the status quo, and the similarities and continuities between mother and daughter—personal as well as professional—provide the structural framework for Shaw's disturbingly dark exposé of the relation between capitalism, prostitution, and the New Woman.

Mrs Warren's Profession, like the "Pleasant" play *You Never Can Tell* (1898), exhibits a tension between the romantic force of comedic convention and the characterization of a New Woman, whose relationship to the opposite sex wavers during the course of the drama. In the latter play, Shaw tips the balance heavily in favor of a traditional ending, reversing the antimarriage stance of "the Woman of the Twentieth Century" (216), while in the former he allows the heroine to remain single, perhaps as much for lack of a suitable mate as for her wish to focus her attention on her actuarial responsibilities. Nevertheless, much of the action between early in act 1, when Vivie declares her intention to go to London to work (217), and act 4, when she decides in typical New Woman fashion that "brother and sister would be a very suitable relation for [her and Frank Gardner] . . . the only relation I care for" (271),[10] revolves around Vivie's somewhat ambiguous amorous relationship with her neighbor Frank and the courting and marriage proposal of Sir George Crofts. In other words, this play, like *You Never Can Tell*, is dramaturgically divided; here, the drama of the New Woman attempts to assert itself, to surround and overcome the story of the older generation's attempts at conventional marriage market machinations. Shaw makes it very clear that the pressure of these romantic complications, on top of her disillusionment with her mother's life and livelihood, literally drive Vivie to London at the close of act 3, forcing her to assume her conveyancing operations for more personal reasons than those expressed to her mother's friend Praed in act 1. Immediately following Frank's chivalrous rescue of Vivie at gunpoint from Croft's clutches, and the older suitor's declaration of the possibly incestuous relation of the two young people, Frank attempts to renew the intimacy between them:

> Frank (coaxingly) Take it ever so easy, dear Viv. Remember: even if the rifle scared that fellow into telling the truth for the first time in his life, that only makes us the babes in the wood in earnest. (He holds out his arms to her). . . .
> Vivie (with a cry of disgust) Ah, not that, not that. You make all my flesh creep.
> Frank. Why, whats the matter?
> Vivie. Goodbye. (She makes for the gate).
> Frank (jumping up) Hallo! Stop! Viv! Viv! (She turns in the gateway) Where are you going to? Where shall we find you?
> Vivie. At Honoria Fraser's chambers, 67 Chancery Lane, for the rest of my life. (She goes off quickly in the opposite direction to that taken by Crofts).
> Frank. But I say—wait—dash it! (He runs after her).
>
> (267)

Mrs Warren has also been operating under the assumption that Vivie will conform to "her ideal" (219) of conventional womanhood by marrying and experiencing an adulthood quite different from her own (243), and Shaw plays with the motif of conventionality throughout the drama to highlight the surface differences, but essential similarities, between Mrs Warren and her daughter. Unlike *You Never Can Tell*'s Mrs Lanfrey Clandon and Gloria, Mrs Warren wants Vivie to be her opposite: educated and socially acceptable, but still espousing her traditional Victorian values of womanliness, marriage, and the assumption that "the only way for a woman to provide for herself decently is for her to be good to some man that can afford to be good to her" (251). She believes she has arranged for Vivie to be like "any [other] respectable girl brought up . . . to catch some rich man's fancy and get the benefit of his money by marrying him" (249).

The irony of Mrs Warren's wishes for her daughter lies, of course, in the parallel voiced by John Stuart Mill, Shaw, and others between marriage and prostitution: the only distinction between Mrs Warren's profession and the marriages she tries to negotiate is the legality of the arrangement; Vivie is to be "sold" to a man who can afford to pay for her, and despite Frank's declaration that "this is ever so mercenary," Crofts makes the situation perfectly clear: "I suppose you dont want to marry the girl to a man younger than herself and without either a profession or twopence to keep her on" (235).[11]

Vivie, conveniently out on a walk with Praed during this discussion, is unaware of the financial dealings that have transpired, nor is she apprised of them during her confrontation with her mother at the end of act 2. Having established Vivie's own desire for, and pleasure in, "working and getting paid for it" (218), Shaw instead uses this scene to reveal not only the social and economic atrocities of Mrs Warren's past and present life, but also to illuminate the similarities between Vivie and her mother—similarities inherent to their natures, since there has been virtually no contact between them during Vivie's life to date (219).

Many critics have noted such shared traits in Vivie and Mrs Warren as business sense, the enjoyment of work, the appreciation of financial independence, and the value placed on choice of lifestyle. Shaw acknowledges these with a "recognition scene" similar to those found elsewhere in the canon: Vivie perceives the resemblance between herself and her parent, as do children like Gloria Clandon or Barbara Undershaft. She explains, "I am my mother's daughter. I am like you: I must have work, and must make more money than I spend" (284). Her ultimate realization is that Mrs Warren is "a conventional woman at heart," a status that is juxtaposed, and perhaps linked in her mind, to the hypocrisy of having "lived one life and believed in another" (286). Vivie cannot be accused of this, which certainly distinguishes the two women, but Praed's early appraisal, that Vivie is "not conventionally unconventional" (215), must be questioned. She conforms to the profile of the New Woman in behavior, dress, and beliefs, and in that sense is just as "conventional" as her mother, although the two conventions seem distinct, and the audience probably sees Vivie as finally having made a complete break from familial influence.

But Shaw scatters throughout the play some other resemblances between the women and their work that prove haunting in the aftermath of reading or performance. At the top of act 1, Vivie explains to Praed that for relaxation "I like a comfortable chair, a cigar, a little whisky, and a novel with a good detective story in it" (218). At the opening of act 2, after an invigorating stroll in the evening air, Mrs Warren exclaims, "I could do with a whisky and soda now very well" (231), although she has no inkling that Vivie shares her taste for strong spirits. Shaw conveys no value judgment in connection with the women's predilection, although he himself rarely drank alcohol. But it is interesting that he should generate an association between the New Woman and the Fallen Woman through this partiality. Marked as an unwomanly and unconventional (if not degenerate) taste, the consumption of liquor would provide yet another point of attack for the detractors of both groups, who most often focused on the sexual activities of women in each category.

Similarly, the distinctions between Vivie's career and Mrs Warren's may not be so clear-cut. Mrs Warren erroneously associates the remuneration of Vivie's profession with that of her two half-sisters, whom she has described in act 2 (247): "And what are you here? A mere drudge, toiling and moiling early and late for your bare living and two cheap dresses a year" (281).[12] Actually, Shaw constructs the circumstances around both women's early professional careers quite similarly. Both first went into partnership with another woman already established in the business, who showed them the desirability, profitability, and suitability for themselves of the field. And both women operate within the patriarchal structure, Vivie and Honoria organizing their office along traditional hierarchical lines, with a male clerk and with no mention of their partnership as in any way distinct from that of other businessmen's, and Mrs Warren, enmeshed in a capitalist, profit-making network recognized by, but not discussed in, good society (265).

Although Vivie acknowledges the dispositional link between herself and her mother, neither sees the larger social implications of their association. Although superficially Vivie appears independent and content—a New Woman success story without the inevitable moral retribution of so many fictional depictions—this portrait is darkened by the subtle connections between mother and daughter, Fallen Woman and New Woman.[13] This association seems to add another dimension to Julie Holledge's connection of dramatic New Woman heroines with the sexual promiscuity of Pinero's Paula Tanqueray (35). Shaw, who claimed to have based *Mrs Warren's Profession* in part on *The Second Mrs. Tanqueray* and in part on Shelley's *The Cenci* (*Collected Letters* 1:403), clearly wanted to shift the impact of sexuality from titillation to pragmatism. Sexuality is far from missing in Shaw's version; however, it is tied overtly to finance, which intentionally robs it of its romanticism.

Clarifying this dramatic theme may be part of Shaw's rationale for the revisions to the end of act 3, the scene between Frank and Vivie after Crofts's departure. In the original holograph manuscript, the scene ends quite differently:

> Frank (after a pause of stupefaction, raising the gun) You'll testify before the coroner that its an accident, Viv (aims at Crofts).
>
> Vivie (pushing the barrel gently up) Yes, dear, without hesitation if it were necessary. But I forgive him now. Listen to me, dear (she puts the rifle against the stone and draws him beside her on it). Oh Frank, I'm so glad.
>
> Frank. Indeed?
>
> Vivie. All this morning a great cloud of horror has been gathering over me like a storm after the moonlight last night. From moment to moment it has been growing on me that I must get away from it all—away from the sentimental tie I formed under the spell of that ghastly moonlight, away from the very air breathed by my mother and that man, away from the world they are part of. I thought of killing myself—
>
> Frank. My *dear* Viv—what about little Frank?
>
> Vivie. Frank was the most unbearable thought of all; for I know that he would press on me the sort of relation that my mother's life had tainted for ever for me. I felt that I would rather die than let him touch me with that in his mind. Never that for me—never while I live. I shrank from you more than from him when you came to rescue me; and then—oh my

darling little boy, then the blackest cloud vanished. Our affection is innocent: we are brother and sister, the babes in the
wood really and truly. (nestling against him) Oh, now it is I
who am ready to get covered up with leaves.
Frank (rocking her) The wise little girl with her silly little boy.
Vivie (almost sobbing) The dear little boy with the dowdy little
girl (quite sobbing)
Frank (smothering the sobs) Sh-sh-sh—little boy want to see his
darling little girl quite happy in her play (lifts her face and
presses his lips on hers)

(204–6)

Vivie makes it clear here that she has separated her intimacy with
Frank from the kind of sexuality she associates with her mother.
Vivie, as a New Woman, must emerge in purer form than her
mother, the Fallen Women.

In excising the physical intimacy from his later published version,
Shaw disrupts this continuity of mother to daughter, but cannot
eliminate it altogether. Rather, Vivie's revised response appears as
an aggressive repudiation of sexuality with Frank—a dismissal that,
by the extremity of the rejection, conveys an atmosphere of negative
sexual charge, as Vivie contemplates the possibilities that viscerally
"make all [her] flesh creep" (267).

Shaw has Vivie close out this world in act 4, moving the scene to
her office on Chancery Lane. She dismisses Frank, rejects her
mother, and appears content to plunge into her life as a working,
single New Woman. As in the ending of You Never Can Tell, the
problems here are eliminated with relative ease and dramatic dis-
patch, symbolized by Vivie's tearing up and tossing away Frank's
note (286). But this conclusion, like that of the more "Pleasant" play,
belies the personal issues that have come before. Structurally, the
play mirrors the characterization of the figure who opens and closes
it. Vivie, whose outer frame is that of a New Woman, holds within a
sexually and emotionally troubled core.

3

The New Woman in Love

Barbara Bellow Watson describes Gloria Clandon as "glorious Gloria, queen of fatal fascination" (*Shavian Guide* 19). The role has been played by actresses who have tackled other Shavian heroines noted for physical appeal, for example, Raina Petkoff and Aurora Bumpas (*Collected Letters* 3:63). Gloria's brother Philip neatly affiliates her with these Life Force women by noting her initial effect on the dentist, Valentine: "Did you observe? Love at first sight. Another scalp for your collection, Gloria. Number fifteen" (222). Valentine has, of course, been set up to succumb by the first "dithyrambic" depiction of "the Woman of the Twentieth Century: . . . Gloria":

Dolly. Nature's masterpiece!
Philip. Learning's daughter!
Dolly. Madeira's pride!
Philip. Beauty's paragon!

(216)

What, exactly, does Shaw want his audience to think "the Woman of the Twentieth Century" means? As with other fin de siècle uses of "the twentieth century," it connotes a certain progressiveness, a certain advance toward an ideal—in Gloria's case the embodiment of physical and intellectual perfection. But it also seems reasonable to associate "the Woman of the Twentieth Century" with the New Woman, especially given Gloria's upbringing by Mrs Lanfrey Clandon, "a veteran of the Old Guard of the Women's Rights movement" (219).[1] Gloria's selected vacation text, *The Subjection of Women* (258), positions her neatly as an "aspiring New Woman," for whom "Mill and Spencer are prescribed reading" (Cunningham 47), while Mrs Clandon's assertion of their bond, reminding her " 'we' used to mean you and I, Gloria" (225), reinforces the sense of the daughter as the inheritor of her mother's struggle for independence and equality. Ellen Jordan reminds us that

> the New Woman was born in the 1880's, and it was the second generation of English feminists, those women who had profited from the educational and vocational opportunities won by the pioneer feminists of the sixties, who acted both as parents and midwives. It was they who endowed the New Woman with her hostility to men, her questioning of marriage, her determination to escape from the restrictions of home life, and her belief that education could make a woman capable of leading a financially self-sufficient, single, and yet fulfilling life. (19)

Gloria's early interaction with Valentine likewise sounds like a prototypical New Woman's speech on marriage:

> Pray let us be friends, if we are to be friends, in a sensible and wholesome way. I have no intention of getting married; and unless you are content to accept that state of things, we had much better not cultivate each other's acquaintance. . . . I do not think the conditions of marriage at present are such as any self-respecting woman can accept. (266)

Gloria, very much the product of her mother's upbringing, has taken the matriarchal "Bible" (Mill's treatise) as well as Mrs Clandon's adverse stance on matrimony for her own (219). But as Shaw points out in his initial description of Gloria, "Unlike her mother, she is all passion" (220). As early as 1926, decades before feminist critics codified the structure of New Woman fiction, one female critic of Shaw identified his adherence to the literary patterns examined here:

> A favorite Victorian plot was the New Woman, the cold high-minded lady, forfeiting all at last for love, undone by her own surging womanliness (Such a character is Shaw's own Gloria . . .). (Barnard 273)

On a characterological level, the tension between Gloria's inherent self and the identity she projects as a result of her mother's tutelage underlies much of the play's action; structurally, Shaw recapitulates this struggle by pitting the demands and confines of a West End comedy *"de nos jours"* (*Collected Letters* 1:801), which can only be met with a complicated but ultimately happily resolved love affair, against the dramatization of Mrs Clandon's disastrous marital relations and her subsequent attempt to shield Gloria from similar pain by raising her as a New Woman. Shaw was clearly aware of the structural conflict in the piece, for he described some of the character dynamics as tragic (*Collected Letters* 1:583), and the work overall as "a very serious comedy, dancing gaily to a happy ending round the grim earnest of Mrs Clandon's marriage" (*Collected Letters* 2:471).

The fancy dress ball with which Shaw closes the last act neatly illustrates the metatheatrical role-play pervading the comedy. Characters whirl about in false noses and harlequinade just as they have danced around each other in their social personae (as with Dolly and Phil, who "discard their style" upon "missing their audience" [219]). Gloria also realizes her identity has been a charade—a process that completes her *Bildungsstück*, and polarizes her from her mother's precepts by emphasizing what they neglected:

Gloria (sinking upon the bench) Mother!
Mrs Clandon (hurrying to her in alarm) What is it, dear?
Gloria (with heartfelt appealing reproach) Why didnt you educate me properly?
Mrs Clandon (amazed) My child: I did my best.
Gloria. Oh, you taught me nothing: nothing.
Mrs Clandon. What is the matter with you?
Gloria (with the most intense expression) Only shame! shame!!

shame!!! (Blushing unendurably, she covers her face with her hands and turns away from her mother).

(271)

Although Gloria never reveals to her mother the origin of her rather melodramatic "shame," she does intimate that she may contribute her own experiences with love to her mother's revised volume on the *Twentieth Century Woman* (273). Mrs Clandon, who has never had a love affair and never been in love (276), has omitted any such discussion from her treatise, and thus also from her children's education, and it is this singular lack that becomes all-consuming for Gloria. Her surprise at the discovery of her own sexuality and emotions, awakened by Valentine at the end of act 2, prompts the central conflict between her upbringing as a sexless New Woman[2] and the realization of her inherently emotional nature.

Shaw enmeshes Mrs Clandon in this conflict so that it becomes a battle between her modern precepts and the conventions of romance represented by Valentine (and more darkly by Crampton). "The duel of sex" (278) thereby involves Mrs Clandon in a contest she cannot win; she is up against the power of the Life Force as well as the structure of a West End romantic comedy. Valentine embodies the patriarchal dominance of English social mores as well as of the theatrical genre; a woman who has spent the past eighteen years raising her children progressively, literally marginalized from the British mainstream in exile in Madeira, is no match for such a romantic hero. Mrs Clandon inhabits a problem play that cannot overpower the English seaside resort setting of a nineteenth-century farce (Meisel 256).

Dolly and Philip make this extremely clear in their humorous debunking of their mother's usually advanced behavior:

Mrs Clandon (much troubled) Children: you must not be here when Mr Valentine comes. I must speak very seriously to him about this.

Philip. To ask him his intentions? What a violation of Twentieth Century principles!

Dolly. Quite right, mamma: bring him to book. Make the most of the nineteenth century while it lasts.

(275)

Mrs Clandon is forced to assume the pose of a marriage market matriarch while Valentine reveals how he "learnt how to circumvent the Women's Rights woman before [he] was twenty-three" (279). And although she has "great faith . . . in the sound training [of] Gloria's mind" (277–78), her own lack of emotion leaves her unprepared for her daughter's revelations concerning the conflict of intellect and emotion, a conflict that pits maternal influence against paternal inheritance.

Although she is unaware of it, Mrs Clandon has already lost the battle over Gloria much earlier in the play, in a scene that only retrospectively reverberates as an archetypal patriarchal struggle with its resultant transfer of male power from "father" to "son." Near the end of act 1, Crampton arrives at Valentine's office to have a tooth removed—a farcical situation from the commedia dell'arte tradition that Shaw exploits to the hilt. The relation of Crampton to Valentine, landlord to penniless tenant, is by definition an unequal one. Valentine, in classic comedic form, must outwit Crampton, and the dentist bets his landlord he can painlessly extract his tooth against the six weeks' rent he owes. But the conversation surrounding this wager concerns Valentine's matrimonial intentions toward Gloria, whom he has just met, and Crampton's bitter recollections of his own marriage to Gloria's mother. Even more critical is Crampton's insistence on possession of his children:

Crampton (with grumbling irony) Naturally, sir, naturally. When a young man has come to his last farthing, and is within twenty four hours of having his furniture distrained upon by his landlord, he marries. Ive noticed that before. Well, marry; and be miserable.

Valentine. Oh come! what do you know about it?

Crampton. I'm not a bachelor.

Valentine. Then there is a Mrs Crampton?

Crampton (wincing with a pang of resentment) Yes: damn her!

Valentine (unperturbed) Hm! A father, too, perhaps, as well as a husband, Mr Crampton?

Crampton. Three children.

Valentine (politely) Damn them? eh?

Crampton (jealously) No, sir: the children are as much mine as hers.

(234–35)

As Valentine incapacitates Crampton with his levered dentist's chair and a dose of gas, he gains the power over him to balance their relation. He thereby ensures the financial and interpersonal standing he will need to win Gloria's hand at the conclusion of the play. This power struggle between Crampton and Valentine, conducted in an exclusively male arena, is the contest between a father and future son-in-law for the daughter who will shortly identify herself with her father and patriarchy, and thus the curtain to act 1 structurally anticipates the final reestablishment of male dominance in the next generation. Although Crampton verbally acknowledges a shared filial possession here, the action of the scene, with its archetypal patriarchal significance, seems already to overshadow the maternal claim on the daughter. The physical and economic power of the men overwhelms the moral, attitudinal influence of the mother.

The problem play subplot, the debate over the estrangement of Mrs Clandon and Crampton and its impact on their children, is neatly resolved in the comic whirlwind wrap-up of Bohun, the powerhouse lawyer. But the serious issue of Crampton's paternal "rights" (259)[3] is ultimately settled in Gloria's "recognition scene" earlier in act 4. Her realization that she is, at least temperamentally, more akin to her father than to her mother catalyzes the emotional resolution of the comedy. Physically (through stage directions) and intellectually, Gloria positions herself as an inferior (confirming Valentine's sexist opinion of his superior intellect: "I didnt respect your [Gloria's] intellect: Ive a better one myself: it's a masculine specialty" [281]), ensuring the dominance of the patriarchal order in the Woman of the Twentieth Century.

> Crampton (holding her hand) My dear: I'm afraid I spoke very improperly of your mother this afternoon.
> Gloria. Oh, dont apologize. I was very high and mighty myself; but Ive come down since: oh yes: Ive been brought down. (*She sits down on the floor beside his chair*).
> Crampton. What has happened to you, my child?
> Gloria. Oh, never mind. I was playing the part of my mother's daughter then; but I'm not: I'm my father's daughter. . . . (*She turns to him on her knees and seizes his hands*). Now listen. No treason to her: no word, no thought against her. She is our

superior: yours and mine: high heavens above us. . . . My
feelings—my miserable cowardly womanly feelings—may be
on your side; but my conscience is on hers.

Crampton. I'm very well content with that division, my dear.
Thank you.

(295–96; my emphasis)

Gloria describes her mother in idealized form, superior, in intellect
and her ability to control emotion, to her former husband and her
daughter, who now realizes she is not the New Woman of her
mother's tutelage. By having Gloria affiliate herself with her father,
and having female emotionality triumph through the liberating force
of this connection, Shaw ultimately reveals Gloria as a conventional
woman, a womanly woman whose only "modern" trait is her Shavian sexual aggressiveness,[4] a quality shared with her dramatic
predecessor Julia Craven and their ultimate descendant, Ann Whitefield. Mrs Clandon and her belief in the New Woman of high intellect
and controlled emotion are abandoned, left as lofty, unrealizable ideals from another era that have no place in the thoroughly English
environment of the comedy.

Shaw follows a similar pattern of ultimate regard for the womanly
woman in *The Philanderer*, this time using a more complex matrix of
characters and English locales—especially the conventional London
club setting, which he makes topical with its fundamental devotion
to Ibsenism. In the preface to *Plays Unpleasant* (1898), Shaw states
that "the New Theatre would never have come into existence but for
the plays of Ibsen" (11), and explains that

> In . . . 1893, when the discussion about Ibsenism, "the New
> Woman," and the like, was at its height, I wrote for the Inde-
> pendent Theatre the topical comedy called The Philanderer. (14)

Two years earlier, Shaw had published the first edition of his *The
Quintessence of Ibsenism* (1891), which featured a prefatory discussion
of the "womanly woman": her characteristics, how she was molded
by Victorian male-dominated society, and how she must "repudiate
her womanliness" to "emancipate herself" and achieve "equality for
women and men" (61–62). Shaw then opened his first examination

of an Ibsen play, *Brand*, with the assertion, "We are now prepared to learn without misgiving that a typical Ibsen play is one in which the leading lady is an *unwomanly* woman" (64; my emphasis)—in other words, a woman who has successfully repudiated the womanly behavior connected with her "sphere," the domestic, romantic environment in which she is traditionally placed.

Shaw details the emotional nexus surrounding this womanly ideal and gestures toward a definition of liberated behavior that he feels essential for a more egalitarian relation of the sexes:

> Although romantic idealists generally insist on self-surrender as an indispensable element in true womanly love, its repulsive effect is well known and feared in practice by both sexes. The extreme instance is the reckless self-abandonment seen in the infatuation of passionate sexual desire. Everyone who becomes the object of that infatuation shrinks from it instinctively. Love loses its charm when it is not free; and whether the compulsion is that of custom and law, or of infatuation, the effect is the same; it becomes valueless and even abhorrent, like the caresses of a maniac. The desire to give inspires no affection unless there is also the power to withhold; and the successful wooer, in both sexes alike, is the one who can stand out for honorable conditions, and, failing them, go without. (*Quintessence* 56)

It is noteworthy that here, at least two years before the composition of *The Philanderer*, Shaw has already formulated the emotional argument of its action, an argument he explicitly ties to his concern with the status of marriage under English law in the preface to *Plays Unpleasant*:

> In The Philanderer I have shewn the grotesque sexual compacts made between men and women under marriage laws which represent to some of us a political necessity (especially for other people), to some a divine ordinance, to some a romantic ideal, to some a domestic profession for women, and to some that worst of blundering abominations, an institution which society has outgrown but not modified, and which "advanced" individuals are therefore forced to evade. The scene with which The Philanderer opens, the atmosphere in which it proceeds,

and the marriage with which it ends, are, for the intellectually and artistically conscious classes in modern society, typical; and it will hardly be denied, I think, that they are unpleasant. (26)

These same "'advanced' individuals" populate the Ibsen Club in the play, and as noted above, Shaw associates Ibsenism with other "New" and advanced notions: "we of course called everything advanced 'the New' at that time: see The Philanderer, the second play in this volume" (11). But as Shaw pointed out to Golding Bright, the play really intertwines the New and advanced with sexuality: "In 'The Philanderer' you had the fashionable cult of Ibsenism and 'New Womanism' on a real basis of clandestine sensuality" (*Collected Letters* 1:632). Some years later he wrote William Archer:

The Philanderer is a tragi-comedy . . . on the very subtle subject of the operation of the Ibsenist changes in feeling about marriage and sexual relations in a society mainly quite impervious to Ibsen, even when it tried to be fashionably advanced in his name. (*Collected Letters* 3:838)

It would seem that, for Shaw, within the clearly defined socioeconomic world of his characters (middle or upper-middle class), the main thrust of the progressive views and behavior in the 1890s was sexual, and he used this thesis as the central theme of his play.

More insidious, however, is the tension between the portraits of the womanly woman and the unwomanly or New Woman in *The Philanderer*. It appears that Shaw's privileging of the latter in *The Quintessence* is undermined by the dynamic of the relation between women who represent each type in the drama. Shaw's ambivalence toward the women in the play very possibly stems from the biographical basis of the initial plot sequence. Shaw claimed the idea for *The Philanderer* came from a late-night scene caused by Jenny Patterson, his first sexual lover, who burst in on Shaw and Florence Farr in Farr's home (*Collected Letters* 1:295–96). In the play, this characterological ambivalence evolves into the promotion of sympathy for and a virtual ennobling of the womanly woman at the close of act 3. Margot Peters comments on this problematic conclusion:

Philanderers, Shaw tried to show, are not born but made by the artificial relations society enforces between men and women.

And yet the character of the philanderer half defeats Shaw's case for new and honorable relationships between the sexes, because Charteris emerges as that timeless misfortune: the person who evokes deep feeling while remaining immune to it him- or herself. . . .

The Philanderer was thus a bitter-comic drama, with a heroine too understated to win the cause for the New Woman, a "heavy" too sympathetic to dash the case against the Old, and a hero who cannot be trusted with either. It is as ambiguous as Shaw's own feelings about the duel of sex, and its interest stems not so much from its topical case against sexual politics as from its unresolved tension between the woman who wants and the man who eludes. (115–16)

The plot resolution, with its focus on enforced reinstatement of patriarchal order between women through marriage and the social codes surrounding it, raises questions simultaneously about gender roles and about the future social order Shaw is projecting.

Given the theatrical and public associations of Ibsenism with the figure of the New Woman in the 1890s, it is not surprising that Shaw should populate his "Topical Comedy" with variations on this character—albeit in the service of his social theme. Julia Craven, Grace Tranfield, and Sylvia Craven, the only female characters, fall along an axis of womanly to unwomanly behavior, the Craven sisters representing the extremes, while Grace treads middle ground as an advanced but also pragmatic woman.

Barbara Watson calls Julia Craven one of "the most unloving of the early portraits" (*Shavian Guide* 53) of Shaw's aggressive women, and Julia shares with her immediate dramatic predecessor Blanche Sartorius a tendency toward physical violence as well as sexual forwardness. This characteristic of frank sexuality immediately clouds the distinctions between womanly and New Women in Shaw, for he diverges from the traditional Victorian view of woman as having little sexual drive in his presentation of feminine women as instruments of the Life Force (within the confines of the socially acceptable institutions of courtship and marriage). The New Woman, usually depicted in literature as free and open in her decision to explore or reject her sexuality regardless of social convention, is thus conflated with the otherwise womanly woman through the expression of sexual desire.

Shaw's fusing of character types here colors the comedy through-out. Even the designation "New Woman" becomes confused in the hypocrisy of Julia's efforts to mask her conventionality by her association with Ibsenism. Referring to Julia, Charteris explains to her father that a New Woman does not wait for a man to make "advances to her" before declaring her feelings (*Plays Unpleasant* 133), while the opening moments of the play feature the legitimate New Woman figure in a virtual parody of a romantic clinch with Charteris:

> Charteris (impulsively clasping Grace) My dearest love.
> Grace (responding affectionately) My darling. Are you happy?
> Charteris. In Heaven.
> Grace. My own.
> Charteris. My heart's love.
>
> (100)

We soon learn that Grace is a widow, a convenient social status that most probably allows her both personal and financial independence, as well as prior sexual experience. She can thus "play it both ways"; she can behave as freely as a New Woman would without moving radically beyond the confines of accepted social behavior in her status as a widow. She has not had to suffer through a bad marriage or leave it (and be subsequently "left behind" socially and amorously, as is Mrs Clandon). She need not reject social convention to achieve freedom; Mr Tranfield, whose only notable characteristics were his love of Grace and his money (100), has conveniently died, leaving her free to love elsewhere off her inheritance.

The expression of affection between Charteris and Grace is integrally connected with the "advanced views" that they share as Ibsenists. Shaw plays with the adjective "advanced" throughout the play, using it both to explain Grace's true stance on the relation of the sexes and to expose the hypocrisy of Julia's assumption of those views to attract Charteris and gain social standing. Shaw also plays with the sexual connotations of the nominative form "advances" (133), which creates a revealing tension between the liberal views and private desires of the Ibsenists. Charteris, a "founding father" of the club, most often exploits this duality in his relations with Julia, propounding the former sense in service of the latter. The primary focus of the Ibsenists' advanced views is the current legal status of women in marriage, as explained by Charteris, "the famous Ibsenist philosopher" (115). In a speech remarkably similar in tone to the attitude of Mrs Lanfrey Clandon, Charteris reminds Julia:

> As a woman of advanced views, you were determined to be free. You regarded marriage as a degrading bargain, by which a woman sells herself to a man for the social status of a wife and the right to be supported and pensioned in old age out of his income. Thats the advanced view: our view. Besides, if you had married me, I might have turned out a drunkard, a criminal, an imbecile, a horror to you; and you couldnt have released yourself. Too big a risk, you see. Thats the rational view: our view. Accordingly, you reserved the right to leave me at any time if you found our companionship incompatible with—what was the expression you used?—with your full development as a human being. I think that was how you put the Ibsenist view: our view. (107–8)[5]

Yet Julia never voices these beliefs independently; she learns her Ibsenism from Charteris and parrots it back to him to retain his affections, as he takes advantage of these open-ended relationships to further his philandering ends. Grace, who seems to have developed her views on her own, nevertheless also learns how to identify herself from a man, her father: "I'm an advanced woman. . . . I'm what my father calls the New Woman" (141).

Thus *The Philanderer* introduces a pattern of paternal (or older male)[6] influence on and instruction of younger women in Shaw—a pattern not historically unfounded, given the history of women's education. Yet it is questionable here because Shaw uses it to reassert patriarchal dominance by the end of the play, as the fathers insist on the reconciliation of Julia and Grace and the conventional matrimonial conclusion to the comedy. It is also interesting that, although we learn the background story of Cuthbertson's and Craven's marriages, their wives are never alluded to in their maternal context. None of the women ever mentions a mother; it is as if each were sui generis or solely the product of paternal upbringing. This motif of absent, outdated, inconsequential, or impotent mother figures, prevalent throughout the canon, thus also finds early demonstration here and will be discussed at greater length in part 3.

The issue of paternal influence and control and the father/daughter dynamic (also treated more fully in part 3) are directly related to the domestic environments of *The Philanderer*. In act 1, Charteris tells Julia they are in "Mrs Tranfield's house" (105), and yet the furnishings clearly belong to "the leading representative of manly sentiment in London" (119), her father Mr Cuthbertson, the drama critic who invites his old friend Craven to take his "place, by [his] fireside" (116). For some inexplicable reason, Craven had "got it into [his] head that your [Cuthbertson's] name was Tranfield" (116). Although Cuthbertson explains, "Thats my daughter's name. She's a widow, you know" (116), this clarification in no way accounts for Craven's confusion over the identity of such a close friend. Even if his exchange of names were ironic, suggesting an emasculation of Cuthbertson by his daughter, his comment highlights the usual subsuming of the female identity into the male through marriage, as well as the traditional ordering of parent/child relations. In the absence of the son-in-law and wife (from whom Cuthbertson is separated [128]), Cuthbertson and Grace have formed a new, undefined alliance in which the "advanced" daughter seems to have the upper hand. Charteris dismisses Craven's concern over a potential offense to Cuthbertson with the comment, "Oh, never mind about him. Mrs Tranfield bosses this establishment" (121). In other words, the New Woman has overpowered the old Adam (132), a turn of events Cuthbertson associates with "the breakup of family life" (116).

Cuthbertson and Craven blame "the advanced ideas in the younger generation" (117) and their association with Ibsenism for this literal movement away from hearth and home. Craven complains that his children are always at the Ibsen Club, but Cuthbertson, who supposedly has joined to protect Grace (118), sees certain advantages to the "New Home":

Well, the fact is, it's not so inconvenient as you might think. When youre at home, you have the house more to yourself; and when you want to have your family about you, you can dine with them at the club. (129)[7]

Not only is the Ibsen Club the alternative domestic environment for "the younger generation," it is also the locus of gender definition. Craven, the embodiment of the Old Order holding out against the

invasion of Ibsenism, struggles with what he has learned of the club
from Jo Cuthbertson and Charteris:

> Craven. . . . Why you [Jo] said the whole modern movement
> was abhorrent to you because your life had been passed in
> witnessing scenes of suffering nobly endured and sacrifice
> willingly rendered by womanly women and manly men and
> deuce knows what else. Is it at the Ibsen club that you see all
> this manliness and womanliness?
>
> Charteris. Certainly not: the rules of the club forbid anything
> of the sort. Every candidate for membership must be nomi-
> nated by a man and a woman, who both guarantee that the
> candidate, if female, is not womanly, and if male, not manly.
>
> (118)

Shaw is, of course, playing here with the issue of the influence of art
(literature, the theater, etc.) on social behavior: have society's senses
of what is (un)manly or (un)womanly been defined by art, or are the
artists of the time reproducing the society they observe, complete
with its sense of gender confusion? Julia, for example, is both theatrical (in the sense of Victorian melodrama) and womanly (105). What
is interesting here, however, is how Shaw knowingly manipulates
this theme while seeming oblivious to his own capitulation to literary
and social conventions of the time by reaffirming manly and womanly behavior and the dominance of patriarchy in the play's conclusion.

Act 1, set in Cuthbertson's home with all its Victorian dramatic
memorabilia, represents the Old Order and traditional behavior, and
introduces the characters more closely related to that environment.
Act 2, at the Ibsen Club, shows how the younger generation, for all
its "advanced views," perpetuates romantic intrigue under the guise
of unmanly and unwomanly conduct, and it is dramaturgically fitting
that Shaw should wait to present characters expressing more "modern" views in this domain. Sylvia Craven, the youngest of the drama-
tis personae, is the New Woman in the extreme, a virtual caricature
of the figure as she was depicted journalistically at the time:

She flouts Love's caresses
Reforms ladies' dresses

And scorns the Man-Monster's tirade;
She seems scarcely human
This mannish New Woman
This Queen of the Blushless Brigade.

(Cunningham 1)

Sylvia exhibits many of the traits of the fictional composite New Woman: she smokes, preferring "cigarets" to "gloves" in payment of a bet (138), and is regarded by all as shockingly outspoken:

> Sylvia (contemptuously) I knew it. Of course it was nothing but eating too much. I always said Paramore was an ass. (Sensation. The group of Cuthbertson, Craven, and Julia breaks up as they turn in dismay).

(146)

She has no interest in Charteris, the object of the other women's affections (176), as anything more than a friend, and it is in her interactions with him that the question of gender identity becomes most obvious:

> Sylvia (knowingly) Oh, I know you, my lad.
> Charteris. Then you know that I never pay any special attention to any woman.
> Sylvia (thoughtfully) Do you know, Leonard, I really believe you. I dont think you care a bit more for one woman than for another.
> Charteris. You mean I dont care a bit less for one woman than another.
> Sylvia. That makes it worse. But what I mean is that you never bother about their being *only women:* you talk to them just as you do *to me or any other fellow.* Thats the secret of your success. You cant think how sick *they get* of being treated with the respect due to *their sex.*

(136; my emphasis)[8]

Sylvia clearly has little use for women; in fact, she obviously prefers not to regard herself as one, identifying more strongly with Charteris than with any member of her own sex. She likes Charteris to refer to her as "Craven, old chap" (135) and "old boy" (139), although she realizes on some level that he is playing with her, and calls his behavior "a little overdone" (135).

The Craven sisters share a certain theatricality, a certain exaggeration of the roles they have chosen to play, and their costumes, like their speech, reflect these personae. Shaw describes Sylvia as "wearing a mountaineering suit of Norfolk jacket and breeches with neat town stockings and shoes" (124). This outfit, reminiscent of the Jaeger designs he perpetually sported, clearly conveys an aura of athletic masculinity. Even more significant is the detail that follows: "A detachable cloth skirt lies ready to her hand across the end of the settee" (124). For Sylvia, the emblem of her femininity, a skirt, is as detachable as that female identity. In the club environment where Sylvia feels most herself, we see she has shed the signifier of social convention, the feminine skirt that synecdochically defines her as a woman. This one gesture sets up a myriad of tantalizing interpretive possibilities: is Shaw suggesting here that the core self, the preferred and better self, is masculine? Or is it only Sylvia in whom Shaw wants to convey the predilection for masculinity? Do the layerings of attire imply a mutual exclusivity of gender identity—an either/or proposition—or is this a situation that fits within the both/and construct that Eric Bentley has identified throughout Shaw?

Sylvia is no less inconsistent than the other female characters, however. Despite her overt masculinity, she bristles at any potential disparagement of herself as a woman, telling the men in the reading room:

> (flustered and self-assertive) You may talk as much as you like if you will have the common consideration to ask first whether the other people object. What I protest against is your assumption that my presence doesnt matter because I'm only a female member. Thats all. Now go on, pray: you dont disturb me in the least. (She . . . again buries herself in Ibsen). (125)

Perhaps most perplexing is her willingness to compromise her own integrity for Charteris, sexually exploiting the femininity she abjures:

> Charteris. . . . Now listen to me: I am going to speak as a philosopher. Julia is jealous of everybody: *everybody*. If she saw

you flirting with Paramore she'd begin to value him directly.
You might play up a little, Craven, for my sake: eh?
Sylvia (rising) Youre too awful, Leonard. For shame! However,
anything to oblige a fellow Ibsenite.

(138)

Cuthbertson, still adapting to the ways of the club, learns that "it's
against the rules . . . to coddle women in any way," and thus he resolves they must "go to lunch in the Ibsen fashion: the unsexed
fashion" (134). Ibsenism, the club, and "advanced views" thereby
become associated with loss of sexual identity, a departure demonstrated by the disparities between professed gender behavior—womanly, unwomanly, advanced, or New Womanly—and speech or action. But this confusion only seems to strike the women; the men in
the play remain remarkably constant, even if that consistency is philandering hypocrisy. Charteris, one of the founding members of the
club, points out that "the unwomanly women who work for their
living, and know how to take care of themselves, never give any
trouble. So we simply said we wouldnt have any womanly women"
(119). Yet despite Grace's "very convenient and businesslike" dress
(139), neither she nor either of the other women work, and indeed
"the unwomanly women who work for their living," women like
Proserpine Garnett and Vivie Warren, would in reality have neither
time nor, at least in Prossy's case, financial wherewithal to belong to
the Ibsen Club, one of the main activities of which seems to be din-
ing.

The men, on the other hand, with the notable exception of Charteris, are all well established professionally. Cuthbertson is a drama
critic, Craven a retired military man, and Dr Paramore, although he
bears the brunt of Shavian medical satire, is a serious physician. Even
the page in the club is male. There is clearly a connection between
professionalism and manliness, an association from which Charteris
is excluded:

Paramore. . . . Er—by the way, do you think is Miss Craven attached to Charteris at all?
Cuthbertson. What! that fellow! Not he. He hangs about after
her; but he's not man enough for her. A woman of that sort

likes a strong, manly, deep throated, broadchested man.

Paramore (anxiously) Hm! a sort of sporting character, you
think?

Cuthbertson. Oh, no, no. A scientific man, perhaps, like yourself. But you know what I mean: a MAN. (He strikes himself
a sounding blow on the chest).

Paramore. Of course; but Charteris is a man.

Cuthbertson. Pah! You dont see what I mean.

(127)

Charteris claims unmanly status for himself to circumvent the conventions of marriage and aid his philandering ends, much as Valentine learns to get around the New Woman in *You Never Can Tell*. But
Shaw never makes clear what defines manly and unmanly behavior;
we have no masculine corollary to the chapter on the womanly
woman in *The Quintessence of Ibsenism*, and Charteris displays none
of the betrayal of professed views that plagues the female characters.

Margot Peters feels *The Quintessence* illustrates Shaw's "sympathy
for the 'unwomanly woman,' since he in his distaste for war, sport,
whisky, cigars, competitiveness, womanizing, and hard facts was
certainly an 'unmanly man'" (76). Shaw's personal notoriety as a
philanderer calls at least part of Peters's assessment into question
(Beatrice Webb *Diary* 2:37, 51, 111, 123; Shaw *Collected Letters* 1:105,
801–2); but more important is the interplay of the qualities of manliness and womanliness he puts forth in *The Quintessence*. Shaw opens
"The Womanly Woman" not with any reference to Ibsen, but with
an extended commentary on the recently deceased female artist
Marie Bashkirtseff.[9] This young painter, whom he identifies as unwomanly, is also manly because she will not conform to the womanly
image of self-sacrifice:

No man pretends that his soul finds its supreme satisfaction in
self-sacrifice: such an affectation would stamp him as coward
and weakling: the manly man is he who takes the Bashkirtseff
view of himself. (*Quintessence* 56)

It would seem that an unwomanly woman, a New Woman, may be
a man, but not necessarily "manly," or she may be something else
altogether. Manliness is only defined through the negation of certain

feminine qualities—a Shavian twist on the usual pattern of female definition by contrast to male. Unmanliness remains unexplained, however, and thus is an enigmatic, tantalizing state that through association with Charteris is not to be idolized (Grace says, "Never make a hero of a philanderer" [177]) but may emerge as the only unexamined, and therefore unattacked, status in the play. Shaw's self-association with the character of Charteris positions the dramatist in this shadowy realm of ambiguous gender definition as well. Although the related issue of Shaw's gender identity will be discussed in part 2, it may be worth noting here the privileging of the "unmanly man" and the flexibility of this status for the portrayal of variations on Shaw's own persona as well as on idealized male characters, such as Caesar *(Caesar and Cleopatra).*

Shaw avoids any hostility between men over issues of sexual self-image, but his scenes of conflict between Grace and Julia highlight the questioning of female gender identity and the relative desirability of being a New or a womanly woman. In the context of their competition for Charteris's affections, Shaw places the women in a prototypical "catfight," replete with accusations and name-calling. He casts Grace here in a didactic role vis à vis Julia, using the "advanced" woman to expose the weakness of the conventional one, but Julia's response turns the tables to take advantage of what she perceives as her strength, rendering Grace's essential female identity problematic:

> Julia (suddenly throwing herself tragically on her knees at Grace's feet) Dont take him from me. Oh dont—dont be so cruel. . . .
> Grace. Do you suppose I am a man, to be imposed on by this sort of rubbish? . . . How I hate to be a woman when I see, by you, what wretched childish creatures we are! Those two men would cut you dead and have you turned out of the club if you were a man. . . . But because you are only a woman, they are forbearing! sympathetic! gallant! . . .
> Julia. . . . Do you think *I* need go down on my knees to men to make them come to me? That may be your experience, you creature with no figure: it is not mine.
>
> (155–56)

Shaw here employs the same physical placement of characters to indicate relative power as he does in the scene between Gloria Clan-

don and her father in *You Never Can Tell*. Julia claims she need not
go on her knees to men; but she has already done so to Charteris in
act 1 (110), and her doing so to Grace promotes the association between that gesture and a masculine object. Her designation of Grace
as a "creature with no figure" is even more telling; on a surface level,
the contrast between the women works to comic effect, as with *A
Midsummer Night's Dream*'s Helena and Hermia. But Grace's absence
of noteworthy secondary sexual characteristics makes her physical
appearance masculine as well. One wonders if there is some latent
"anatomy is destiny" theme at work here: is Julia womanly because
of her physique while Grace is not? Or has Grace developed into a
New Woman because she has not "developed" in ways associated
with male heterosexual definitions of desirable femininity (that is,
with the conventionally womanly figure's ample breasts and hips)?
Finally, Grace's own admission that she "hate[s] to be a woman"
while questioning "do you suppose I am a man" complicates her
gender identity in a Bashkirtseffian manner, and allows her little
room in which to be both "advanced" and female.

Just as the busts of Shakespeare and Ibsen preside over acts 1 and
2, representing the Old and New Orders, so Rembrandt's "School of
Anatomy" hangs over act 3, suggesting the dominance of science as
the latest public idol and guiding social force. Act 3 takes place in Dr
Paramore's combined reception–sitting room, the domain of an established professional and bachelor into which are invited the repre-
sentatives of the play's other distinctive social views. The opening
scene, the strained proposal sequence between Paramore and Julia,
exposes the process by which a womanly woman can compromise
her personal feelings to acquiesce to a less-than-desired marriage,
and how she can come to inhabit a domestic environment thoroughly
under male control.

Julia seems initially to have benefited from Grace's exposé of her
behavior; she seems to want a different type of rapport with men:

> Paramore. I'm afraid I'm a bad entertainer. The fact is, I am too
> professional. I shine only in consultation. I almost wish you
> had something serious the matter with you; so that you might
> call out my knowledge and sympathy. As it is, I can only
> admire you, and feel how pleasant it is to have you here.
> Julia (bitterly) And pet me, and say pretty things to me. I won-

der you dont offer me a saucer of milk at once. . . . Because
you seem to regard me very much as if I were a Persian cat.
Paramore (in strong remonstrance) Miss Cra—
Julia (cutting him short) Oh, you neednt protest. I'm used to it:
it's the sort of attachment I seem always to inspire. (Ironically) You cant think how flattering it is.

(162–63)

But her drive to be married, to mitigate her disappointment over the
loss of Charteris, forces her to compromise herself, although Shaw
makes her repugnance obvious: "Listen to me. If I say yes, will you
promise not to touch me? Will you give me time to accustom myself
to our new relations?" (165).

Grace reads Julia's demonstration that she "can do without" Charteris as a triumph over womanliness and an end to their competitiveness: "Now I take back everything I said" (175), presumably a reference to her castigation of Julia in act 2. But this really reinforces Julia's
womanly self-sacrifice as laudable; she has done nothing more than
abandon her pursuit of the man she loves for the socially acceptable
compromise of marriage (with the potential for ongoing philandering) to a man she finds distasteful but willing.[10] Grace intimates this
resolution of their conflict is far from "a happy ending," but only
because both have given up the shared object of their affections: Julia
to womanly self-sacrifice and Grace to New Womanly spinsterhood.

This theme of self-sacrifice in love relations has strong connotations of masculinity in the play, however. Early in act 2 we learn that
Cuthbertson and Craven formerly loved the same woman, but that
Cuthbertson won out, leaving Craven to "t[ake] [his] defeat well"
(128). Craven sees the triangulation of Charteris, Paramore, and Julia
to be parallel: "Now, Charteris: Paramore and you stand today where
Cuthbertson and I stood . . . thirty-five years ago" (172). In affairs of
the heart, the gentlemanly Old Order prevails. Craven extends this
creed to Julia, however, forcing gentlemanly behavior on her:

(To Julia unanswerably) The test of a man's or a woman's breeding is how they behave in a quarrel. . . . Now you said today, at
that iniquitous club, that you were not a womanly woman. Very
well: I dont mind. But if you are not going to behave like a lady
when Mrs Tranfield comes into this room, youve got to behave

like a gentleman; or as fond as I am of you, I'll cut you dead exactly as I would if you were my son. (174)

Cuthbertson, who arrives at the conclusion of this speech, immediately imposes the same code on Grace, "peremptorily" (175) commanding her to congratulate Julia on her engagement. Thus Julia and Grace are forced to recapitulate their fathers' relationship, to behave "like gentlemen" at the same time that the patriarchal social order is reinstated in the modern, scientific environment through marriage. Julia's womanly self-sacrifice, which Shaw condemns in *The Quintessence*, is virtually revered here, as the other characters feel "the presence of a keen sorrow" (177) at the final curtain. Shaw leaves the other women's stories unresolved; the New Women are marginalized as the comedic structure, albeit conditionally, celebrates union.

Shaw's portraits of New Women, here and throughout the first two volumes of his plays, reveal a thorough familiarity with the type as it appeared in the work of other novelists (and, to a lesser extent, playwrights) and in the popular press. At times bearing the brunt of his humor through caricature (Prossy, Sylvia), at times a vehicle for larger social commentary (Vivie), and at times an exemplar of (inter)personal emotional contradiction (Gloria, Grace), the New Woman is consistently employed as a figure for other dramatic ends, not presented in her own right or focused on as the product of a burgeoning struggle over the status of women in society. Shaw's treatment of the New Woman parallels that of many other writers at the end of the nineteenth century, and the ambivalence reflected in these depictions mirrors that of many male authors of that era.

Michael Holroyd distinguishes among some of the *Plays Pleasant* and *Unpleasant* by designating *The Philanderer* as written with a "man's point of view," while *You Never Can Tell* and *Mrs Warren's Profession* are "from the woman's" (*Search for Love* 288–89, 291). I take this to mean that he feels the reader or audience member will sympathize more with the male characters in the former, the female in the latter. Yet there may also be subtler implications, in terms of authorial tone and style, than Holroyd intended. Shortly after Shaw's arrival in London, he began to ghostwrite music criticism for his mother's voice instructor, George Vandeleur Lee. The editor of *The Hornet* soon caught on, but misidentified Shaw's work as the " 'composition, idea and writing of a Lady'" (Holroyd *Search for Love* 63). The possibility of a connection between Shaw's desire to avoid a conventional gender definition for himself (or, conversely, to be associated with "unmanly" or traditionally feminine traits) and his potential to write in a style identified as feminine is intriguing. The next part, "Shavian Androgyny," continues the discussion of unconventional constructions of gender and takes up the relation of Shaw's own gender identity to his characters and creative technique.

PART TWO

SHAVIAN ANDROGYNY

4

The Late Victorian/Edwardian Context

> . . . taken as a whole a culture's sexual discourse plays a critical role in shaping individuality. It does so by helping to implant in each person an internalized set of dispositions and orientations that governs individual improvisations.
> —Stephen Greenblatt, "Fiction and Friction"

> Defined by man, the conventional polarity of masculine and feminine names woman as a *metaphor of man*. Sexuality, in other words, functions here as the sign of a rhetorical convention, of which woman is the *signifier* and man the *signified*. Man alone has thus the privilege of proper meaning, of *literal* identity: femininity, as signifier, cannot signify *itself*; it is but a metaphor, a figurative substitute; it can but refer to man, to the phallus, as its proper meaning, as its signified. The rhetorical hierarchization of the very opposition between the sexes is then such that woman's *difference* is suppressed, being totally subsumed by the reference of the feminine to masculine identity.
> —Shoshana Felman, "Rereading Femininity"

The "sexual discourse" of the late Victorian/Edwardian period revolves, to a great extent, around the issue of gender identity: on the stage, in the courtroom, and in print—both sensational and learned—questions of sexual orientation and definition abound. Shaw first demonstrates his involvement in this debate in *The Philanderer* and in *The Quintessence of Ibsenism*, both of which consider issues of (un)womanly and (un)manly behavior—

issues intimately connected with concepts of masculinity and femininity and the individual's projection of these characteristics. Indeed, throughout his career as a dramatist, Shaw presented characters exhibiting varying androgynous traits, from subtle mannerisms through overt signs such as cross-dressing and strong opposite-sex identification; his distinctive group of characters mirrors the era's fascination with those whose actions or demeanor seemed at odds with the conventions of gender for their biological sex.

Yet Shaw's was a biased androgyny, in that he virtually ignored this phenomenon in men—who were at the time of equal interest to the scientific community—focusing almost exclusively on instances in women. The next three chapters seek to identify the Shavian plays and characters that display androgyny, to explore the sexual imbalance in Shaw's choice of androgynous subjects, and to account for the various cultural and scientific influences that may have informed these dramas.

Although Stephen Greenblatt's observation in the first epilogue to this chapter refers to the Renaissance, it is equally valid for the nineteenth century, particularly with regard to Shaw, as his self-proclaimed links to Shakespeare create a dramatic bridge between the texts from the two eras. Greenblatt's essay concerns "the relationship . . . between medical and theatrical practice . . . a shared code, a set of interlocking tropes and similitudes that function not only as the objects but as the conditions of representation" (46). He locates this connection in the investigation of androgyny, hermaphroditism, and transvestism as they appear in medical/legal records and separately, but coincidentally, in the cross-dressing found in dramatic texts. The late nineteenth and early twentieth centuries mark another strategic moment in the development of this sexual discourse: the medical/ psychoanalytic theories and writings of Krafft-Ebing, Edward Carpenter, and Havelock Ellis, among others, establish this period as one of heightened sexual consciousness, and the literature of the time reflects this preoccupation with gender identity.

Felman's comments, written in conjunction with an analysis of Balzac's novella *The Girl with the Golden Eyes*, theorize about a moment much closer to Shaw's; the Balzac text, which features both homo- and heterosexuality as well as cross-dressing, demonstrates for Felman the male bias of the patriarchal culture, an orientation observed widely by other critics of literary and theatrical androgyny, and one to which Shaw's androgyny conforms. As Shaw often uses the attire of characters as an indicator of androgyny, Felman's ideas on dress are also relevant:

> If it is clothes, the text seems to suggest, if it is clothes alone, i.e., a cultural sign, an institution, which determine our reading of the sexes, which determine masculine and feminine and in-sure sexual opposition as an orderly, hierarchical polarity; if indeed clothes make the *man*—or the *woman*—, are not sex roles as such, inherently, but travesties? Are not sex roles but travesties of the ambiguous complexity of real sexuality, of real sexual difference? (28)

I identify three distinct influences at work in Shavian depictions of androgyny: the Shakespearean model of the cross-dressed woman who will abandon her masculine attire in the plot resolution; the cross-dressed principal boy figure from the pantomime who often appeared in warrior guise, but was always known by audiences to be female "underneath"; and the androgynous woman discussed in the psychological literature in both homo- and heterosexual variants.

Immediately after the Restoration, women had begun to appear on stage for the first time in England, and soon performed cross-dressed in male attire—in the "breeches parts" that became a main-stay of the eighteenth- and nineteenth-century theater. Felman's questions pertain directly to the investigation of sexuality and culture as it developed during this period, for society's view of cross-dressing needed to incorporate first the theatrical and literary incarnation of the androgynous female, then later her public identity in male attire. Literary tradition privileges the female character who assumes male attire, like Shakespeare's Rosalind *(As You Like It)*, at the same time it denigrates the male corollary, as with Euripides's Pentheus *(The Bacchae)*. But the female cross-dresser became an object of both fasci-nation and controversy after the Restoration, as she was not only a sex symbol but also a threat to patriarchal control through her usur-pation of male attire and action.

The drama resolved this conflict in various ways, by emphasizing the feminine sexual allure in the male disguise, by interpreting the female aspiration to male identity as a recognition of male superior-ity, and/or by incorporating the cross-dressing in a comic context that would diffuse the anxiety surrounding the issue of sexual difference.[1] The sexual component of dramatic cross-dressing distinguished theatrical transvestism from that of female modernists who made their sporting of male attire a political act more overtly threatening to the dominant male culture.[2]

The Shakespearean plot device of the male-disguised female stands as a touchstone for subsequent dramatic instances of male impersonation. Traditionally, audiences have responded more positively to female characters' assertiveness when cloaked in male attire, but the temporary nature of this sartorial transgression is integral to the resolution of the social disruption that shapes Shakespearean comedy (Park 108). In other words, the restitution of order in the Shakespearean world must always include a return to conventional gender roles. Nina Auerbach interprets this phenomenon for nineteenth-century audiences:

> Perhaps because they flirted with the forbidden, Portia, Rosalind, and Viola, who act men for a while but gaily relinquish their masquerade at the end of the play, were loved by Victorian audiences who basked in a transvestism displaced into disguise. None of these women is transformed into a male. . . . Each remains a woman underneath, claiming male prerogatives only in order to educate the fatuous hero she loves. Such plays challenged Victorian audiences just enough to allay their more far-reaching fears. (65)

Robert Kimbrough sees female cross-dressing in Shakespeare as an attempt to expose these conventions of gender and allow a character to grow "into a fuller human self" (23). Kimbrough continues, "Just as an actor's role is a disguise, so also is gender a disguise, and all disguises must be removed for people to be themselves" (27). But Kimbrough's analysis features discussion of only the seven "girl-into-boy" disguises in Shakespeare (21). He does not mention the farcical counter-instance of female impersonation, Falstaff in *The Merry Wives of Windsor*, which suggests that—for Kimbrough, or Shakespeare, or both—the movement toward fuller humanity need be accomplished only by women.

Stephen Greenblatt posits that the dominance of female androgyny in the English theater is integrally related to Renaissance conceptions of the emergence of male identity. The female characters' assumption and subsequent relinquishing of male costume provide a mirror image for the process by which a maturing male distinguishes himself from the female (51). Bernard Shaw, who saw himself as a descendant of Shakespearean tradition, may well have adopted this motif for reasons similar to those suggested by Greenblatt. Shaw employs the trope of the cross-dressed female frequently in his one-act, as well as full-length, comedies, and the Shakespearean model may have affected, or even suggested, Shaw's figuration of cross-dressing.

But the Shakespearean trope of the woman in male disguise relinquishing this role to return to more conventional femininity, which may have its most jarring version in the violence of the transformation in act 5 of *Cymbeline*, also has a direct parallel in the Victorian pantomime. When women took over the roles of female impersonators after the Restoration, they not only portrayed the cross-dressed Shakespearean heroines, they also took on certain younger male roles in Restoration and eighteenth-century drama, and branched out into the popular theater, especially the pantomime. Between 1815 and 1819, the first breeches roles—those filled by actresses in male disguise—entered the English pantomime. These roles evolved over the next few decades into the Victorian pantomime fixture known as the "principal boy": the young male hero portrayed by an actress (usually of noteworthy sexual appeal) cross-dressed to accentuate feminine allure while suggesting traditional boyish appearance (Senelick 32).

In the pantomimes of Shaw's time, the actress in the principal boy role cavorted in boyish fashion throughout the main action of the performance, which was usually based on fairy tale or legend. The productions ended, however, with an extravaganza of theatricality, a harlequinade unrelated to the main action, but which usually united the hero and heroine in their commedia dell'arte incarnations. The transition from pantomime action to the harlequinade, called the Transformation Scene, always included the replacement of the principal boy actress by a male actor, so that a man as Harlequin and a woman as Columbine would resolve any romantic action. Although two women had "set the stage" in the pantomime, essentially representing what we might now think of as a lesbian couple masquerading as a heterosexual unit, neither audiences nor critics viewed them this way then because of the theatrical conventions that had essen-

Fig. 2. Sybil Arundale appeared as Dick Whittington in Birmingham, England, in 1908. Note the conventional features of the principal boy costume: close-fitting bodice, designed to show off the female figure, and exposed legs, which simultaneously suggest a boyish demeanor and reveal more of the female anatomy.

tially reversed the tradition of male actors in all roles, but maintained the illusion of heterosexuality that defined the form of "suspension of disbelief" for the stage.

This trope of female replacement structurally resembles the patterns for New Woman fiction traced in the previous chapters. In the more fantastical pantomime incarnations, the woman is similarly returned to her "proper role" at the play's conclusion: actresses only appear in the costume and character proper to their sex. The external transgressions of women's appropriation of male dress and behavior in Shakespeare and the pantomimes are resolved in the return to traditional female costume and demeanor.[3] The significance of the outcome here—the restitution of male authority and the correct social order—is thus the same as before, although the rationale for assuming the disguise initially is not as threatening to the patriarchy here as was that of the New Women, who made conscious efforts to subvert male authority and privilege.

This strategic difference, that the women assume their disguise in the service of love or the interests of men, lies at the heart of their acceptability in a society as concerned with gender identity as the Victorian. Susan Gubar has identified three categories of female cross-dressers: "woman warrior, Byronic hero, and androgyne" (479), and it is the first that is not only most socially acceptable and widely depicted, but also most frequent in Shaw. In her 1893 history *Women Adventurers*, Ménie Dowie expresses forthrightly her opinion of these women:

> It is difficult to take them quite seriously, these ladies of the sabre; they are to me something of a classic jest: their day is done, their histories forgotten, their devotion dead, and they have left us no genuine descendants. The socialist woman, the lecturing woman, the political woman, the journalising woman—none of these must call them ancestress. . . . Their high, stern code leaves no room for the qualities of "the female soldier." . . .
>
> I am struck, too, in reading of them, by the insistence on their motives: . . . there was ever a man at the root of their ardour. That is as it should be. . . .
>
> For to-day, women make war for themselves; as a rule for themselves and other women, less often for themselves alone.

These in our book followed husbands and lovers—for love, so
they say. (x–xii)

Dowie's attitude toward "the female soldier" is perplexing. By seeing
them humorously, she undermines their bravery and accomplish-
ments. Yet there is also a nostalgic tone to her pronouncement of
their decease, as she misses the colorfulness of these historic women
when she compares them to the stricter, more narrowly active
women of her own era. The New Woman types to which she juxta-
poses her adventurers are denied their "qualities," and an opposition
is established between, on the one hand, feminine bonding and feminist activity and goals—which may be symbolically and/or realisti-
cally militant—and, on the other, Dowie's sense of the only proper
type of female martial activity—that done for love of men. It is clearly
her rejection of homosocial bonding, and of the unspoken alternative
of lesbian love as a contemporary motivation for other forms of female militarism, that attracted Havelock Ellis and John Addington
Symonds to Dowie's text as an affirmation that cross-dressing and
homosexuality were not necessarily mutually inclusive (*Sexual Inversion* 94).[4]

   This literary/historical reference within a medical/psychoanalytic
text illustrates the distinction between Renaissance and fin de siècle
considerations of androgyny and cross-dressing. As the Greenblatt
essay shows, there are remarkable correlations between the independent depictions of the phenomenon in medical/legal and literary writings of the Renaissance. But by the time of *Women Adventurers*, medi-
cal/psychoanalytic researchers were aware of literary parallels to their
studies, and creative writers seem also to have become familiar with
the scientific literature, resulting in a closer connection between the
genres. Greenblatt's argument, that "a culture's sexual discourse
plays a critical role in shaping individuality" (34), may therefore be
even more compelling for this time, for the discourse is now better
integrated: writers such as Shaw have close political and personal
connections with psychologists and theorists such as Ellis and Edward Carpenter, and the possibility of each informing and influencing the other's work becomes even more probable.

   Ellis, Carpenter, and Shaw all belonged to the Fabian Society in its
early years. Shaw contributed the essay "Illusions of Socialism" to

Carpenter's volume *Forecasts of the Coming Century* (1897) (*Collected Letters* 1:637), and both had essays in the collection *Hand and Brain* published by the Royscroft Shop in America.

Ellis had asked Shaw to contribute a volume on rent and value for his Contemporary Science series, although financial disagreements and other commitments precluded Shaw's fulfillment of the request (*Collected Letters* 1:190, 201; Grosskurth 115). Ellis had attended Eleanor Marx's private performance of *A Doll's House* in 1885, in which Shaw played Krogstad, and both became early champions of Ibsen—Shaw writing his *The Quintessence of Ibsenism,* while Ellis wrote a preface to the first cheap edition of Ibsen in English (Grosskurth 109–10). Many years later, Ellis and Shaw, like other Fabians, pursued a growing interest in eugenics, and both men published and lectured on the topic (Grosskurth 410–12).

Ellis and Carpenter also wrote extensively on sexuality, particularly the phenomenon of "sexual inversion," the designation given to those individuals who were either homosexual or who exhibited characteristics associated with their sexual opposite. Shaw knew these writings, and knew their personal connections to their authors, for Carpenter was homosexual, as was Ellis's wife. Shaw believed in Carpenter's and Ellis's authorial freedom to publish theoretical works on the subject; in 1898 he sent a letter to Henry Seymour and joined the Free Press Defence Committee, a group organized to support George Bedborough, who was on trial for selling Ellis's *Sexual Inversion* (Grosskurth 194–96; *Collected Letters* 2:57–58).

Almost ten years earlier, Shaw had advocated the repeal of the law prohibiting homosexual contact between consenting male adults:

I appeal now to the champions of individual rights—to Mr Herbert Spencer, Mr Auberon Herbert, Lord Bramwell, Mr Leonard Courtney, Mr John Morley, Mr Bradlaugh and the rest—to join me in a protest against a law by which two adult men can be sentenced to twenty years penal servitude for a private act, freely consented to and desired by both, which concerns themselves alone. There is absolutely no justification for the law except the old theological one of making the secular arm the instrument of God's vengeance. (*Collected Letters* 1:231)

But by 1909, fourteen years after the 1895 Wilde conviction, Shaw seems to have changed his mind about advocacy in this matter. In a letter to Louis Wilkinson about these efforts, Shaw remarks:

No movement could survive association with such a propaganda. I can sympathize with E[dward] C[arpenter]'s efforts to make people understand that the curious reversal in question is a natural accident, and that it is absurd to persecute it or connect any general moral deficiency with it. . . . [A]bnormal people . . . are unable to conceive how frightfully disagreeable—how abominable, in fact—it is to the normal, even to the normal who are abnormally susceptible to natural impulses. (*Collected Letters* 2:890)

Shaw makes a clear distinction between public support of freedom of the press—including literature with homosexual content—and his private attitude toward homosexuality. In a letter to the Dean of Windsor, who along with Shaw and other prominent cultural figures signed a statement in support of the publication of Radclyffe Hall's *The Well of Loneliness*, Shaw expresses this forthrightly:

The letter we sent to the papers was drafted by me very carefully so as to keep us completely off the ground of any sympathy with the propaganda of homosexualism (I write *ism* advisedly) which goes on, and not to commit us even on the point of the book's appeal for the humane consideration of inversion as a natural misfortune. It might have been signed by persons who had not read the book, and did not know nor care what it was about.

We had better leave it at that. It would be impossible to go further without involving ourselves and one another in the discussion we have evaded. We are in the difficulty that the least expression of emotional abhorrence contributes to the morbid atmosphere in which all sexual aberrations flourish and make their practitioners feel heroic, whilst anything less than that—unless at volume length on the Havelock Ellis scale—is interpreted as sympathetic. (*Collected Letters* 4:118)

Shaw's stated distaste for the practice of homosexuality was equally forceful. In an essay on Oscar Wilde, Shaw expresses his "disgust at 'the man Wilde,'" noting that his behavior "represented a real degeneracy produced by his debaucheries." Shaw adds, "I have all the normal violent repugnance to homosexuality—if it be really normal, which nowadays one is sometimes provoked to doubt" (*Pen Portraits* 302–3). Shaw had learned at an early age of his Uncle Walter's horror at the rampant homosexuality in the English public schools (*Sixteen Self Sketches* 31–32), and carried this abhorrence with him thereafter. He made a point of declaring that neither his vegetarianism nor his abstinence from alcohol was an indication of effeminacy (Holroyd *Search For Love* 87, 90), and he also assured his biographer Frank Harris of his sexuality:

If you have any doubts as to my normal virility, dismiss them from your mind. I was not impotent; I was not sterile; I was not homosexual; and I was extremely susceptible, though not promiscuously. (*Sixteen Self Sketches* 175)

Shaw was aware of the homosexuality of Carpenter and their mutual friend Kate Salt, and could not condone it in either.[5] In his preface to Stephen Winsten's book on Henry Salt, Shaw states:

Kate (Mrs. Salt) loved me as far as she could love any male creature. . . . She was a queer hybrid. I never met anyone in the least like her, though another friend of mine . . . Stewart Headlam, also had a wife who was a homo. (9)

In a 1939 letter to Salt's second wife, Catherine Mandeville, Shaw said Henry initially "was married to a queer wife who fell in love with every woman who was kind to her" (*Collected Letters* 4:529). Shaw's most telling comments on Kate Salt come in a 1932 letter to his friend Nancy Astor, whose son had been briefly imprisoned for homosexual activity. This note reveals Shaw's ultimate understanding of homosexuality—comprehension that came late in life, after the composition of most of the writing considered here. Yet it also shows a lingering resistance to homosexual identity and practice, and the perpetuation of certain Victorian notions of the excesses and perversions associated with that sexual orientation. Shaw maintains his prescription of work was integral to Kate's recovery from a near nervous breakdown, although he admits Carpenter's aid in Kate's realization of her true identity and the nature of her "illness."

> At last she [Kate] was troubled and on the verge of a nervous breakdown, and couldnt tell why. I told her to go and get a job in a factory, as factory girls cannot afford nerves and havn't time for them; and to my astonishment and dismay she took me at my word and went and did it. The result was excellent, though of course, being a lady, she very soon got pushed up into literate and managing work.
>
> But she also found salvation by learning what was really the matter with her. I presume that it was Carpenter who enlightened her: anyhow she told me with great exultation one day that she had discovered the existence of the Urnings; that she was herself an Urning; and that she was very proud of it and understood everything that had puzzled and worried her before. And so she dropped the factory and sublimated her desires into harmless raptures about music and poetry and platonic adorations of Carpenter and of me and of all the nice people she came across.
>
> This gave me a serious and humane view of the subject. It was clear that Carpenter, understanding his condition scientifically and poetically, was not degraded by it. It was equally clear that the lady, when he enlightened her, at once passed from a state of mind that threatened her reason and destroyed her happiness to ease of mind and a new and respectful interest in herself. Neither of them were in the least danger of falling into the debauchery which is a possibility of their condition exactly as it is a possibility of the normal condition. (*Collected Letters* 4:285)[6]

Shaw knew another lesbian, the wife of his friend Sydney Olivier. In an 1898 letter to Charlotte, Shaw explains

> [Olivier] requests five minutes private conversation with me. In this we settle, as between man & man, that the romantic

arrangements made by Mrs Salt & Mrs Olivier are not to be carried out, though appearances are to be kept up so as to secure us against all suspicion of being too conventional to be worthy of the New Age & the New Light. Thus are women deceived: thus do men stand by one another in the war of the sexes. (*Collected Letters* 2:17)

Although there is clearly a certain irony of tone here, the harshness of the designation "homo" and "queer" for Kate Salt and "degeneracy" for Wilde, coupled with the patriarchal homosociality of the male bond against lesbian sexuality, point to a homophobic attitude in Shaw, one that conflicts with his public egalitarianism on matters of sexuality. In the same letter to Nancy Astor quoted above, he reflects on this earlier stance:

When I was young and ignorant I had the usual thoughtless horror of it; for though I had absolutely no scruples or reticences where women were concerned, any sort of sexual relation within my own gender was repugnant and impossible: in fact I never thought of such a thing and did not want to hear about it. (*Collected Letters* 4:284)

Shaw's conflicting feelings about lesbian sexuality appear in scenes of violence and/or conflict between women tinged with sexual aggression. He never makes these relations overt; indeed, he buries them in heterosexual contexts, masking lesbianism as he no doubt saw it, and wanted it to be, suppressed by women such as Kate Salt.[7]

As Carpenter (*The Intermediate Sex*) and Ellis and Symonds (*Sexual Inversion*) make clear, the designation *inversion* comprises a wide range of social and sexual behavior. Ellis and Symonds in particular stress that appearances of inversion do not necessarily imply homosexuality:

a "mannish" woman . . . may imitate men on grounds of taste and habit unconnected with sexual perversion, while in the inverted woman the masculine traits are part of an organic instinct which she by no means always wishes to accentuate. (87–88)

The opening of Carpenter's study merits quoting at length, for it captures the climate of advanced thinking about gender, and its final sentence has particular relevance to Shaw's self-conception:

> In late years (and since the arrival of the New Woman amongst us) many things in the relation of men and women to each other have altered, or at any rate become clearer. The growing sense of equality in habits and customs . . . have brought about a *rapprochement* between the sexes. If the modern woman is a little more masculine in some ways than her predecessor, the modern man (it is to be hoped), while by no means effeminate, is a little more sensitive in temperament and artistic in feeling. . . . It is beginning to be recognised that the sexes do not or should not normally form two groups hopelessly isolated in habit and feeling from each other, but that they rather represent the two poles of *one* group—which is the human race; so that while certainly the extreme specimens at either pole are vastly divergent, there are great numbers in the middle region who (though differing corporeally as men and women) are by emotion and temperament very near to each other. . . . Nature, it might appear, in mixing the elements which go to compose each individual, does not always keep her two groups of ingredients— which represent the two sexes—properly apart . . . if a severe distinction of elements were always maintained the two sexes would soon drift into far latitudes and absolutely cease to understand each other. As it is, there are some remarkable and (we think) indispensable types of character in whom there is such a union or balance of the feminine and masculine qualities that these people become to a great extent the interpreters of men and women to each other. (189–90)

In later writing on the same topic, Ellis similarly maintains that the presence of feminine traits in men or masculine traits in women "by no means necessarily indicates the existence of sexual inversion. . . . genius in either sex frequently involves the coexistence of masculine, feminine, and infantile traits" (*Studies* 196).

Ellis's notion of "genius" coincides with the Coleridgean dictum that a great mind must be androgynous (J. Watson 44):

The man who most completely contains the feminine principle
and the woman who most completely contains the masculine
principle—while at the same time being the gender that he or
she is—is the individual within whom the power of life is most
intense. (J. Watson 40–41)

Carpenter's idea that individuals with this balance often become "interpreters of men and women to each other" corresponds to these
other two statements, and can be taken as a theoretical confirmation
for Shaw's understanding of his success at drawing characters different from himself.

One intriguing element of the discourse of gender in the Victorian
and Edwardian eras is the uniform assumption, on the part of the
theorists, of the stability and universally shared understanding of the
connotations of "masculine" and "feminine." Ellis, Carpenter, and
others use the terms as shorthand, as codes standing in for a catalogue of polar distinctions which, for them, comprise in the aggregate
gender identity.

In her discussion of androgyny, Carolyn Heilbrun comments on
the longevity of these assumptions:

If we are still, in our definition of sexual roles, the heirs of
the Victorian age, we must also recognize that our definitions
of the terms "masculine" and "feminine" are themselves little
more than unexamined, received ideas. According to the conventional view, "masculine" equals forceful, competent, com-
petitive, controlling, vigorous, unsentimental, and occasionally
violent; "feminine" equals tender, genteel, intuitive rather than
rational, passive, unaggressive, readily given to submission.
The "masculine" individual is popularly seen as a maker, the
"feminine" as a nourisher. (xiv)

Heilbrun's sense of the ongoing impact of the Victorian conception
of gender is well supported by the work of Dr. Beatrice M. Hinkle,
who published the essay "On the Arbitrary Use of the Terms 'Masculine' and 'Feminine' " in *The Psychoanalytic Review* in 1920:

Masculine immediately brings the collective picture of strength,
aggressiveness, courage, a fighting, dominating, conquering

figure, sexually polygamous, with vigourous action in both the physical and intellectual spheres. The creative, constructive, adventurous, independent human being is, of course, the male.

Obversely, the feminine characteristics are presumed to be passivity, submissiveness, timidity, weakness, emotionalism, with instability and perverseness as the most dominant traits; gentleness, sweetness, spirituality, chastity as her great virtue; in short, all the qualities with which we associate infantilism, which is another word for the ideal feminine character. (18)

Shaw clearly understood these culturally shared notions of gender, invoking them from such early essays as *The Quintessence of Ibsenism* forward. In both dramatic and nondramatic writings dealing with gender identity, Shaw depends on this common understanding, working against the assumptions about gender in creating "unwomanly" women or "unmanly" men. Furthermore, Shaw assumes shared knowledge of the larger cultural implications of this coding, the "separate spheres" that distinguish forms of social activity by these same gender markers, as, for example, military duty for men and domestic labor for women. Vocations and avocations thus become gendered as well, and Shaw counts on audience familiarity with all these codes for the recognition and comprehension of those characters who defy them.

Independent of the scientific writings, Shaw had constructed a theory of human similarity, developed from his culture's sense of gender codes. Rather than identify the feminine and masculine elements dominant in any individual, Shaw propounds an essential likeness among all people. He expresses an early version of his notion of shared human traits in a letter to his first (platonic) lover, Alice Lockett:

If you tell a human being, male or female, that he or she has more in common with the most antipathetic other human being on earth of the same age, than he (or she) can possibly have that is unique, you will offend them. Nevertheless, this is so. The reason I know so much about you (and about everybody else) is that at least nine tenths of me is a simple repetition of nine tenths of you. (*Collected Letters* 1:158)

And to Florence Farr, he voices a sensibility close to the Platonic concept of androgyny, calling her "my other self—no, not my other self, but my very self" (*Collected Letters* 1:296).

In Plato's *Symposium*, Aristophanes presents his lesson on the nature of man and his development:

> In the first place, there were three kinds of human beings, not merely the two sexes, male and female, as at present: there was a third kind as well, which had equal shares of the other two and whose name survives though the thing itself has vanished. For "man-woman" was then a unity in form no less than name, composed of both sexes and sharing equally in male and female. (135)

Some Shaw critics do not see him in the same light in which he presents himself in his letter to Lockett. Warren Sylvester Smith contends he "needed the feminine response to complement his own masculine assertiveness" (221), suggesting an absence of feminine components in Shaw. Arthur Ganz theorizes that Shaw was unconsciously attracted to such myths as "Pygmalion and Galatea" because they reveal male fear of feminine difference (184–85). If this is indeed the case, then Shaw may have constructed his notion of human similarity to efface difference—to eliminate the threat of the Other and present women in a fashion in which they can be understood by him, that is, as men. His most striking statement of an androgynous nature comes in his essay "Woman—Man in Petticoats":

> People are still full of the old idea that woman is a special creation. I am bound to say that of late years she has been working extremely hard to eradicate that impression, and make one understand that *a woman is really only a man in petticoats*, or if you like, that *a man is a woman without petticoats*. People sometimes wonder what is the secret of the extraordinary knowledge of women which I shew in my plays. They very often accuse me of having acquired it by living a most abandoned life. But I never acquired it. *I have always assumed that a woman is a person exactly like myself,* and that is how the trick is done. (*Platform and Pulpit* 174; my emphasis)[8]

This quotation merits close analysis for several reasons. First, Shaw attributes the source of this sexual distinction to women: *"she has been working extremely hard to . . . make one understand."* But his transcription may, or may not, accurately record the sense these unnamed women have of the differences and/or similarities between themselves and men. Shaw's version of the equation neatly coincides with his own sense of sexual identity, however. Essentially, if one puts petticoats on a man one gets a woman; or, conversely, if one takes the petticoats off a woman, one has a man. In either case, the fundamental identity is male, which corresponds to Shaw's sense that a woman is a person like himself, albeit with the addition of petticoats, that is, with certain external, unimportant distinctions. William Archer once called Vivie Warren nothing " 'but a Shaw in petticoats' " (quoted in Holroyd *Search For Love* 266), perhaps giving Shaw the idea for this conceit.

Several years before this essay appeared, Shaw had published an article ostensibly on the recent history of female dress and behavior (but of course equally reflective of Shaw and his views) entitled "Woman Since 1860 as a Wise Man Sees Her."[9] The humorous condescension of the title notwithstanding, the piece sheds light not only on the better known talk quoted above, but on the complex issue of Shaw's sense of gender identity. Shaw opens his analysis with reflections on his youth, and then proceeds to establish the crucial sartorial connections between himself and women:

> I was born in the year 1856. Shortly after this I became conscious of women as immense mounds of flounced dress fabric with waists at the top of the mounds, and above the waists *figures more or less like men,* but with ampler bosoms. . . . *I was dressed like a woman myself,* as boys were not then distinguished from girls in dress in their early years. I wore a frock, under the frock a white petticoat, under the white petticoat a flannel petticoat, under the flannel petticoat a pair of loose white drawers and stays, which were no more than a thick ribbed shirtwaist; under the drawers a chemise, also called a shift or shimmy, and under the chemise my unshiftable skin.
>
> *And all this a grownup woman wore also,* with . . . the difference that her frock came down to the ground and concealed the fact . . . *that she had legs and used them just like a man. . . .*

It must not be inferred that because I wore stays as part of *my feminine costume,* women's stays were necessarily like mine. (10; my emphasis)

Although the tone of this narrative maintains a certain intentional naïveté, its repeated emphasis on dress, age, and gender identity is striking. Dressed like a woman, Shaw realizes at an early age the essential similarities and observable differences between himself and the opposite sex. He perceives the association of adult women with children of both sexes in the Victorian era, but also needs to align himself with the male sex that he embodies by observing his appearance as similar to the Other's, but not indistinguishable from it. Thus his later statement concerning the interchangeability of men and women with or without petticoats seems a synthesis of these childhood observations.

In this same 1920 article Shaw also alludes to feminine dress reform, and clearly prefers the sensible attire that became fashionable for women after the necessities of the war:

In the nineties, when the bicycle became fashionable and practicable for women, an attempt was made to discard skirts. It failed for a very obvious reason which nevertheless nobody seemed to see. When a woman borrowed her husband's or brother's Norfolk jacket and breeches, and they fitted her reasonably well, she looked perfectly correct, natural, and often very smart.

Unfortunately, she seldom did this. . . . Not until the war came did women in attire bifurcated with masculine frankness and unconsciousness become familiar objects throughout the country. (11)

Shaw does not fully explain the "very obvious reason" why earlier attempts at dress reform failed, but he seems to hold women responsible for their own vain unwillingness to adopt the sensible male attire they finally sported during and after the war. The article contains no suggestion that patriarchal opposition to women's appearing in male attire—until political conflict necessitated it—lay at least in part behind their reticence to don men's more practical designs. Shaw does not mention here that he held a contradictory view as far as his own wife was concerned:

> I remember when we went to the first Fabian Summer School she was dressed in a very masculine costume, tailor-made, with a stiff white collar; and I said, not to her but to the assembled gathering, how much I disliked the way women had of dressing like men: it detracted from their charm and made them look ridiculous. That evening she appeared in a lovely dress with a low-cut chiffon bodice, through which her skin showed very attractively, and she never reverted to the masculine garb again. (quoted in B. Watson *Shavian Guide* 23)

These comments reveal Shaw's predilection for only a certain variant of masculine style in female clothing, which is reflected in his descriptions of characters like Sylvia Craven *(The Philanderer)*, who wears breeches she can cover with a skirt, as well as the connection he establishes between female cross-dressing and political change within patriarchal society. In other words, Shaw's version of women's sartorial history here views change as solely male-determined: women only appropriated male attire when it became socially propitious to do so, not as a statement of their own independence or autonomy, which was of course the historical reality.

This sensibility carries over to the latter portion of "Woman Since 1860," in which Shaw discusses the behavioral changes he has observed. He opens this section with the statement: "Masculine affectations were always a mistake" (11), and goes on to group the female followers of John Stuart Mill and Henry Fawcett as "mannish above the waist whilst remaining quakerish below it" (11)—an interestingly hermaphroditic image of a creature half male and half female. Not only does this description echo his initial remarks on the relative similarity of men and women above the waist, it creates an interesting opposition between the masculine display of "waistcoats and shirtfronts and watch chains" above the waist and the feminine neatness or simplicity—or perhaps even sexual frigidity ("quakerish")—below. More important, this focus on masculine dress and gender detracts from the political significance of the garb's selection by women who wear it as part of their way of life, which includes protest against unfair marriage laws and advocacy of professional and educational reform for women. Shaw concludes this section with an acknowledgment of the onset of the women's rights movement: "Still, it was inevitable that the movement should begin with women insisting on doing everything that men did" (11).

He continues with what he feels is a better alternative for the self-assertion of women:

> It was clear to me that what women had to do was not to repudiate their femininity, but to assert its social value: not to ape masculinity, but to demonstrate its insufficiency. That was the point of my play *Candida* (1895), in which it is made quite plain that the husband's masculine career would go to pieces without the wife's feminine activity. (11)

Shaw does not explain what "the social value" of femininity is, but what does become clear here is his avowal of the patriarchal thematics of "women's spheres," where the woman exerts influence in the domestic space that is her realm, as opposed to the masculine public "career." In *Candida* we do indeed see masculine "insufficiency," but Candida reveals this within the home, in private, so that her "feminine activity," running the household, remains the secret shared by only Marchbanks, Candida, and her husband. The world at large never learns the woman's superior strength and ability; the play is the perfect demonstration of what the women's movement sought to expose. And as Shaw knew, the bevy of "Candidamaniacs" who did not see the play in any way as an exposure of Victorian hypocrisy, but rather as the story of an ideal woman keeping the secret every woman should keep, outnumbered by far those who may have interpreted the play differently. Furthermore, this statement of Shaw's, which points to his own work as a "solution" to the issue of women's appropriation of male appearance and behavior, implicates him in the debate in a very contradictory way.

His depiction of the suffragettes suffers from a similar interest in shaping women's history to fit his own purposes. According to Shaw, these women "obliterated the would-be manly woman" and "insisted on their womanliness" (11). The outcome of their efforts was, for Shaw, a "great increase in companionship between men and women during that period." This in turn led to an androgynous blending of gender attributes, as women became "roughened" by male influence, men "refined" by women's: "The feminine refinement, which was only silliness disguised by affectation, has gone; and women are hardier and healthier, and the stock size of their clothes are [sic] larger in consequence" (11). Shaw neatly conflates biology with the social construction of gender here, implying that women's loss of refinement has had a physiological impact, making them healthier and bigger. In part, he may be right, simply in that the change in fashions led to a letting out of the formerly popular cinched waists, resulting in both larger sizes and less fainting. But he does not suggest this is the result of change in costume alone; in fact, his preceding point about the suffragettes' return to "womanliness" would directly contradict such an argument, as he thought popular fashion returned to a more feminine trend.

Shaw's distinctive blending of biology with social philosophy continues with his analysis of the feminists' opposition to maternity:

> There is . . . *a rebellion against nature* in the matter of the very unequal share of the burden of reproduction which falls to men and women in civilized communities. . . . But I can testify that among the women brought up amid the feminist movement of the second half of the nineteenth century, there was a *revolt* against maternity which went deeper than that revolt against excessive maternity which has led to birth control. . . . I suggest that when a woman is found in complete revolt against maternity, *the proper treatment for her apparent mania* is not to revile her as a monster, but to explain to her *that her instinctive antipathy* is a creditable movement toward an end that will one day be reached, though it cannot relieve her from the necessity for making the best of the existing provisional arrangements. (11, 27; my emphasis)

Shaw uses a medical rubric here, as if the conscious, political choice (indicated by the term "revolt") that some women made not to have children should be categorized as a biological problem, their "instinctive antipathy" to their "natural" role and responsibility as childbearers. He proposes "treatment"; not only in the medical sense, however, as the foregoing argument might imply, but also in the sense of consideration. The "end" that he foresees is ambiguous, though, for it is uncertain whether he is thinking of the biological state of menopause, or his own eschatological, more politically and philosophically utopian world in *Back to Methuselah*, where children are hatched full-grown from eggs, freeing the Ancients from the responsibility to perpetuate the race. Regardless of the interpretation, it is clear that Shaw associates feminism and the mixing of gender attributes with the rise in antipathy to maternity, which, although not condemned here outright, does conflict with his own philosophy of the Life Force, the energy that controls the actions of most Shavian women, including those who display masculine qualities.

Shaw closes his article where he began it, with comments on his birth, origins, and beliefs, mixed with a final view and interpretation of the changes he has seen over sixty years:

> And now I shall be asked whether I have anything to say about Woman in Thought, in Art, in Shakespeare, in the Musical Glasses, and in the glow of her soul. Have I noticed nothing but the position of her stays, the shape of her boots, and the fashion of her dress? *I reply, nothing whatever except the changes that have come to the race without distinction of sex. [If there has been a specifically feminine change of soul, I, being masculine, cannot know anything about it; for I am too old to have inherited a share of it from my mother; besides, if it could be inherited by a male, it would not be specifically feminine.]* I do not regard women as animals of another species. I have no difficulty, as a playwright, in making female *dramatis personae* as easily as male ones; and I conclude that *I could not do this if I had not a first-hand knowledge of both, being my mother's son as much as my father's.* The sexes wear different boots and bonnets, not different souls; that is why I have left the soul out, and concentrated on the boots and bonnets. (27; my emphasis)[10]

This concluding paragraph reveals a number of intriguing ideas. Here as elsewhere, Shaw confirms his belief in an essentially identical humanity, that men and women do not have sexually differentiated "souls," only external distinctions. Yet at the same time he asserts this view, he admits the possibility of a feminine soul he cannot know because, being male, he essentially rejects it. There is the tantalizing possibility that at a younger age, he might have understood this feminine essence through maternal inheritance[11] (again, the biological construct at work in a nonscientific context), but that his old age now precludes this potential.[12] This statement continues the theme of Victorian childhood with which he opened the article; Shaw's masculine maturation has been a process of loss of the feminine identity he had as a child. But he maintains he still holds the ability to draw male and female characters equally well, as he has inherited a sensitivity to both sexes as the biological product of each. The only way that Shaw can resolve this contradiction is to deny inherent sexual difference.

The suggestion that a feminine-identified youth matures to masculinity will be discussed in part 3. For purposes of the examination of Shavian androgyny, this chapter highlights his concerns with the nature of gender identity, and particularly its relation to the pressing biological issue of reproduction. The problem of the feminist woman who may also be associated with mannishness, and/or the rejection of maternity, combines his interest in expressions of androgyny with his belief in the Life Force—essentially an exclusively heterosexual philosophy.

Catharine R. Stimpson makes a crucial distinction between the homosexual and the androgyne—a distinction that may account for Shaw's ability to characterize the latter, while feeling great discomfort with the former:

> The androgyne is nothing more, or less, than an idea. . . . The androgyne . . . may reject the patriarchy, but not heterosexuality, home, and babies. It gives itself permission to think that biological men, even if they have both feminine and masculine traits, and biological women, even if they have both feminine and masculine traits, will continue to sleep together, have children, and marry. (242)

A. J. L. Busst, in "The Image of the Androgyne in the Nineteenth Century," notes that the fictional and artistic depiction of androgyny was particularly evident in the fin de siècle, and quotes from the novelist and critic Péladan, who had observed an androgynous theme in Wagner's version of the Tristan and Isolde story (57). Shaw also seems to have perceived this Wagnerian motif, and he chooses to quote Wagner's affirmation of heterosexual love as well as his androgynous sensibility in The Perfect Wagnerite:

Love in its most perfect reality . . . is only possible between the sexes; it is only as man and woman that human beings can truly love. . . . Now a human being is both *man* and *woman:* it is only when these two are united that the real human being exists; and thus it is only by love that man and woman attain to the full measure of humanity. (278–79)

Shaw sees in these Wagnerian expressions not only a confirmation of the desirability of heterosexual union, but also the elucidation of the Platonic notion of the ideal human coming from the reunion of the male and female principles that were separated in the mythic past—a conjunction now only possible through (sexual) love.

Péladan also identified a "*'troisième sexe,'* the category of the androgyne . . . whose souls are of a different sex from their bodies" (Busst 57). Krafft-Ebing, Freud, and Ellis had all isolated this figure, and associated it "with female lust and with feminist revolt against traditional roles" (Newton 18). Shaw finds his own revolutionary example of "the third sex" in the artist Marie Bashkirtseff, the publication of whose diary caused a sensation in England in 1890.

In an essay from *The Quintessence of Ibsenism*, "The Womanly Woman," Shaw refers to an article on the diary that appeared in the *Review of Reviews* in June 1890. The article intersperses excerpts from the diary with comments by editor William Stead that reveal why Shaw identified Bashkirtseff with the individuals who had been labeled inverted. Stead comments:

If Mdlle. [*sic*] Marie be the genuine revelation of the ultimate product of the women of femininity in the nineteenth century, the cynical opponents of woman's rights would have much to say for themselves. For Marie Bashkirtseff, although a genius, is as wayward as fitful, as passionate, as imperious, as vain, and, withal, as indifferent as any coquette of any age. *"It is only the envelope of me that is feminine, deucedly feminine,"* she says, and the envelope does not go deep down. Of the distinctively womanly there is in her but little trace. (*Review of Reviews* 544; my emphasis)

Stead later quotes these additionally telling passages from Marie's diary:

As a man, I should have conquered Europe. Young girl as I was, I wasted it in excesses of language and silly eccentricities. . . .

Curse it all; it is this that makes me gnash my teeth to think I am a woman! I'll get myself a *bourgeois* dress and a wig, and make myself so ugly that I shall be as free as a man. It is this sort of liberty I need, and without it I can never hope to do anything of note. (548)

Bashkirtseff, who seems to have been quite selfish and self-assured, stands out for Shaw as a model of opposition to the prevalent view of the womanly woman in her procreative, domestic sphere:

Hence arises the idealist illusion that a vocation for domestic management and the care of children is natural to women, and that women who lack them are not women at all, but members of *the third, or Bashkirtseff sex.* Even if this were true, it is obvious that if the Bashkirtseffs are to be allowed to live, they have a right to suitable institutions just as much as men and women. (*Quintessence* 60; my emphasis)

Stead's description of Bashkirtseff markedly resembles that of many of Shaw's strong women, whose outward femininity belies a hard, aggressive core. Shaw clearly values these traits in a woman, yet he seems to have fictionalized Bashkirtseff and turned her into a symbol that he provocatively manipulates. Through the designation "the third . . . sex," Shaw makes the identification of Bashkirtseff with those women scientific theorists of the time had labeled as inverted. Clearly, Marie's frustration with her feminine appearance and desire for masculine freedom suggested this linkage, and the categorization resonates with late Victorian concerns surrounding the matrix of inversion, homosexuality, and female aversion to childbearing. According to George Chauncey, doctors at this time "attributed the supposed increase in inversion to the repudiation of motherhood by women influenced by feminism" (141). Shaw's commentary also hints at the homophobic hysteria of the period, with the exterminationist phrase, "if the Bashkirtseffs are to be allowed to live." Although Shaw does not embrace this kind of homophobia, the passage indicates a sensitivity to the sentiment in his society.

Shaw also uses Bashkirtseff in comparison with male behavior, as noted in the discussion of *The Philanderer* above:

No man pretends that his soul finds its supreme satisfaction in self-sacrifice: such an affectation would stamp him as coward and weakling: the manly man is he who takes the Bashkirtseff view of himself. (*Quintessence* 56)

Although this construction appears distinctive for its positive depiction of a male via association with a female (rather than the usual positive comparison of female with male), it must be considered within the Shavian context of (un)manly and (un)womanly behavior. The womanly woman, given to self-sacrifice, is condemned by Shaw, while he lauds selfishness for men and women, as in his didactic epistolary work *My Dear Dorothea*.

Thus Bashkirtseff stands for both the unwomanliness associated with sexual inversion and the masculinity of a "real" man. She positively embodies a male essence at the same time her masculine identification makes her a threatening image of female inversion. The contradictory messages Shaw sends in conjunction with this figure reveal a tension between the desirability of an androgynous identity—female exterior, male sensibility—for women, and the homophobia connected with the image of "the third sex." The heterosexuality of Bashkirtseff, attested to in the *Review*, makes her a safe model for Shaw, however. She becomes an attractive figure because she can be discussed in the *language* of inversion without the threat of its homosexual behavior, just as Shaw's contemporary Ellis spotlights reassuring examples of female heterosexual cross-dressing.

Shaw projects his own Bashkirtseff view of selfishness onto many of his female characters, creating a person "like [him]self," an androgynous woman whose center would ideally be male. Shaw's attraction to Bashkirtseff, and the interesting contradictions in his textual treatment of her, correspond to the dramatic characterization of Shaw's androgynous women, who embody the tension between feminine sexuality and traits associated with inversion. The heterosexual paradigm demanded by the Life Force dramatically overpowers the homosexual association with "intermediacy," however; Shaw neutralizes the sexual activity or desirability of female characters in whom masculinity and the rejection of maternity appears dominant, as in *Saint Joan* and *Back to Methuselah*, so that sexual orientation is never the explanation for, nor associated with, traces of inversion.

The male basis on which Shaw builds female characters may be at the center of much criticism of Shaw's women. As Toni Block succinctly states, "We have all heard the old complaint that Shaw could not create a woman in any of his plays without making that woman a female Bernard Shaw" (133). In a letter to Max Beerbohm that links Rosalind to the principal boy tradition, Shaw attacks the critic for making some version of Block's "complaint":

> Years ago Stead said eloquently of Marie Bashkirtseff "A woman she was NOT." You laughed; but you are now explaining my creations away in the same fashion. In vain do I give you a whole gallery of perfectly miraculous life studies. (*Collected Letters* 2:373)

The connection of the attack on Shaw's female characters with the figure of Bashkirtseff confirms the nature of the problem. Shaw's assumption of a male center, as he feels Marie has, for his strong women makes them for him "perfectly miraculous life studies" which conform to his theory of essentially unisexual humanity. His critics, who may not share this view, simply cannot see these characters as Shaw does.

The next two chapters explore the range of Shaw characters and plays featuring androgyny. The Shakespearean model of the cross-dressed woman appears in Shaw's revision of *Cymbeline*, variants of the pantomime principal boy inhabit a number of his one-acts and lesser known works, and his depiction of the (female) androgyne enlivens such pieces as *Misalliance* and *Saint Joan*. In addition, some of Shaw's eschatological dramas such as *Back to Methuselah* echo depictions of androgyny found in mythic and religious texts, and these same sources may inform other isolated instances of androgynous characterizations, such as the twins Dolly and Phil in *You Never Can Tell*.

5

Shakes vs. Shav: *Cross-Dressing in*
Cymbeline Refinished *and*
the Pantomime Tradition

Shakespearean plays featuring the woman in male disguise were winning ever greater Victorian audiences at the same time the pantomime principal boys were drawing large crowds to their theaters. Shaw's connection to the last Shakespearean work to feature this motif—the late romance *Cymbeline*—dates at least to 1896, when he corresponded at length with Ellen Terry about her performance as Imogen, the heroine who disguises herself as the boy Fidele. During this period Shaw served as theater critic for the *Saturday Review* and attended all sorts of stage entertainments, including the pantomime. Judging from the frequency with which he incorporated cross-dressed female characters in his plays, one can assume this popular figure made a strong impression on Shaw. His dramatization of female characters wearing male attire shows great consistency across a span of fifty years, indicating that his view of cross-dressed women, formed in his youth, remained constant over time. He clearly associated them with the questions of gender identity and female appropriation of male authority that also concerned Victorian and later audiences.

Ironically, however, Shaw chose not to discuss the phenomena of women cross-dressing on stage or the figure of the principal boy in anything other than passing remarks. Shaw, usually so vocal about actresses, is peculiarly quiet about the distinctive presence of women in these forms of entertainment. Yet the consistent presence of cross-dressed female characters in his work necessitates the examination of this silence, as well as the history of the principal boy figure and its variants in his work.

One rare comment shows Shaw's clear appreciation of the connection between the Shakespearean tradition and the performances of his own day. In a letter to Max Beerbohm, he accuses the critic of believing "Rosalind the pantomime 'leading boy' is a real woman" (*Collected Letters* 2:373). Michael Holroyd recounts Shaw's early contact with the stage, but discusses his attendance at only one of the two major Dublin theaters, the Theatre Royal, home of "serious pantomime, farces, and melodramas" (*Search For Love* 56). Holroyd focuses on the impact on Shaw of such actors as Barry Sullivan, who specialized in Shakespearean heroes, and does not discuss the importance of any other performers or performance genres to the playwright. Martin Meisel, in his study of the dramatic antecedents of and influences on Shaw, includes a discussion of pantomime, burlesque, and related theatricals, but notes that Shaw claimed to have spent little time during his youth at Dublin's other important theater, the Queen's Theatre, the house for more popular entertainment. Although Meisel remarks that Shaw "remembered [the theatre], not quite accurately" (15), he does not overtly question Shaw's dismissal of this theater and its potential influence. He does, however, observe that during Shaw's young adulthood in Dublin, another new theater, the Gaiety, featured a visit by Mrs. John Wood and her company from London, which specialized in an alternating repertory of legitimate drama and burlesque (15–16). Meisel later describes burlesque and pantomime and their influence on *Androcles and the Lion*. In this section Meisel refers specifically to the work of Planché, the creator of numerous spectacles based on fairy tales and/or fables that prominently featured principal boy actresses (384–88).

Kathy Fletcher, in her study of Planché and Madame Vestris, notes: "The form which extravaganza assumed was largely the result of a collaboration between James Robinson Planché and Madame Vestris" (10). Vestris (1797–1856), one of the foremost male imper-

Fig. 3. An illustration of Madame Vestris as Captain MacHeath in John Gay's *The Beggar's Opera* (1728), produced at London's Haymarket Theatre in 1820. Note the duplication of male attire in her costume, which, although it does not disguise the female anatomy, is neither designed to emphasize it, as was the principal boy's. This feature separates female stage transvestism from the pantomime figure.

sonators of the nineteenth century, was also an actress-manager whose career included operating London's Olympic Theatre. Her attractive figure, singing voice, and dancing abilities suited her ideally to principal boy roles; Fletcher counts "twenty-two major transvestite roles in the Planché extravaganzas" and "numerous minor roles as well" of which "Vestris created the greatest number" (24). Meisel makes no mention of Vestris or cross-dressing in relation to Shaw, although he discusses at length the way that male and female character types from the popular theater—but not the sex that performed them—appeared in Shaw's plays. He also quotes one review of a pantomime at the Theatre Royal that mentions the names of the actresses in the principal boy roles (330), but offers no commentary on this element of those productions, perhaps because *Androcles* has no cross-dressed characters, although a number of other Shaw plays do.

Finally, Margery Morgan dismisses this influence entirely: "Significantly, Shaw avoided the music hall as a model" (48). It would be more accurate to say that Shaw spoke of the music hall as a *negative* model, one that could be perceived as influential on his plays if they were acted *incorrectly*. It would appear Shaw wanted to efface the potential association of his work with this form of popular entertainment, but this negative identification and repeated denial point to the actual strong relation of Shaw's work with the female transvestism of the popular stage. In a letter to the actress portraying Lina, the androgynous character in *Misalliance*, he explains,

> I am writing to Tarleton to say that if he would work less conscientiously for a Vesta Tilley success, with you as the representative of "the girls—the Gy—erls," he would find the scene easier for himself as well as for you. (*Collected Letters* 4:181)

Vesta Tilley (1864–1952) transported the techniques of male impersonation to the vaudeville and music hall stages from their origins in breeches parts and in the pantomime, where she performed principal boy roles early in her career. The foremost male impersonator of her era, Tilley sported dapper costumes that reputedly set the tone for offstage fashions, blurring the line that originally separated actresses from female cross-dressing modernists, and even from the men who adopted Tilley's trend-setting attire.

Margery Morgan's insightful reading of Shaw incorporates much analysis of the importance of the commedia dell'arte for his work. But the source of Shaw's knowledge of the commedia goes unexamined. The filtration of these character types through Shakespeare is well documented, but the most direct lineage emerges in the popular theater. Michael Booth notes:

> Early nineteenth-century pantomime directly descended not only from the traditions of *commedia dell'arte* as they had evolved for centuries, but also from the distinctively English pantomime of the eighteenth century, an amalgam of serious scenes from classical and modern legend or fable with unrelated harlequinade episodes. (2)

In a footnote, Booth calls his readers' attention to two Shaw reviews of pantomimes, both contained in the third volume of *Our Theatres in the Nineties*, on 1 January and 9 April 1898 (53n; 55n). Interestingly, Shaw makes no mention in these pieces of the figure of the principal boy, although he does praise the performance of several actresses whose roles are unspecified. In Shaw's preface to William Archer's *Theatrical "World" of 1894*, he mentions the above-named Mrs John Wood as a "theatrical manageress" (xvi), but makes no reference to her other identity as "Queen of the Burlesque" (Meisel 16). In that same volume Archer reviews two pantomimes, *Cinderella* and *Jack and the Beanstalk*, and he praises the actresses playing specifically identified boy roles in each (5, 8).

Mander and Mitchenson's history of pantomime features a lengthy extract from a review by Shaw in *The Era*, 30 December 1937. In the article, Shaw reveals his view of the form: "I have seen dozens of them; and not one has amused me since I was a very small child and thought it all real" (quoted in Mander and Mitchenson 44). He directs his comments to an analysis of the deterioration of technique in actors portraying the harlequin role, and again makes no mention of actresses or the tradition of the principal boy. He refers to J. M. Barrie's *Peter Pan* as well as his own play, *Androcles and the Lion*, as "attempt[s] to get Christmas pieces out of their groove" (44). Shaw makes no mention, however, of the fact that *Peter Pan* differs markedly from his piece by the centrality of its principal boy role.[1]

The prominence of the principal boy role in the pantomime (for example the Prince in *Cinderella* and Jack in *Jack and the Beanstalk*), coupled with the stature of the actresses in these roles, could not have gone unnoticed by Shaw, who clearly had ample opportunity to observe their performances. Shaw's silence on these characters may account for Meisel's not mentioning them, but it is interesting that Meisel does not connect the incidence of cross-dressing in Shaw's plays with this tradition. In fact, Meisel makes no mention of this dramatic phenomenon in Shaw.

Shaw is equally silent on Ellen Terry's association with breeches parts, despite their long, close connection. Terry's career started with these roles (Auerbach 50), although Shaw first encountered her work after she had begun predominantly to act parts for mature women. He makes no mention of these roles in his semibiographical preface to their correspondence (St. John vii–xxviii), nor does the male disguise of Imogen have any place in Shaw's extensive communication with Terry about her performance in the Irving production of Shakespeare's romance *Cymbeline.*

Yet it is hard to believe that Shaw would not have been highly conscious of this aspect of Imogen's story, for only the year before (1895), he had created his first cross-dressed female character, the Strange Lady in *The Man of Destiny.* Shaw sustained his interest in such portraits through 1945, when, with a moderate touch of irony, he joined the ranks of such nineteenth-century artists as Henry Irving by rewriting Shakespeare. Shaw maintains he wrote *Cymbeline Refinished,* a revision of the last act of the late romance,[2] when a revival of *Cymbeline* was proposed at the Shakespeare Memorial Theatre at Stratford-upon-Avon, and concern was expressed about the length and complexity of act 5 (133). He claims he wanted to see how "Shakespeare might have written [the last act] if he had been post-Ibsen and post-Shaw instead of post-Marlowe" (136).

Shaw probably alludes to the modern dramatists' concerns with domestic themes of women's roles and marital relations—themes that in part lie behind the controversy surrounding cross-dressed women. He refers to Charles Charrington's comment that "Posthumus [was] Shakespeare's anticipation of his Norwegian rival," because

> after being theatrically conventional to the extent of ordering his
> wife to be murdered, he begins to criticize, quite along the lines

of Mrs Alving in Ghosts, the slavery to an inhuman ideal of marital fidelity which led him to this villainous extremity. (135)

Shaw's sense of the contemporary relevance of the Shakespearean drama makes his revision important as an indicator both of the parallels to his era he saw in the Renaissance text and of the reflections of his own dramatic concerns he perceived in the Shakespearean scenario. That these revisions center on the moment of reinscription of the cross-dressed heroine into her properly gendered role and domestic sphere shows the preoccupation of Shaw with this plot resolution in literary (as well as contemporary social) contexts.

The plot of *Cymbeline* may have appealed to Shaw for its similarity to one of his own favorite dramatic situations: the love triangle between two men and a woman, found in such plays as *Candida*, *The Philanderer*, and *How He Lied To Her Husband*, among others. Indeed, the tone of Shaw's dialogue between Imogen, Posthumus, and Iachimo resembles that of the final discussion scene between Candida, Marchbanks, and Morell, while Imogen's comments at the conclusion echo Grace Tranfield's ironic remarks to her former rival Julia about the "happy ending" for all concerned: "They think this a happy ending, Julia, these men: our lords and masters!" (*Philanderer* 175).

In Shaw's revision, Imogen's lines point to the fallacies in her husband's logic that led to his jealously ordering her murder:

Imogen. . . . My husband thinks that all is settled now
    And this a happy ending!
Posthumus. Well, my dearest,
    What could I think? The fellow did describe
    The mole upon your breast.
Imogen. And thereupon
    You bade your servant kill me.
Posthumus. It seemed natural.
Imogen. Strike me again; but do not say such things.
(145)

Shaw's Imogen is much spunkier, wittier, and more modern than her Shakespearean predecessor. As Sally Peters recently observed, "There are no Shakespearean lines retained for Imogen because Shaw remakes her character" (307). Shaw remains true to the original ending, where Imogen and Posthumus renew their marital union, but in his refinished conclusion, his audience is much more aware of the conventions of women's roles within marriage.

> Cymbeline. God's patience, man, take your wife home to bed.
>   You're man and wife: nothing can alter that . . .
>   (To Imogen) Go change your dress
>   For one becoming to your sex and rank.
>   Have you no shame?
> Imogen.   None.
> Cymbeline.   How? None!
> Imogen.   All is lost.
>   Shame, husband, happiness, and faith in Man.
>   He is not even sorry. . . .
>   I must go home and make the best of it
>   As other women must.
> Posthumus.   Thats all I ask.
>
> (148–49)

As in *The Philanderer*, the father here is the voice of tradition, prescribing proper dress and behavior for a woman. His daughter understands the constraints of her role; she must "make the best of it" even though she realizes the inherent hypocrisy of the story's outcome. Central to her father's decree is the edict to "change [her] dress for one becoming to [her] sex and rank"—a dictum indicative of hostility toward her alternate identity both as a male and as the serving boy, Fidele. In this, Shaw evokes some modernist male authors' concern with costume. According to Sandra Gilbert, these men

> see false costumes as unsexed or wrongly sexed, transvestite travesties, while true costumes are properly sexed. In defining such polarities, all are elaborating a deeply conservative vision of society both as it is and as it should be . . . for most male modernists the hierarchical order of society is and should be a pattern based upon gender distinctions. (195)

In the Shakespearean original, however, Cymbeline makes no mention of Imogen's attire, nor is there any overt suggestion that her behavior conflicts with her identity (although this may have been understood by the Renaissance audience). Throughout that text, she behaves modestly and passively, taking suggestions for action from others, in contrast to earlier comic heroines such as Rosalind, whose choices are more autonomous (Park 107). Her very passivity excuses her; she is clearly a victim and becomes an object worthy of sympathy rather than rebuke. The male attire she assumes is interpreted as a necessary part of Pisanio's plan, and when her brothers learn her true identity, they marvel not at her sexual identity, but at the transcendent fraternal bond they felt from their first meeting.

Yet Shaw makes this sexual identification a central part of his "éclaircissement" (136):

> Guiderius. Enough of this. Fidele: is it true
> Thou art a woman, and this man thy husband?
> Imogen. I am a woman, and this man my husband.
>
> (148)

Imogen, still dressed in male disguise, must reassure them of her femaleness. Cymbeline's association of Imogen's dress with shameful, inappropriate behavior and her resignation to the problems of women's marital roles are additions that simultaneously point to the hypocrisies in these social roles and reinforce them. Posthumus's satisfaction with Imogen's resignation resembles Crampton's mollification when Gloria accepts the patriarchal order in *You Never Can Tell*: "I'm very well content" (296).

The return to proper gender roles is inherent to the structural resolution of Shakespearean drama that features male impersonation. Thus, structurally, *Cymbeline Refinished* parallels the Shakespearean form. Yet the questions of blatancy and stridency of tone remain. Why does Shaw make Imogen a more active heroine, closer in independence of character to Rosalind, at the same time he introduces the sense of unacceptability of her male impersonation? Shaw projects through Cymbeline's displeasure at Imogen more responsibility on her part for her appearance and behavior. Imogen indeed appears to be much more like an Ibsenian or Shavian woman—a knowledgeable, independent thinker. It would appear that for that very reason she must be kept in check, and the chastisement for appropriation of male identity must be more blatant. The social order must be maintained more forcefully because the female threat to it is stronger; cross-dressing cannot be compatible with a woman's "sex and rank."[3] Another late play that sets forth the theatrical context in which to consider the issues surrounding female transvestism is "In Good King Charles's Golden Days" (1939). This work features the fanciful, fictional meeting of the historic figures Isaac Newton, George Fox (founder of the Quakers), and Charles II—several of whose mistresses confront each other in farcical comic relief at intervals throughout the action. The most notorious of these, Nell Gwynn, was, as Shaw puts it, "a lively and lovable actress" (153), who shortly after the Restoration specialized in the breeches roles that influenced the development of the pantomime principal boys. Although Shaw characterizes her only in her private, amatory capacity, he incorporates several interesting references to Nell's theatrical career in the play. The first of these, uttered before Nell's initial entrance, highlights the ironies of the tradition of boy actors in women's roles. Through the character Mrs Basham (one of Shaw's classic female servant figures who is comically outspoken, in the vein of Emmy from The Doctor's Dilemma), Shaw dramatizes the central historical debate over female impersonation: for an audience with certain puritanical (or patriarchally inspired) views, a male actor makes a more appropriate, "better" woman, because he projects and can therefore perform the male feminine ideal.[4] The other side (the Restoration view) perceives male cross-dressing as obscene, feeling women in women's parts are less titillating. Interestingly, Shaw gives the expression of the patriarchal view to a woman, underlining the female perception of her role through male definition:

> Mrs Basham. I do *not* disapprove of the playhouse, sir. My grandfather, who is still alive and hearty, was befriended in his youth by Mr William Shakespear, a wellknown player and writer of comedies, tragedies, and the like. Mr Shakespear would have died of shame to see a woman on the stage. It is unnatural and wrong. . . .
>
> Charles. Still, the plays are more natural with real women in them, are they not?
>
> Mrs Basham. Indeed they are not, Mr Rowley. They are not like women at all. They are just like what they are; and they spoil the play for anyone who can remember the old actors in the

women's parts. They could make you believe you were listening to real women.

(171)

George Fox perpetuates the sense of impropriety connected with female cross-dressing and the stage in general, responding with horror to Nell's repeated references to her breeches roles (201, 203, 213–
14, 218). Yet Nell has earlier noticed a connection between herself
and Fox—one he either does not grasp or upon which he chooses
not to comment. When King Charles asks Fox (who was historically
noted for his leather clothing) to pass judgment on the behavior of
another of the monarch's mistresses, Barbara Villiers, Villiers remarks:

Barbara. What does this person know about women?
Fox. Only what *the woman in myself* teaches me.
Nell. Good for *leather breeches!*

(176–77; my emphasis)

Nell responds favorably to this androgynous sensibility in Fox, but
there are certain clear distinctions in the realization of this sensibility
in each of the two characters. For Fox, the sensibility is internal or
spiritual, an asset to his understanding of human nature but never
an element of conflict in his external presentation of a masculine self.
With Nell, the lines of gender definition blur through costuming; she
more overtly expresses a sense of masculinity that is threatening to
Fox. The hypocrisy of the acceptability of male androgynous sensibility versus the unacceptability of male impersonation goes unexamined, however. It would seem that, for Fox at least, a spiritual sensitivity to both sexes is a positive, empowering thing, but he cannot
tolerate the physical demonstration of this same capacity in a woman.
Even when Charles draws verbal parallels among the characters, his
speech does not really resolve the debate; instead, Shaw uses it to
establish connections among historic figures and point out the similarities between such unconventional institutions as the stage and the
meeting house:

Nell. . . . I never was an orange girl; but I have the gutter in my
blood all right. I think I have everything in my blood; for

when I am on the stage I can be anything you please, orange
girl or queen. Or even a man. But I dont know the reason
why. . . .

Charles. It is because in the theatre you are a queen. I tell you
the world is full of kings and queens and their little courts.
Here is Pastor Fox, a king in his meeting house, though his
meetings are against the law. Here is Mr Newton, a king in
the new Royal Society . . . who would be mere dukes and
duchesses if they could be kings and queens?

(218)

Shaw's equation of Fox and Nell may, or may not, relate to their
individual androgynous capacities. Fox's tone of disapproval toward
Nell certainly overpowers her admiration for him, and the fact that
we see her in her feminine capacity as Charles's mistress, rather than
in her theatrical guise, may influence audience perception of these
roles. Shaw skews the thrust of the play toward larger political issues, and concerns with sex and gender devolve to a consideration
of women only as amatory companions. The theme of androgyny in
"In Good King Charles's Golden Days" takes a subsidiary role, perhaps
included only because of the historic coincidence of Nell Gwynn's
professional identity and private connection with the male character
more central to Shaw's interests. Nevertheless, the presentation of
androgyny here, with its distinctions between male and female incarnations, shows that for Shaw this concept was not sexually balanced.
Men and women do not symmetrically reflect each other's characteristics; androgyny is already part of the sexually determined behavior
that distinguishes men from women.

Although Shaw wrote this "true history that never happened"
(151) late in his career, it is nevertheless very much of a piece thematically with his earlier short plays that feature female cross-dressing.
Each strong woman character who wears male attire also appears in
relation to an amatory role suggested or demonstrated in the body
of the play. Moreover, the costuming of the actresses in these roles
(martial and pastoral) reveals their connection to the pantomime principal boys. Although Shaw opted for less flaunting of their physical
charms than was the norm in pantomime, with its stockings, short
breeches, and tight tunics, he more subtly emphasized the actresses'
sexual potential through speech and action. The prominence of fe-

male heterosexuality in these plots neutralizes the threat of male impersonation; furthermore, Shaw selected for these plays outstanding women, real or fictional, whose leadership role or social standing allows them unusually great autonomy and/or power.

Great Catherine, "whom glory still adores" (*Great Catherine* [1913] 265), is never seen on stage cross-dressed, but her habit of reviewing her troops in "hussar uniform" (293) becomes a central issue in the second scene. We first see her here at her *"petit lever"* (288), dressed only in a nightgown, holding court from her bed. Her lady-in-waiting, Varinka, rhapsodizes on the splendor of the queen in her ceremonial military attire, and then questions the visiting English dignitary, Edstaston, on his reaction:

> Varinka. What else did you presume to admire her Majesty for, pray?
> Edstaston (addled) Well, I—I—I—that is, I—(He stammers himself dumb).
> Catherine (after a pitiless silence) We are waiting for your answer. . . .
> Edstaston. Well, I—naturally—of course, I cant deny that the uniform was very becoming—perhaps a little unfeminine—still—. . . Well, let me put it this way: that it was rather natural for a man to admire your Majesty without being a philosopher.
> Catherine (suddenly smiling and extending her hand to him to be kissed) Courtier! . . . Courage, Captain: . . . We are *greatly* pleased. (She slaps his cheek coquettishly).
> (293–94)

Later in the next scene, Edstaston chastises the queen for displaying her ankles when she tickles him, calling her behavior "not ladylike" (304). Edstaston's satirized British prudery notwithstanding, Shaw clearly depicts Catherine as a flirtatious and yet domineering monarch. More important, he connects these qualities with theatricality in the preface to the play, and positions Catherine in a pantomime tradition, although he does not discuss her cross-dressing as a part of this dramatic form:

> But Catherine as a woman, with plenty of character and (as we should say) no morals, still fascinates and amuses us as she

fascinated and amused her contemporaries. They were great sentimental comedians, these Peters, Elizabeths, and Catherines who played their Tsarships as eccentric character parts, and produced scene after scene of furious harlequinade with the monarch as clown, and of tragic relief in the torture chamber with the monarch as pantomime demon committing real atrocities, not forgetting the indispensable love interest on an enormous and utterly indecorous scale. (268)

This humorous emphasis on love may be part of Shaw's satiric purpose in *Great Catherine*. As a theater reviewer, Shaw often criticized the amoristic nature of historical costume dramas, which made a pretense of depicting characters of greatness or elevated social stature. By consciously avoiding the heroic inflation of these pieces, while blatantly exploiting the amoristic content, Shaw may be using his short farce as an exposé of the popular theater. But Shaw's contemporary, the actress Elizabeth Robins, attacked both the playwright and the piece with wry irony in her initially anonymous feminist treatise, *Ancilla's Share*. She condemned the amoristic content, and believed Shaw's comic manipulation of the historic figure of Catherine merited her serious rebuttal. At the conclusion of her review, Robins not only exonerates the actress Gertrude Kingston, for whom Shaw wrote the bravura piece, but also acutely notes Catherine's connection with the pantomime stage tradition, in the sexually provocative roles associated with the genre:

Catherine called the Great suffered yet again a little while ago in England.
  Mr. Bernard Shaw pleases us by the admission in his preface that he had been taken to task for his abuse of the perhaps sufficiently besmirched name of one "whose diplomacy, whose campaigns and conquests . . . enabled her to cut such a magnificent figure in the eighteenth century."
  "In reply," says Mr. Shaw, "I can only confess that Catherine's diplomacy and her conquests do not interest me."
  Quite so.
  "If," he goes on, "Byron leaves you with an impression that he said very little about Catherine, and that little not what was best worth saying, I beg to correct your impression by assuring

you that what Byron said was all there really was to say that is worth saying."

Therefore, Mr. Shaw tells us, he proceeded to write a play about this person, as to whom anything worth saying had already been said by that authority upon womankind, Lord Byron. . . .

The result is a sketch which leaves Great Catherine's greatness not only clean out of sight but disavowed in order, he would have us believe, to fit an actress with a part. . . . ourselves cannot accept his explanation of avoidance of all that was notable in a notable character. . . . He should have fabricated some Shavian Queen of Zenda to go through the motions of his little farce. . . . We should have liked him to be warned that the label "great" attached to a woman acts as a challenge to the attention of others besides the groundlings whose interest must be proved by box office receipts. . . .

To say that the true ground of Catherine's greatness . . . did not "interest" Mr. Shaw, is to say but half. The true ground slightly offended him. . . .

With his boring lay-figure Miss Kingston and we are to be content—content, at least, to leave it. But content to call it Catherine of Russia . . . ? Better content to call it the Kitten of the Adelphi, or Puss in Boots. (130–32)

Robins's attack calls into question Shaw's view of this historic figure and his rationale for dramatizing this fictional moment in her life. Robins observes that Shaw pays no attention to, and includes no details of, her significant achievements as a woman ruler. Rather, he positions her as a comic character in a romantic story, with any notion of the basis of her political greatness left solely to the imagination of the audience. Robins is not explicit about "the true ground" of Catherine's stature that "offended" Shaw, but he might have responded negatively to the contention that she was bisexual, and that her attire and sexual habits placed her among those prominent women Havelock Ellis identified as masculine female inverts (Ellis 196). Shaw's characterization safely removes her to a purely heterosexual realm[5] and, by making her virtually a farcical figure, diffuses her impact as a woman of political and personal power. Her cross-dressing, rather than an integral element of her personality, becomes an offstage image, while Shaw initially displays her in a locus and costume of feminine weakness, vulnerability, and allure: in bed in a nightgown. Shaw's depiction of Catherine suggests the tension between his attraction to a woman of power and his hesitancy to portray her with the full force of her public identity. His presentation reflects the way he must position this compelling historic individual to project her heterosexual femininity and contain the strength and prominence he admires.

In her theatrical memoir *Myself and My Friends*, Lillah McCarthy lovingly describes her costume for Shaw's *Annajanska, The Bolshevik Empress* (1919): "a gorgeous white uniform half covered by an enormous green overcoat trimmed with black fur" (190). An actress familiar with the demands of male impersonation, McCarthy had portrayed Viola in *Twelfth Night:*

> As Viola I had to solve one of the most difficult problems which can confront any actress. . . . Viola must be mannish. Is she not disguised as a boy! . . . During rehearsal I must have stressed too much the poetry of the part, and by so doing let Viola betray the woman in her. . . . I must play the man—that is the youth that Viola pretends to be. . . . [quoting from her own diary] "Viola is a big strain played as a leading man, which the producer insists on." (160–61)

Shaw made no such demands on McCarthy when she originated the role of Annajanska in 1918. The elaborate Panderobajensky Hussar uniform Annajanska wears, although integral to the dramatic action, is only displayed at the climax, when her alternate identity as a male officer is revealed. During most of the action, Annajanska appears "enveloped from head to foot by a fur-lined cloak" (133) that conveniently hides her disguise. Here, as with the uniform alluded to in *Great Catherine*, the costumes resemble those of pantomimes with military themes, such as a 1905 production of *Aladdin* that featured a Boer War setting for the design concept, or the 1828 production of *The Invincibles*, in which Madame Vestris appeared as one of a regiment of uniformed actresses (Fletcher 20).

But Shaw's use of the actress in male disguise is sparing in his short pieces. He clearly wants the visual impact of male impersona-

Fig. 4. Lillah McCarthy in her costume for *Annajanska*, produced at London's Coliseum in 1918. Note the sexual ambiguity of the image: with headdress and baggy jacket, McCarthy's female identity is masked, generating a different sense of character from the principal boy, whose true sexual identity was never in question.

tion for theatrical effect but prefers to emphasize androgyny through character rather than costume. In *Annajanska* in particular, dramatic irony is heightened through the opposition of the behavior and speeches of the Grand Duchess to the characteristics of her presumed male companion. This double identity, conflated in actuality in one character who is female but has masculine strength and goals, epitomizes Shavian androgyny, which is most frequently found in the characterization of a woman externally (physically) female or feminine, but with certain masculine components to her personality or sense of self.

Before the audience first sees Annajanska, it learns of her tremendous physical strength, which has overwhelmed two officers who have captured her. We hear they were "not men enough to hold her" (133), a comment that introduces the theme of gender identity by calling their masculinity into question. But we also learn that Annajanska uses conventionally female techniques in conflict: she bites one of the officers to make him release her. Like Great Catherine, whom Shaw describes as a "pantomime demon" (268), Annajanska is referred to as "a devil incarnate" (132)—a designation that will also apply to the "Satan[ic]" Strange Lady in *The Man of Destiny* (190).[6]

Shaw had had McCarthy in mind as well when he created the notably androgynous character of Lina Szczepanowska in *Misalliance*, and Annajanska yearns for a circus career like Lina's as an acrobat. Although General Strammfest finds the bare costume of an acrobat (which is not dissimilar to that of a principal boy) indecent (141), the Grand Duchess longs for the freedom it represents—a freedom similar to that of the masculine attire she sports under her cloak. Both costumes would allow her to express more of her potential and innate self, rather than the identity that has been thrust upon her at court (140–41).

Annajanska's realization of her true identity includes her embracing of Bolshevism. She has escaped from confinement as a member of royalty to join the Revolution, and much of the humor of the piece revolves around the mistaken assumption that she has eloped with an officer in uniform who was traveling with her on her passport. The officers cannot conceive of her traveling alone in male disguise and thus fabricate the scenario of her secret marriage. General Strammfest in particular has very fixed notions of the aristocracy and women's roles, all of which Annajanska explodes during the course of their dialogue. He wishes for a man of her strength, vitality, and leadership qualities to unite the people, but cannot envision a woman in that capacity:

> The Grand Duchess. . . . Only a great common danger and a
> great common duty can unite us and weld these wrangling
> factions into a solid commonwealth.
> Strammfest. . . . what can *I* do? I am only a soldier. I cannot
> make speeches: . . . they will not rally to my call.
> The Grand Duchess. Are you sure they will not rally to mine?
> Strammfest. Oh, if only you were a man and a soldier!
> The Grand Duchess. Suppose I find you a man and a sol-
> dier? . . .
> Strammfest. Then who is he?
> The Grand Duchess. . . . He is under your very eyes.
> Strammfest (staring past her right and left) Where? . . . (. . . The
> Grand Duchess takes off her cloak and appears in the uni-
> form of the Panderobajensky Hussars). . . .
> The Grand Duchess. Here, silly.
> Strammfest (turning) You! Great Heavens!
>
> (143–44)

Annajanska reveals the uniform that more accurately represents the concept of her own identity: a masculine self capable of leadership and the admiration of the people. Her removal of her cloak here echoes the image of the detachable skirt in *The Philanderer*; Shaw's androgynous women dress in keeping with the identity they feel or wish to project, as with Sylvia's insistence on her masculine persona at the Ibsen Club. That Annajanska's revelation comes at the climactic, final moment of the piece emphasizes her male identification even further and creates a lasting image of her as the masculine soldier she can and has become.

Annajanska thus functions on two levels: as "variety theatre" entertainment (127), a staple of which was cross-dressing, and as a more thoughtful study of gender conventions and presumptions. The avuncular relation of General Strammfest to the Grand Duchess parallels similar character patterns elsewhere in Shaw, where an older male figure who represents traditional views must come to terms with the evolving independence of a young woman who does not conform to standard patterns of womanly behavior. The older man's wish for the younger woman to be male exposes the binary opposition of gender categories in Shaw and points toward an attempt to maintain conventions of masculinity and femininity in their "proper" sexes.

As in the Victorian pantomime theater, the emphasis on the heterosexuality and/or sexual appeal of the cross-dressed actress mitigates concern about the appropriation of male power implied by the assumption of masculine attire. Shaw's earliest play with a cross-dressed female character, *The Man of Destiny* (1895), resembles *Annajanska* in that the cross-dressing initially occurs offstage and tricks foolish officers who cannot comprehend the deception; the actress only appears in male attire near the end, once her feminine identity has been clearly established by the preceding action and dialogue. In remarks on each play, Shaw alludes to their connection to the popular theater, calling *Annajanska* "a 'turn' for the Coliseum theatre" (127), while admitting that the actress in *The Man of Destiny* "*must look well in a man's uniform*. Such are the opera bouffe depths to which I have descended" (*Collected Letters* 1:553).

The premise under which the Strange Lady assumes her French uniform appears a bit weak, but dramatically intriguing: she has agreed to intercept a letter sent to disgrace Napoleon by revealing his wife's involvement with the government official Barras. That Shaw should motivate the Strange Lady by the desire to protect the honor of a female friend whom she knew in school taken one way reveals a unique example of female bonding in Shaw; but taken another, it echoes (ironically?) Ibsen's *Hedda Gabler*, a play that features a strong heroine who hypocritically makes much of a schoolgirl friendship with a woman she later exploits.

Much of the dialogue between Napoleon and the Strange Lady concerns their respective forms of bravery, selfish and altruistic. In keeping with the thrust of the "womanly woman" essay from *The Quintessence*, the self-sacrificing inclinations of the Lady receive a designation of "womanish" and "slavish" (182), while Napoleon's personal, selfish drive for power and glory garners praise. They each recognize the other's theatrical prowess as well and realize that each assumes roles with the other and the world at large.

This theatrical role play incorporates cross-gender impersonation, but as in *"Good King Charles,"* the male exhibits only feminine behavior, retaining his masculine form, while the woman changes appearance and demeanor. Early in the play, Napoleon realizes the Strange Lady has fooled his lieutenant, and tells her, "You disguised yourself as a man. I want my despatches. They are there in the bosom of your dress" (178). Later, the final technique that convinces her to turn over the letters is his admission of his clearly undesirable potential to be feminine:

> . . . Now attend to me. Suppose I were to allow myself to be abashed by the respect due to your sex, your beauty, your heroism and all the rest of it? Suppose I, with nothing but such sentimental stuff to stand between these muscles of mine and those papers which you have about you . . . were to falter and sneak away with my hands empty . . . sparing you the violence I dared not use! would you not despise me from the depths of your woman's soul? Would any woman be such a fool? Well, Bonaparte can rise to the situation and act like a woman when it is necessary. (185–86)

The Strange Lady's rejection of his "woman's part" parallels her displeasure with her own "womanliness" discussed above. From the opening of the play, she is a character physically identified with gender conflict:

> She is very feminine, but by no means weak: the lithe tender figure is hung on a strong frame: the hands and feet, neck and shoulders, are useful vigorous members of full size in proportion to her stature, which perceptibly exceeds that of Napoleon and the innkeeper, and leaves her at no disadvantage with the lieutenant. Only, her elegance and radiant charm keep the secret of her size and strength. (175)

When the lieutenant first sees her, he immediately identifies the likeness between the Strange Lady and the officer who has recently tricked him into handing over the despatches: "So Ive got you, my lad. So youve disguised yourself, have you? (In a voice of thunder . . .) Take off that skirt" (176). The audience, with only the benefit of a well-known actress's name to guide their interpretation, could

indeed be confused at this first humorous exchange. Are they viewing extremely realistic female impersonation, as the lieutenant assumes in his order to reveal the male attire hidden beneath female
garb, or do they already know the Lady is really a male impersonator,
in the tradition of women whose higher voices could be mistaken for
those of male youths?

The Lady maneuvers her way around the lieutenant's insistence
that she's no "lady! He's a man!" (176) by maintaining the lieutenant
must have mistaken her for her twin brother, an explanation he readily accepts (176–77). This convenient fiction, perpetuated throughout
the drama, ties *The Man of Destiny* to the literary and religious tradition of androgynous twins (Heilbrun 34–45), which Shaw had recently encountered in productions of Shakespeare's *Twelfth Night*
(Shaw *Diaries* 2:1006, 1084) and perhaps in Dickens's unfinished
novel *The Mystery of Edwin Drood*, as well as in Sarah Grand's novel
The Heavenly Twins (S. Weintraub "G.B.S. Borrows" 288–97). These
literary corollaries all feature opposite-sex twins who are physically
indistinguishable and frequently function knowingly or unknowingly
as each other's counterparts to advance the action.[7] But here, the
fictional twin has another resonance with Shaw's belief in uniform
gender identity. Excusing himself for the confusion, the lieutenant
remarks, "Madam: my apologies. I thought you were the same person, only of the opposite sex" (177).

In *The Man of Destiny*, the fiction of a male twin only thinly covers
the reality of the trick of male impersonation. As in *Annajanska*, when
the Strange Lady ultimately returns in her man's uniform, Shaw uses
the opportunity to further the demonstration of parallels between his
leading male and female characters. He points up Napoleon's sexual
conventionality, by exposing the hypocrisy behind it:

> Napoleon. You are guilty of indelicacy: of unwomanliness. Is
>   that costume proper?
> Lady. It seems to me much the same as yours.
> Napoleon. Psha! I blush for you.
> Lady (naively). Yes: soldiers blush so easily.
>
> (202–3)

The Lady's sexual desirability has been highlighted earlier by a blush
that spreads "all over her body," appearing from beneath the fichu

Fig. 5. The 1925 New York Theatre Guild production of *The Man of Destiny* was recorded by the famous theatrical photographer Vandamm. Here he captures the actors' (Tom Powers and Clare Eames) efforts to mirror each other physically, aided by their similarity of costume.

that barely covers her décolletage (176). This tension between the characters as sexual duelists and opposite-sex doubles pervades the play, adding a twist to the fiction of the male twin the Lady creates. As she and Napoleon manipulate the lieutenant in their power struggle, Bonaparte metaphorically takes the role of the brother, by lying to and tricking the officer just as the Lady has before the start of the action.

Shaw's final image of these characters emphasizes their likeness: both in uniform, they sit in identical poses at the table looking at each other, as if each were gazing at a reflection in a mirror:

> Lady (taking up the snuffers and holding the letter to the candle flame with it). I wonder would Caesar's wife be above suspicion if she saw us here together!
> Napoleon (echoing her, with his elbows on the table and his cheeks on his hands looking at the letter). I wonder!
> *The Strange Lady puts the letter down alight on the snuffers tray, and sits down beside Napoleon, in the same attitude, elbows on table, cheeks on hands, watching it burn. When it is burnt, they simultaneously turn their eyes and look at one another. The curtain steals down and hides them.*
>
> (207–8)

The sexual overtone contained in the last speeches teases the audience, as it has been teased all along with various forms of role-play (the casting of Josephine Bonaparte as "Caesar's wife" incorporates her in this motif as well). In keeping with Victorian theatrical tradition, the homosexual appearance of this closing moment, which includes the Lady's "ventur[ing] to rest her hand on his shoulder, overcome by the beauty of the night and emboldened by its obscurity" (206), gives way to the secure knowledge of the gender and sexual orientation of these characters. Yet the emphasis on the superiority of masculine (martial) courage and behavior (established in Napoleon's speech rejecting traditionally "womanly" behavior, quoted above), reinforced by the final image of male dress, and coupled with the symbolic narcissism of the closing tableau, all contribute to a sense of privilege and preference for the male component in Shavian androgyny.

In a letter to Janet Achurch, Shaw says of *The Man of Destiny*, "It is not exactly a burlesque: it is more a harlequinade, in which Napoleon and a strange lady play harlequin & columbine" (*Collected Letters* 1:546). The costumes of Harlequin and Columbine, characters from both the commedia tradition and the English pantomime, appear in the final scene of *You Never Can Tell* on Phil and Dolly, who have donned them for a fancy dress ball. Shaw suppresses the romantic/sexual component traditionally associated both with these commedia figures (Morgan 91) and with the mythology of opposite-sex twins androgyny (Heilbrun 34), choosing instead to highlight the behavioral similarities and theatrical potential of these characters for entertainment.

From their first entrance, Dolly and Phil function like a music hall comedy team—two patter and repartee experts whose rapid-fire exchanges demonstrate a sense of timing, naturalness, and spontaneity that could only come from years of experience:

The Young Gentleman. Am I in time?
The Young Lady. No: it's all over.
The Young Gentleman. Did you howl?
The Young Lady. Oh, something awful. Mr Valentine: this is my brother Phil. Phil: this is Mr Valentine, our new dentist. (. . . She proceeds, all in one breath) He's only been here six weeks and he's a bachelor the house isnt his and the furniture is the landlord's but the professional plant is hired he got my tooth out beautifully at the first go and he and I are great friends.
Philip. Been asking a lot of questions?
The Young Lady (as if incapable of doing such a thing) Oh no.
Philip. Glad to hear it. (To Valentine) So good of you not to mind us, Mr Valentine. The fact is, weve never been in England before; and our mother tells us that the people here simply wont stand us. Come and lunch with us.

(214)

The unflappable exuberance of the twins gives way, however, at Phil's injunctions for silence:

Dolly. You were going to improve our minds, I think.
Valentine. The fact is, your—

Philip (anticipating him) Our manners?
Dolly. Our appearance?
Valentine (ad misericordiam) Oh *do* let me speak.
Dolly. The old story. We talk too much.
Philip. We do. Shut up, both.

(217)

Phil has clearly taken upon himself the dominant role; he gives Dolly orders, and also tries to take the upper hand with his mother and older sister, reminding them often of his "knowledge of human nature" (223, *passim*), which guides his judgments. Although the audience sees the comic irony behind the limited worldly expertise of an eighteen year old who has spent most of his life on the island of Madeira, within his immediate family Phil does exercise a certain controlling influence. This may be explained in part by Phil's unspoken realization that, as the only male in the household, he must assume the patriarchal role. His habituation to an air of dominance may also account for Phil's discomfort with the notion of his real father's identity finally being revealed—an act that would remove him from his position as the only male in the family, and eliminate the sui generis atmosphere that has surrounded their upbringing. Phil announces unequivocally, "No man alive shall father me" (219), but later, when he confronts his father, Phil challenges him with his sexual identity: "Whose fault is it that I am a boy?" (251). Phil cannot claim responsibility for his sex, yet it is interesting that in a household run by an advanced woman like Mrs Clandon, Phil should have emerged as such a conventional Victorian male.

The pattern of the Clandon household—a mother of two daughters and a son who leave their father—of course resembles Shaw's own. The fact that the death of Shaw's younger sister allowed him to move to London and achieve his literary goals may have a subtle impact on the dynamics of Phil's relation to his family. But the dominance of Phil in his identity as the male half of opposite-sex twins may simply exemplify the social construction of gender in Shaw, pointedly demonstrating the strength of the male components in the total of humanity represented by the androgynous characterization of Dolly and Phil, "in tandem . . . the hermaphrodite ideal" (Holroyd *Search For Love* 386), who as twins must have a certain significance beyond that accorded to the more common treatment of sibling relations.

Shaw uses female impersonation much less frequently in his plays, although this tradition was longstanding in English popular entertainment. In fact there is only one example of male cross-dressing in the canon, found at the opening of the one-act *Press Cuttings*. Shaw wrote this short piece for the West End, but for political reasons it was initially refused a license by the censor. Eventually the Actresses' Franchise League toured the production, which received significant press coverage. Yet, as Julie Holledge points out,

> there is a marked difference in his treatment of the sexes [in the play]: the men are ludicrous because of their political prejudices while the women are ridiculed for being ugly, aggressive predators. (68)

This is especially clear in the opening scene, in which Prime Minister Balsquith disguises himself as a militant suffragette to gain entrance to the War Office unmolested by the real suffragettes demonstrating outside the building.

The Orderly. Another one, sir. She's chained herself.

Mitchener. Chained herself? How? To what? Weve taken away the railings and everything that a chain can be passed through.

The Orderly. We forgot the doorscraper, sir. She lay down on the flags and got the chain through before she started hollerin. She's lying there now; and she downfaces us that youve got the key of the padlock in a letter in a buff envelope, and that youll see her when you open it. . . .

Mitchener (who has been reading the letter . . .) This is a letter from the Prime Minister asking me to release the woman with this key . . . and to have her shewn up and see her at once. . . .

The Orderly [outside] In you go. (He pushes a panting Suffraget into the room) The person, sir. . . . (The Suffraget takes off her tailor-made skirt and reveals a pair of fashionable trousers.)

Mitchener (horrified) Stop, madam. What are you doing? you must not undress in my presence. I protest. Not even your letter from the Prime Minister—

The Suffraget. My dear Mitchener: I *am* the Prime Minister. (He takes off his hat and cloak; throws them on the desk; and confronts the General in the ordinary costume of a Cabinet Minister). . . .

Balsquith. . . . It has come to this: that the only way the Prime Minister of England can get from Downing Street to the War Office is by assuming this disguise; shrieking "VOTES FOR WOMEN"; and chaining himself to your doorscraper. They were at the corner in force. They cheered me. Bellachristina herself was there. She shook my hand and told me to say I was a vegetarian, as the diet was better in Holloway for vegetarians.

(226–28)

Shaw's use of drag here fits the comic depiction of female characters in the pantomime "dame" roles—those taken on by male actors who portray spinsters, witches, and other older women's roles. It may also owe something to Shakespeare, as Falstaff is farcically disguised as a woman in *The Merry Wives of Windsor*, or to the larger classical tradition, where a male's assumption of feminine attire is characterized in a humorous but derogatory fashion. The dialogue and action surrounding the disguise in *Press Cuttings* clearly differ from those used for Shaw's female characters, however. Here, the cross-dressing occurs for opening comic effect, and then is abandoned to move on to the more serious issues that the men must discuss. The female impersonation has nothing to do with the character's identity or personal goals; it is purely a ruse to circumvent a disruptive obstacle, namely the true suffragettes protesting outside. There is no sexuality associated with the temporary male transvestism; it neither appears in conjunction with a heterosexual relationship nor has any connection to a discussion of its wearer's gender identity.

Although the stage direction of the "suffragette's" removal of "her" skirt to reveal trousers underneath would seem the companion to the description of Sylvia Craven's attire in the Ibsen Club, the moment in *Press Cuttings* has no other connection with the "Unpleasant" play so concerned with the issue of gender identity. It would seem that Shaw's use of cross-dressing is not only a theatrical motif he prefers to associate with his female characters, but also one that has distinct gendered resonances. The male components of the female identity privileged through male costume do not find a counterpart in Prime Minister Balsquith. The androgyny depicted in all of these predominantly short plays thus heavily favors masculine qualities and appearance, both in the strong characterization of women in male disguise, and ironically in the rapid rejection of the feminine depicted in *Press Cuttings*.

6

Instances of Inversion and Eschatological Androgyny

The plays in which attributes of
gender are implied externally through cross-dressing have subtler
dramatic counterparts that feature characterological androgyny—a
behavioral manifestation of the traits identified by Ellis, Carpenter,
et al. connected with sexual inversion. In these plays, Shaw portrays
individuals who voice or embody his personal unisexual sensibility
and who represent the mixed natures (masculine women and feminine men) described by the sexual theorists.

In the late short piece *Village Wooing* (1933), Shaw engages two
"voices" (145) in a series of "conversations" (147) that replicate "the
duel of sex" found throughout his dramas. Shaw chooses to designate these otherwise nameless characters "A" (the male) and "Z" (the
female). This "genericizing" suggests numerous interpretive possibilities: the distance between the characters, the primacy and origi-
nality of the male (which are integral to the female's attempt to gain
some control over him through marriage), and the sense of ending
connected with the female (hence the male desire to escape legal
entrapment), to name a few. Shaw uses these possibilities to generate
one of his twists—a humorous overturning of audience expectation.

125

He plays off the sense of sexual difference assumed by the audience to surprise them with androgynous identity:

> A. I am not Everyman. Everyman thinks that every woman that steps into a railway carriage may be the right woman. But she is always a disappointment.
> Z. Same with the women, isnt it? If you were a woman youd know.
> A. I *am* a woman; and you are a man, with a slight difference that doesnt matter except on special occasions.
> Z. Oh, what a thing to say! I never could bring myself to believe that.
>
> (150)

As with Alice Lockett, whom Shaw informed that "nine tenths of me is a simple repetition of nine tenths of you" (*Collected Letters* 1:158), so here the better-educated man instructs the ingenuous woman about their essential similarity. This speech reflects the didactic dominance of male characters in Shaw and exemplifies the heterosexual context in which the playwright explores issues of sex and gender. At the same time that gender appears indeterminate—men can be feminine and women masculine—conventional gender distinctions are reinforced, as the male character flaunts his intellectual superiority in the midst of exposing traditional gender opposition.

Shaw projects his masculine sense of female-identification in other ways, occasionally choosing a female persona to serve his epistolary ends, as in this amusing example from the *Pall Mall Gazette* (*Agitations* 9):

> Sir,—Can you tell me why it is that the newspapers are always so interesting at this season of the year? I have often noticed that in August and September the articles begin to grow fresher and more varied; the hackneyed political subjects are dropped; anecdotes, descriptions of new scientific inventions, pretty accounts of the country, and deep thoughts about life take the place of the ordinary routine matter which no one ever reads. Is it because the gentlemen who write go away for autumn? Because, if it is, I am sure we should be quite content

if they stayed away altogether. . . . I never enjoy the papers so much as in August; and I am sure there are plenty of people who think just the same. . . . I feel certain that a great deal of money is wasted by newspaper proprietors on literary refinements and cleverness that only bore commonplace people like yours truly,

Amelia Mackintosh

Shaw's satiric, stereotyped female persona here indicates his ability to create readily identifiable, conventionally feminine and masculine voices, a skill he uses in the creation of characters of both sexes in his dramas of inversion. He perhaps realized, at the time of the discovery of his ghostwriting for Vandeleur Lee, that he had some ability to write in a style identified as "feminine"—to conceive personas that (male) editors and publishers, drawing on their own fixed, conventional views of the sexes, perceived as female.

In *A Room of One's Own* (1929), Virginia Woolf explicates her understanding of the Coleridgean great mind—one that is androgynous. She insists that Coleridge "certainly did not mean . . . that it is a mind that has any special sympathy with women; a mind that takes up their cause or devotes itself to their interpretation" (102). She points to "Shakespeare's mind as the type of the androgynous" but admits "it would be impossible to say what Shakespeare thought of women" (102–3). It would appear that Woolf held a different view from that of her contemporaries Havelock Ellis and Edward Carpenter, who saw genius precisely as the ability of artists to be "interpreters of men and women to each other" ("Intermediate Sex" 190). Shaw's sense of his ability to create believable female characters drawn from his self-knowledge affiliates him more with the Carpenter school of androgyny. Yet Woolf's further comments on the current status of male authors draw Shaw back into her analysis. She notes, "No age can ever have been as stridently sex-conscious as our own" (103) and asserts that, as a result, "virility has now become self-conscious" (105). More recently, Peter Schwenger has analyzed the "masculine mode" in writing, and observes:

To think about masculinity is to become less masculine oneself . . . [for a man] to consider his own sexuality at any length would be to admit that his maleness can be questioned, can be revised, and, to a large degree, has been created rather than existing naturally and irresistibly as real virility is supposed to. (110)

This dilemma may in part account for Shaw's reluctance to define masculinity in such works as *The Quintessence of Ibsenism* and *The Philanderer*, as well as his concern about establishing the conventional masculinity of some of his male characters who fit slightly more androgynous profiles.

In his early full-length plays, Shaw often depicts young, sensitive, highly emotional male characters such as the poet Marchbanks *(Candida)*, the intellectual Bentley Summerhays *(Misalliance)*, and the artist/consumptive Dubedat *(The Doctor's Dilemma)*. Shaw reveals concern over the reception and/or performance of these male characters, however, in his prefatory description of the last of these, Dubedat: "He is a slim young man of 23, physically still a stripling, and pretty, though not effeminate" (127). Shaw clearly does not want the traits associated with a male's feminized nature or appearance to be interpreted as indicative of the socially disdained effeminate behavior often linked to homosexuality. Critics have suggested the possibility of this interpretation for the character of Praed in *Mrs Warren's Profession*—particularly given his affection for the "pretty" Frank Gardner (225). It may be partly for this reason that Shaw regretted making Praed a single, older gentleman, seemingly immune to Mrs Warren's charms, a Pateresque "sentimental artist" (199).

Perhaps to avoid potential difficulties with the stage censor, who would have prohibited any theatrical activity suggestive of homosexuality, Shaw often places those characters who project gender traits associated with their sexual opposites in safely heterosexual contexts. Perhaps the best example of this comes in his 1913 "piece of utter nonsense" (153), *The Music Cure*, which Shaw called "not a serious play: it is what is called a Variety Turn" (154). This short farce, still topical for its plot of ruin following the discovery of insider stock trading, features a man and a woman exploring their attraction to each other through the realization that they would make an ideal couple since the woman wants to behave as a man, and the man prefers the occupations of a woman.

Reginald. They call me a Clinger. Well, I confess it. I *am* a Clinger. I am not fit to be thrown unprotected upon the world. I want to be shielded. I want a strong arm to lean on, a dauntless heart to be gathered to and cherished, a bread-winner on whose income I can live without the sordid horrors of having to make money for myself. I am a poor little thing, I know Strega; but I could make a home for you. I have great taste in carpets and pictures. I can cook like anything. I can play quite nicely after dinner. Though you mightnt think it, I can be quite stern and strongminded with servants. . . . And I shouldnt at all mind being tyrannized over a little: in fact, I like it. It saves me the trouble of having to think what to do. Oh, Strega, dont you want a dear little domesticated husband who would have no concern but to please you, no thought outside our home, who would be unspotted and unsoiled by the rude cold world. . . .

Strega. . . . My child: I am a hard, strong, independent, muscular woman. How can you, with your delicate soft nature, see anything to love in me? I should hurt you, shock you perhaps—yes: let me confess it—I have a violent temper, and might even, in a transport of rage, beat you.

Reginald. Oh do, do. Dont laugh at this ridiculous confession; but ever since I was a child I have had only one secret longing, and that was to be mercilessly beaten by a splendid, strong, beautiful woman.

(166–67)[1]

Shaw blends the profile of sexual inversion here with a parody of stereotyped characters and traditional gender roles in society to expose humorously the very conventions that define masculinity and femininity for his culture. Yet he simultaneously subtly reinforces convention with these characters. By calling the female "Strega," Italian for witch, he suggests that she fits one of the long-standing molds for women characters—one at times associated with a kind of masculine aggression or appropriation of male roles that Strega exemplifies. Yet "Reginald," the evocation of dominance and kingly rule, is the ironic opposite of this image. These characterizations reinforce the notion of Shavian gender flexibility in female personas, but relative fixity for males. In other words, the inversion in Strega's character does not transcend gender coding with the same degree of irony (or perhaps even comedy?) as Reginald's, despite the fact that each is based on extant gender conventions.

By dramatizing the exaggerations of the masculinized woman and feminized man, Shaw also effectively demonstrates the real problems with marriage roles and the financial institution of matrimony of his time, playing on a theme that lies at the center of his earlier disquisitory work, *Getting Married* (1911). Shaw gives a provocative name to the female character in *Getting Married* who adamantly refuses to accept the current state of the institution of marriage, particularly the necessity of having a husband. Lesbia Grantham, "a tall, handsome, slender lady" (116) like many of Shaw's unwomanly women, regrets that she cannot be a mother in society without taking a husband, and chooses to sacrifice maternity:

> I'm a regular old maid. I'm very particular about my belongings. I like to have my own house, and to have it to myself. I have a very keen sense of beauty and fitness and cleanliness and order. I am proud of my independence and jealous for it. I have a sufficiently well-stocked mind to be very good company for myself if I have plenty of books and music. The one thing I never could stand is a great lout of a man smoking all over my house and going to sleep in his chair after dinner, and untidying everything. Ugh! . . . I ought to have children. I should be a good mother to children. I believe it would pay the country very well to pay *ME* very well to have children. But the country tells me that I cant have a child in my house without a man in it too; so I tell the country that it will have to do without my children. If I am to be a mother, I really cannot have a man bothering me to be a wife at the same time. (119)

Barbara Bellow Watson remarks, "One might suppose the lady's name to be a euphemistic hint at the reasons for her intransigence. It is more likely that Shaw means us to reconsider our judgments of real women who live as she does" (*Shavian Guide* 90). To call a character "Lesbia" in 1911 may indeed have suggested a certain sexual orientation to some readers/audience members. Scientific literature on sexuality had begun to use the designation "lesbian" for female homosexual relationships by this time (Chauncey 127), and Shaw's depiction of Lesbia incorporates some of the traits associated with this orientation. Her repeated rejection of a husband, her expression of minimal heterosexual desire, and her strongly independent nature are all characteristic of the attitudes sexual theorists connected with inversion.[2]

Although Shaw gives Lesbia a name that suggests her possible sexual preference, he never has her admit any sexual desire, even in a veiled way. The constancy of the General's entreaties for her hand place her in a heterosexual context, yet the determination with which she repeatedly rejects him allows room for interpreting her inclinations differently.

> The General. I'm afraid, Lesbia, the things you do without are
> the things you dont want.
> Lesbia. . . . Thats not bad for the silly soldier man. Yes, Boxer:
> the truth is, I dont want you enough to make the very unrea-
> sonable sacrifices required by marriage.
>
> (194)

The concerns with marriage expressed in the interactions of Lesbia and the General, and ironically in the conversation between Reginald and Strega, carry over into Shaw's slightly later "debate" *Misalliance* (1914). The hothouse atmosphere of social concern with heterosexual and familial alliances that pervades Victorian and Edwardian drama finds neat literalization here in the "glass pavilion" setting (113), in which all the conversation "is about lovemaking" (201). Lina Szczepanowska, the Polish visitor who stands in opposition to the English preoccupation with mating, calls the environment "a rrrrrrrabbit hutch" (202) after she has had to reject the advances of virtually every man in the cast.

More than perhaps any other of Shaw's female characters, Lina epitomizes the fascination and appeal of the exotically foreign "Other"—a woman in whom issues of difference and similarity are dramatized around the theme of androgyny and sexual attraction. Just about halfway through the play, Lina literally and metaphorically crashes onto the scene, as the airplane in which she has been a passenger makes an emergency landing, smashing into the greenhouse immediately offstage. A dea ex machina, Lina strides onstage totally covered by an aviator suit, helmet, and goggles, thus unrecognizable as a woman. When she removes her helmet and goggles,

however, she also reveals her sexual identity, which causes general
consternation, as the other characters have assumed through her
costume that she is a man.

> Tarleton. I must apologize, madam, for having offered you the
> civilities appropriate to the opposite sex. And yet, why oppo-
> site? We are all human: males and females of the same spe-
> cies. When the dress is the same the distinction van-
> ishes. . . . Szczepanowska! Not an English name, is it?
> Lina. Polish. I'm a Pole.
> Tarleton. (dithyrambically) Ah yes. What other nation, ma-
> dame, could have produced your magical personality? Your
> countrywomen have always appealed to our imagination.
> Women of Destiny! beautiful! musical! passionate! tragic! You
> will be at home here: my own temperament is pre-eminently
> Polish.
>
> (154)

The recognition of similarity and difference demonstrated here
shows interesting connections between views of the idealized woman
and of common humanity. Tarleton's speech on dress echoes Shaw's
designation of woman as man in petticoats, and what stands out here
is the assumption of the male base for this remark. In other words,
Shaw places these statements of sexual identicalness in his male characters' mouths (or expresses them himself nondramatically), and the
motivation for these comments is always the recognition of masculine
behavior or appearance in a woman. Humans are all the same, therefore, because the woman is just like the man. Significantly, Shaw
does not present dramatic examples of the inverse of this equation;
a woman such as Nell Gwynn may recognize her similarity to men
through dress, but she never extends this to an equation of female
and male identity.

The women who behave and look masculine in Shaw are often
foreign: Lina from Poland, the Russians Catherine and Annajanska,
and the French Saint Joan. Shaw called Lina "the St Joan of Misalliance" (Collected Letters 4:180), cementing their connection. There is
clearly some association between geographical otherness and the
strangeness of women in male attire; it would seem that for Shaw the
foreign woman who breaks English womanly conventions is more

intriguing, and capable of more, than her British counterpart, who is frequently portrayed as the males' antagonist, the character opposite from themselves in beliefs and behavior who wants to trap them in the duel of sex. Barbara Bellow Watson believes Shaw modeled Lina "to some extent on Marie Bashkirtseff" (*Shavian Guide* 159), and if this is true then Lina may well inhabit Shaw's category of "the third sex" as well as exemplify Bashkirtseff's blend of masculine independence and heterosexual desire and desirability.

Shaw quickly establishes Lina in a heterosexual context. When questioned about her motives for attempting the flight, Lina is tricked into giving her marital status:

> Mrs Tarleton. I hope it wasnt to spite your mother?
> Percival. (quickly) Or your husband? . . .
> Hypatia (aside to Percival) That was clever of you, Mr. Percival.
> Percival. What?
> Hypatia. To find out.
>
> (156)

But she demonstrates her opposition to the conventions of interpersonal relationships by discussing them all as business transactions, as bids on her worth.

> Tarleton. . . . I want to make a fool of myself. About you. Will you let me?
> Lina. (very calm) How much will you pay?
> Tarleton. Nothing. But I'll throw as many sovereigns as you like into the sea to shew you that I'm in earnest.
> Lina. Are those your usual terms?
>
> (161–62)

Just as she will have no truck with the false romanticism of the male characters' propositions—although she sincerely values, if rejects, Tarleton's offer—she similarly has no interest in exchanging her male flight gear for traditional female dress, which is equally false with its padding and stays.

> Mrs Tarleton. . . . Hypatia will lend the lady a gown.
> Lina. Thank you: I'm quite comfortable as I am. I am not accus-

tomed to gowns: they hamper me and make me feel ridiculous; so if you dont mind I shall not change.

(157)

Like Shaw's other androgynous women, Lina displays remarkable
physical strength—a quality that establishes her as more masculine
than some of the male characters in the play. Recounting Lina's brilliant feat of strength in the airplane, saving Joey Percival from harm
in the crash, Lord Summerhays tells the pilot before his passenger's
identity is revealed:

I saw it. It was extraordinary. When you were thrown out he
held on to the top bar with one hand. You came past him in the
air, going straight for the glass. He caught you and turned you
off into the flower bed, and then lighted beside you like a bird.
(153)

When we learn Lina is a professional acrobat, her physical prowess
makes perfect sense. Like Annajanska, who ran away to the circus
to become an acrobat (141), Lina embodies the magical freedom and
power of the high wire. She resembles the character Miss Urania in
Huysmans's A rebours (1884), a novel much admired at the fin de
siècle (also known to English audiences through references in Wilde's
The Picture of Dorian Gray):

This was Miss Urania, an American, with a vigorous body, sin-
ewy limbs, muscles of steel and arms of iron.
    She had been one of the most celebrated acrobats of the Cir-
cus . . . her power and strength . . . had for him all the charm of
masculinity. Compared with her, Des Esseintes seemed to himself a frail, effeminate creature. (Huysmans 158)

Like the foreign Miss Urania—a name associated with androgyny
from the theoretical writing of K. H. Ulrichs (Carpenter 190–91)—
Lina's strength and predilection for male attire associate her closely
with the inverted women depicted by Havelock Ellis and Edward
Carpenter. Shaw makes her androgynous identity readily apparent
through Hypatia's designation of her as "the man-woman or woman-
man or whatever you call her" (165). And again like Huysmans's

acrobat, Lina brings out the feminine in the men around her, by overpowering them physically and emotionally, reducing them to tears (164) or figures of impotence (175). After disarming "Gunner" (the name given to the intruder who tries to shoot Tarleton) Lina proposes, "Come to the gymnasium: I'll teach you how to make a man of yourself" (175). Through the instruction of Lina—a masculine woman—men will learn how to realize their correct masculinity, as with the men of *The Quintessence* who should take the Bashkirtseff view of themselves (56).

Lina's stirring speech at the end of the play makes her appear an ideal woman—one with strength, independence, and a definite sense of self:

> . . . I am an honest woman: I earn my living. I am a free woman: I live in my own house. I am a woman of the world: . . . I am strong: I am skilful: I am brave: I am independent: I am unbought: I am all that a woman ought to be. (202)

Nevertheless, Shaw closes *Misalliance* with the pairing off of Lina and Bentley, the "sensitive" (114), effeminate youth whose nickname is "Bunny." This resolution of the earlier potential misalliance of Bentley and Hypatia seems thematically appropriate—a union of the masculine woman and feminine man into an androgynous whole, a more realistic ending than that of *The Music Cure*. Yet as witty as this pairing may appear, it is strange that Lina should want both to escape the "rrrrrrrabbit hutch" and to take off with the character identified as Bunny. Perhaps Bentley's potential for growth under Lina's tutelage ("You must learn to dare" [204]) implies a transition in his personality, and the vagueness of their future relationship leaves the ending ambiguous as to the sort of alliance they will make. Equally puzzling is the need for Lina, "the divine androgyne, emblem of human nature restored to unity" (Morgan 196), to mate with anyone. If Lina is already an androgynous whole and the representation of a goddess, then why pair her with a superfluous human mate? Is this an affiliation of two androgynes, or another misalliance?

Within the play itself, Shaw leaves these questions unresolved. Many years later, however, he wrote an essay entitled "Biographers' Blunders Corrected," in which he comments on some of these androgynous women, partially clarifying his view of their sexuality:

Have I really conveyed to you that when it comes to the relations of the sexes there is no female but the spider female? Ann Whitefield in Man and Superman does not fill up my field of vision as completely as she has filled up yours. . . . Major Barbara, Lesbia Grantham, and Lina Szczepanowska you have noted in subsequent passages as getting quite as far from the bee and the spider as my least philoprogenitive men. It seems to me that what is in your mind is the vast mass of people who are as nearly neuter in sex as it is possible for human beings to be. (*Sixteen Self Sketches* 156)

Shaw does not make clear exactly what the "blunder" in this biographers' assumption is, moving the discussion on to a slightly different plane, remarking "I am not sure that I shall not deal dramatically with the anti-maternal woman some day" (157). This comment seems to reinforce Catharine Stimpson's sense that the literary androgyne, as opposed to the homosexual, retains the potential for heterosexuality and maternity (242).

Surely this potential lurks behind Shaw's portrayal of one of his best known characters, Saint Joan. In her groundbreaking study, *Toward a Recognition of Androgyny*, Caroline Heilbrun says of Shaw's Joan:

Shaw was able miraculously to portray in one person a female being with masculine aptitudes who, in her sainthood, reminded humanity of the need for feminine impulses in the world. Joan is an entirely androgynous figure. (111)

A woman's potential for these "masculine aptitudes" indeed seems to have been realized by Shaw with the composition of *Saint Joan*. In a letter to his artist friend Bertha Newcombe, Shaw remarks:

All the attempts to shew that Joan was a hypersuggestible lunatic in the hands of priests and intriguers are mere Anti-Feminist methods of dodging the glaring truth that her success was a genuine success of ability of the kind supposed to be exclusively masculine. (*Collected Letters* 3:858)

To John Middleton Murray Shaw repeats this opinion and explains the key failing in Anatole France's characterization: "he was completely disabled as to Joan herself by a simple disbelief in the existence of *ability* (in the manly sense) in women" (*Collected Letters* 3:876). But perhaps most telling is his letter to Dame Ethel Smyth, a woman composer ("who was notoriously lesbian" [Faderman 310]) whose work Shaw had followed since 1893:

You are totally and diametrically wrong in imagining that you have suffered from a prejudice against feminine music. On the contrary you have been almost extinguished by the dread of masculine music. It was your music that cured me for ever of the old delusion that women could not do men's work in art and other things. . . . But for you I might not have been able to tackle St Joan, who has floored every previous playwright. Your music is more masculine than Handel's.

When have the critics and the public ever objected to feminine music? Did they object to Arthur Sullivan, whose music was music in petticoats from the first bar to the last? . . . You scorned sugar and sentimentality; and you were exuberantly ferocious. . . . And now you say we shrink from you because you are "only a woman." Good God! (*Collected Letters* 3:868–69)

Although Shaw displays his usual charm to Dame Ethel here, the content of the letter nevertheless stands out for its recognition not only that women can function in traditionally male arenas, but also that the work that people do can be described in gendered ways that have nothing to do with the sex of their producers—that is, Arthur Sullivan's feminine music, which is synecdochically depicted "in petticoats," Shaw's recurrent image of womanliness. Shaw also implies a certain value inherent in the gendered description of art. Widely performed, if uninteresting, instrumental music, such as Arthur Sullivan's, is linked with the feminine, whereas Smyth's less conventional "masculine" music clearly challenges its audience. Thus the genders are maintained, unquestioned, in their traditional forms, with connotations intact, although their perpetrators (the composers) may be of either biological sex. Shaw contends his recognition of Smyth's ability to produce music—an artistic function he associated with men—coupled with his realization of the independence of artists' sex and the gender of their productions enabled him to dramatize Joan—a character of both androgynous personality and masculine action. Shaw does not comment on the composer's personal, sexual notoriety, yet the tantalizing questions of its possible impact on Shaw's view of her music, and its potential connection to his characterization of Joan, remain.

In choosing to write the story of Joan, Shaw recognized the need to confront other well-known depictions of her, not only Shakespeare's, but also the relatively more recent interpretations of Schiller, Mark Twain, Andrew Lang, and Anatole France.[3] Shaw finds fault with each of these authors' versions, seeing in them a subjectivity reflective of their era:

> Before Schiller came Voltaire, who burlesqued Homer in a mock epic called La Pucelle . . . its purpose was not to depict Joan but to kill with ridicule everything that Voltaire righteously hated in the institutions and fashions of his own day. . . . But the publication by Quicherat in 1841 of the reports of her trial and rehabilitation placed the subject on a new footing. . . . Typical products of that interest . . . are the histories of Joan by Mark Twain and Andrew Lang. . . . Andrew Lang and Mark Twain are equally determined to make Joan a beautiful and most ladylike Victorian. (24–25)

Shaw lays the blame for their misinterpretations on their unfamiliarity with the history of the Middle Ages and the significance of Joan for that time: "To understand Joan's history it is not enough to understand her character: you must understand her environment as well" (25). He also points out their failure to see the nineteenth-century context through which they interpret her:

> Her ideal biographer must be free from nineteenth century prejudices and biases; must understand the Middle Ages, the Roman Catholic Church, and the Holy Roman Empire much more intimately than our Whig historians have ever understood them; and must be capable of throwing off sex partialities and their romance, and regarding woman as the female of the human species, and not as a different kind of animal with specific charms and specific imbecilities. (11)

By implication (the failure to say anything good about any of these other authors) he lumps together all her biographers to date: "If a historian is an Anti-Feminist, and does not believe women to be capable of genius in the traditional masculine departments, he will never make anything of Joan" (10).[4] Thus Shaw implies that as a feminist, with the proper historical perspective other authors have missed, he is that "ideal biographer."

Yet Shaw's prefatory comments praising Joan as a Protestant and a Nationalist (7), and the associations he makes between her martyrdom and the treatment of suffragettes (27, 37),[5] indicate that he is as guilty of her contextualization, and perhaps anachronization, as her other depictors, although he seems to imply he avoids this problem through his maintenance of a medieval atmosphere. One early critic, John MacKinnon Robertson, notes Shaw's relative failure in this attempt and draws a significant parallel between Joan and other figures that Shaw associates with unwomanliness or gender indeterminacy:

> The difference here between Shakespeare and Mr. Shaw is that the former would never have pretended to be recovering the atmosphere of the Middle Ages; while Mr. Shaw, professing to be doing so, is in the main a great deal further from doing it. . . . Mr. Shaw's blend of Jeanne and Marie Bashkirtseff and George Eliot is true for neither the fifteenth nor the twentieth [century]. ("Mr. Shaw and 'The Maid'" 86–87)

It is undoubtedly the associations between historical and contemporary issues and events that attracted Shaw to Joan, as he indicated in a letter to the Reverend Joseph Leonard in 1922, when he sought background information on her canonization (*Collected Letters* 3:795–96). In the opening paragraph to the preface, after noting her larger religious and political significance, Shaw addresses his sense of Joan's importance to women's history:

> She was the pioneer of rational dressing for women, and like Queen Christina of Sweden two centuries later, to say nothing of Catalina de Erauso and innumerable obscure heroines who have disguised themselves as men to serve as soldiers and sailors, she refused to accept the specific woman's lot, and dressed and fought and lived as men did. (7)

As Catherine Schuler has noted, by opening his discussion of Joan with a remark about costuming, Shaw may be trivializing her significance in the larger realm of revolt against the patriarchal structures of church and state (156). Shaw's description of Joan's historical value here resembles Ménie Muriel Dowie's introduction to the "women adventurers." But his comparison of Joan to Queen Christina raises an interesting, related issue, for in his study of sexual inversion in women, Havelock Ellis also mentions Queen Christina, as well as Catherine II of Russia, as a woman of "homosexual temperament":

> It has been noted of distinguished women in all ages and in all fields of activity that they have frequently displayed some masculine traits. . . . Famous queens have on more or less satisfactory grounds been suspected of a homosexual temperament, such as Catherine II of Russia, who appears to have been bisexual, and Queen Christina of Sweden, whose very marked masculine traits and high intelligence seem to have been combined with a definitely homosexual or bisexual temperament. (196)[6]

Shaw avoids the issue of these queens' sexuality entirely, but his emphasis in the preface on Joan's essential heterosexuality deserves attention. His selection and highlighting of the historical details of her sexuality reveal his concern with this aspect of her character. Shaw's preface to *Saint Joan* is dated 1924, after the initial production of the play in December 1923. The efforts he makes to establish Joan within a conventional framework, with the potential for marriage and the professional explanation for her dress and behavior, stand out in contrast to the implications of the play itself, as if Shaw were working against the relative absence of sexual intrigue in the drama, or making excuses for one of his only female characters not involved in an amatory relation.

Like Lina Szczepanowska and the other female figures Shaw described as "neuter," Joan, too, is considered "neutral in the conflict of sex":

> The evident truth is that like most women of her hardy managing type she seemed neutral in the conflict of sex because men were too much afraid of her to fall in love with her. She herself was not sexless: in spite of the virginity she had vowed up to a

point, and preserved to her death, she never excluded the possibility of marriage for herself. But marriage, with its preliminary of the attraction, pursuit, and capture of a husband, was not her business: she had something else to do. (11)

Noteworthy here is the way Shaw reflects this neutrality: men's fear precluded their attraction to her, although she was open to the possibility of marriage at a later date. Like all aggressive Shavian women, Joan would have had to hunt a husband, a task that conflicted with, and was therefore precluded by, her more compelling nationalistic goals. Shaw entitles this particular section of the preface "Joan's Good Looks," as if he needed to establish her physical attractiveness to assure her heterosexuality. He neatly gets around the historical problem of male testimony to Joan's unattractiveness by his own conviction that a French sculpture of an unidentified model from the fifteenth century must be that of Joan. Shaw claims it has "a wonderful face, but quite neutral from the point of view of the operatic beauty fancier" (11). He closes the discussion with a thrust at those "fanciers," among whom must have also been the men whose historical testimony he read:

> Such a fancier may perhaps be finally chilled by the prosaic fact that Joan was the defendant in a suit for breach of promise of marriage, and that she conducted her own case and won it. (12)

Clearly someone found Joan "attractive" enough to seek her hand, although Shaw's Joan states she "never promised him" (83).

This section of the preface, coupled with the comments on her dress and "unwomanly" (7) behavior, not only links the discussion of Joan with Shaw's views on other nontraditional women in the late nineteenth and early twentieth centuries, but also works to position Joan within the context of the discourse of gender for his readers. Thus although Shaw claims a medieval milieu for the play itself, and within the drama eschews amatory involvements for Joan, he uses the preface to frame the action's relevance and contemporaneity, which, to be compelling on the issue of Joan's full identity, seems to incorporate issues of sexuality (including physical appearance and sexual orientation) that correspond to current aspects of analysis.

Barbara Bellow Watson maintains that in Joan, "for the first and last time, Shaw does get completely away from sexual appeal" (*Shavian Guide* 168), which is partly true, in that Joan neither sexually pursues nor is pursued by anyone in the action of the play. According to Shaw's friend, compatriot, and fellow playwright Lady Gregory, Shaw "chose Joan of Arc because of Bernhardt and others having played so many parts turning on sexual attraction, he wanted to give Joan as a heroine absolutely without that side" (213). But Margery Morgan, who associates Joan with the "Victorian . . . cult of the Principal Boy," notes that "Shaw's view fluctuates and, though it is faint and subtle and shouldn't protrude on consciousness at all, the feminine erotic quality faintly colours the figure [of Joan]" (254).[7]

Morgan's view can be substantiated textually by looking not so much at Joan herself as at her construction by other male characters who interact with her. In the opening scene, Captain Robert de Baudricourt interrogates Monsieur de Poulengey about his "intentions" with regard to Joan:

> Robert. It's about this girl you are interested in. . . . Now no doubt it seems to you a very simple thing to take a girl away, humbugging her into the belief that you are taking her to the Dauphin. But if you get her into trouble, you may get *me* into no end of a mess, as I am her father's lord, and responsible for her protection. So friends or no friends, Polly, hands off her.
> Poulengey (with deliberate impressiveness) I should as soon think of the Blessed Virgin herself in that way, as of this girl.
> Robert. . . . But she says you and Jack and Dick have offered to go with her. What for? . . .
> Poulengey. . . . They are pretty foulmouthed and foul-minded down there in the guardroom, some of them. But there hasnt been a word that has anything to do with her being a woman. They have stopped swearing before her.
>
> (55–56)

For Poulengey, "anything to do with being a woman" clearly means thinking of her only as a sexual object, although there is also the problem of the (Victorian) convention of "not swearing before a lady" that seems to complicate this denial of Joan's gender, but not her religious, identity.[8]

Shaw also makes Joan fully aware of her society's traditionally masculine and feminine roles. This is one of the clearest historical parallels implied in the play, for the Victorian sense of the woman's sphere seems identical to the domestic duties Joan can perform well, but abjures. Shaw connects these activities to the class theme in the drama: "When she was called a shepherd lass to her face she very warmly resented it, and challenged any woman to compete with her in the household arts of the mistresses of well furnished houses" (12).

In her first interview with Charles, the Dauphin, Joan says ironically, "What is my business? Helping mother at home. . . . I call that muck" (77). Later, during her trial, she makes her distinctive calling explicit:

> Joan. Nay: I am no shepherd lass, though I have helped with the sheep like anyone else. I will do a lady's work in the house—spin or weave—against any woman in Rouen.
> The Inquisitor. This is not a time for vanity, Joan. You stand in great peril. . . .
> The Chaplain. If you are so clever at woman's work why do you not stay at home and do it?
> Joan. There are plenty of other women to do it; but there is nobody to do my work.
>
> (128)

Joan here establishes herself as a Shavian superwoman: she can do woman's work as well as any other woman, and she can lead the French to victory and crown the Dauphin, which no one else—male or female—can seem to do.

Shaw aligns Joan's "vanity" with her youthful obliviousness of the proper (womanly) way to manage men:

> If she had been old enough to know the effect she was producing on the men whom she humiliated by being right when they were wrong, and had learned to flatter and manage them, she might have lived as long as Queen Elizabeth. (8)

> We have plenty of managing women among us of that age who illustrate perfectly the sort of person she would have become had she lived. But she, being only a lass when all is said, lacked

their knowledge of men's vanities and of the weight and pro-
portion of social forces. She knew nothing of iron hands in
velvet gloves. (22)

In other words, had Joan been a Candida, she might have survived.
But these womanly skills were not in Joan's repertoire; on the contrary, Shaw clearly identifies her as one of his "unwomanly" women
(20).

At the opening of the preface, Shaw explains that Joan was "judi-
cially burnt . . . essentially for what we call unwomanly and insuffer-
able presumption" (7). Under the heading "Joan's Manliness and
Militarism," he identifies her "abnormality": "her craze for soldiering
and the masculine life" (19). Although Shaw does not condemn this
not-quite-"peculiarity" (19), the categorization of Joan's behavior under "abnormality" gives his depiction a medical/psychoanalytic air.
He has established this way of examining Joan in the preceding paragraph of the preface, addressed to even "the most sceptical scientific
reader" (19). Shaw's use of the designations "abnormality" and "peculiarity" create some ambiguity here; he does not explicitly associate
the terms with others' views of the Maid (in other words, those
familiar with the scientific study of gender in his time), but the scientific context may indicate that these concepts are being thrown back
at those readers, rather than reflecting Shaw's personal attitude.
Shaw sums up Joan's case history—a series of questions he poses
about her desire to cross-dress, maintain constant asexual contact
with soldiers, and perform military functions (19–20)—with the diag-
nosis: "The simple answer to all these questions is that she was the
sort of woman that wants to lead a man's life" (20).

In this, Shaw likens Joan to the writer George Sand and the artist
Rosa Bonheur, both of whom cross-dressed (20).[9] Joan's sporting
male attire is the most obvious manifestation of her male identification, although Shaw makes certain that he accounts for the necessity
of Joan's costuming by her professional function. Like Lina, whose
aviator costume reflects her activity at her arrival, and the women
from the one-acts who disguise themselves during times of military
occupation, Joan, too, has a legitimate reason for cross-dressing—one
that may reflect her personality and sense of self, but that nevertheless has a practical explanation as well, unlike the purely personal
choice to cross-dress of the two female artists Shaw mentions. Placing

Joan in a contemporary context, Shaw likens her to the women who worked for the recent war effort:

> We can all see now, especially since the late war threw so many of our women into military life, that Joan's campaigning could not have been carried on in petticoats. This was not only because she did a man's work, but because it was morally necessary that sex should be left out of the question as between her and her comrades-in-arms. (14)

In an interview published in 1924, Shaw even implies that Joan's choice in dress reflected feminine modesty more than any other motive:

> Her idea in wearing men's clothes was a sensible one; she was a soldier, and could not be bothered with skirts, and as she associated with soldiers constantly it was really more modest to dress as one of them, instead of unnecessarily drawing attention to the difference in sex. (Quoted in Tittle 13)

The remarkable coincidence of Sybil Thorndike, the first English Joan, having just played numerous male roles through the exigencies of the war (Cheshire 246), cannot go unmentioned. Thus Shaw assures the reasonableness and normality of Joan's behavior: she cross-dresses for laudable, necessary purposes, and her male identification indicates no sexual irregularity, as he has established her essential heterosexuality by choosing to underline the relevant details concerning her potential for marriage as well as her distinctive but not unappealing physical appearance from the historical documents he consulted for his play.

Shaw uses the male authority figures who oppose Joan's dress and behavior to highlight the tradition of patriarchal displeasure with female appropriation of conventional masculine dress and occupation. Both church and state voice their contempt, in the figures of the Chaplain and the Inquisitor:

> The Chaplain. . . . But I know as a matter of plain commonsense that the woman is a rebel; and that is enough for me. She rebels against Nature by wearing man's clothes, and fighting.

Fig. 6. Sybil Thorndike played Saint Joan in the first London production in 1924. As with Shaw's other uniformed characters, she appears
androgynous.

> She rebels against The Church by usurping the divine author-
> ity of the Pope. . . . This is not to be endured.
>
> (100)

> The Inquisitor. . . . Mark what I say: the woman who quarrels
> with her clothes, and puts on the dress of a man, is like the
> man who throws off his fur gown and dresses like John the
> Baptist: they are followed . . . by bands of wild women and
> men who refuse to wear any clothes at all.
>
> (121–22)[10]

> The Inquisitor. . . . Now as to this matter of the man's dress. For
> the last time, will you put off that impudent attire, and dress
> as becomes your sex? . . .
> Joan. . . . If I were to dress as a woman they would think of me
> as a woman; and then what would become of me? If I dress
> as a soldier they think of me as a soldier, and I can live with
> them as I do at home with my brothers.
>
> (131–32)

Joan's simple realization here that others will treat her according
to her physical appearance and attire corresponds to her own distaste
for conventionally feminine clothing and behavior.[11] Once she
achieves her goal of convincing Baudricourt to give her a uniform
(62) and appears as a man, complete with a bobbed haircut which she
wears "because [she is] a soldier" (72), she never returns to woman's
dress.[12] She attests strongly to her masculine self-identity, which is
integrally connected to her wish to act and dress like a soldier:

> I will never take a husband. . . . I am a soldier: I do not want to
> be thought of as a woman. I will not dress as a woman. I do not
> care for the things women care for. They dream of lovers, and
> of money. I dream of leading a charge, and of placing the big
> guns. (83)[13]

Furthermore, she makes sure that any seemingly conventional feminine behavior she exhibits has a plausible masculine/soldierly explanation. After their success in battle, Joan addresses Dunois:

Joan. . . . I wish you were one of the village babies.
Dunois. Why?
Joan. I could nurse you for a while.
Dunois. You are a bit of a woman after all.
Joan. No: not a bit: I am a soldier and nothing else. Soldiers
always nurse children when they get a chance.
Dunois. That is true.

$$(103)^{14}$$

Like Lina Szczepanowska, Joan takes charge of the instruction of a weak, somewhat effeminate male, the "poor creature" (65) the Dauphin. In the epilogue, the ghost of Joan asks, "Did I make a man of thee after all, Charlie?" (147). Both of these masculine women know better how to be a man than some of the men they encounter. And their identities—external and internal—are of a piece: their physical appearance coincides with the essential gender orientation they feel, as Joan implies in her earlier comment to the Dauphin: "Dressing up dont fill empty noddle" (76). But Joan also realizes how conventional patriarchal society views her androgynous identity: "I might almost as well have been a man. Pity I wasnt: I should not have bothered you all so much then" (148).

The epilogue, Shaw's dream sequence of Joan's spiritual return in 1456 after the overturning of the verdict against her, and the announcement by a gentleman from 1920 of her canonization, drives home his contemporary message: the world is still not "ready to receive [God's] saints" (159), as evidenced by the repeated abandonment of Joan when she suggests she return from the dead. Following her revelation that she "might almost as well have been a man," she provocatively proposes she "come back . . . a living woman" (158), a possibility that prompts the other spirits' quick departure. After Joan's earlier denials of her femininity and her assertions of masculine identification, this threat to return as a woman is striking. Is Shaw implying here that a woman who behaves "as a woman" is even more dangerous than an unwomanly woman? Or potentially more powerful or damaging to the patriarchal structure? Does this final twist somehow undermine the impact of Joan as a masculine woman, and suggest Shaw can envision a realistic womanly woman of even greater potential? If this were so, then his futuristic, eschatalogical plays would be the locus for this characterization.[15]

Shaw's previous play, excepting his 1923 translation of Siegfried Tre-bitsch's *Frau Gittas Sühne* (*Jitta's Atonement*), had been the "Metabio-logical Pentateuch" *Back to Methuselah* (1921). This sweeping portrait of the progress of civilization from the Creation to its apocalyptic conclusion corresponds to studies identified by A. J. L. Busst from the Romantic period that are "closely associated with" discussions of androgyny: "a work tracing the progress of mankind from a single individual through universal history to the four corners of the mod-ern world, and discussing the general significance of each nation and civilization" (13).

Shaw opens the first of his five plays, "In the Beginning," in the Garden of Eden, with a version of the Adam and Eve story. Depart-ing from Genesis, he dramatizes the conversation of Eve and the Serpent, who here is female in contrast to the usually more masculine depiction. The Serpent tells Eve about the Creation, which she attri-butes to the apocryphal figure of Lilith:

> Listen. I am old. I am the old serpent, older than Adam, older than Eve. I remember Lilith, who came before Adam and Eve. . . . She was alone: there was no man with her. She saw death. . . and she knew then that she must find out how to renew herself and cast the skin like me. . . . And when she cast the skin, lo! there was not one new Lilith but two: one like herself, the other like Adam. You were the one: Adam was the other. (69)

This depiction of Lilith's determination to save humanity seems strong and forceful, but her independent triumph and power are short-lived. Shaw's version of the origin of mankind differs markedly from biblical tradition in that androgynous matriarchal power brings forth human life, rather than the more common patriarchal notion of God extracting Eve from the androgynous potential of Adam via his rib (Busst 7).[16] Nevertheless, male power and potency soon assert themselves, as Lilith determines that "the labor is too much for one. Two must share it" (69). Thus Adam receives the potential to aid in conception, and with the arrival of Cain, male dominance asserts itself in the Shavian rendition as with biblical records.[17] Bram Dijkstra has observed that for Pre-Raphaelite artists, there was a strong con-nection between the figures of the New Woman and Lilith, who were both "intent upon destroying the heavenly harmony of feminine subordination in the family" (309). Thus it is not surprising that, given Shaw's close ties with members of this movement, his work might mirror theirs in its engagement with the debate over the strength and impact of such character types.

The androgynous fecundity of the female Lilith contrasts markedly with the movement toward sterile masculine androgyny figured throughout the rest of the play. In part 2, "The Gospel of the Brothers Barnabas," set shortly after the Great War, discussion focuses on the brothers' theory of extended life potential, and its concomitant loss of gender identity and sexual interest:

> Lubin. By the way, Barnabas, is your daughter to keep her good looks all the time?
> Franklyn. Will it matter? Can you conceive the most hardened flirt going on flirting for three centuries? At the end of half the time we shall hardly notice whether it is a woman or a man we are speaking to.
>
> (143)

In part 3, "The Thing Happens," we see life in the twenty-second century, which is marked by human loss of the ability to reproduce: "Until the twentieth century you could produce children" (151). It is unclear exactly how life is created at this point in the future, but Shaw obviously suggests that a movement toward androgynous appearance is endemic to this era, as the Domestic Minister appears in a costume "not markedly different from that of the men" (168).[18] She has apparently retained her procreative potential; but, as one of the long-lived individuals predicted by the Brothers Barnabas, she no longer has any sexual drive (176, 181). Still, she sees it as her duty to reproduce "if the white race is to be saved" (181).[19]

By part 4, "Tragedy of an Elderly Gentleman," the sexes of long-livers are indistinguishable except "by a slight moustache" (196) that identifies the male sex. The thirtieth century inhabitants of the locale that was once Ireland wear identical "silk tunics and sandals" (190), and their names, Zoo and Zozim, not only give no indication of gender, they have also reversed the usual English distinction of the female signifier as an outgrowth of the male, as with (wo)man, since Zoo is identified as the woman, Zozim as the man.

This sexual indeterminacy carries over into part 5, "As Far as Thought Can Reach." In this last section, Shaw introduces the He- and She-Ancients, the ultimate corporeal form of the human race, who devote themselves exclusively to intellectual pursuits. They have no interest in sexual identity:

> The Youth. You old fish! I believe you dont know the difference between a man and a woman.
> The Ancient. It has long ceased to interest me in the way it interests you. And when anything no longer interests us we no longer know it.
>
> (252)

Even more telling is the physical uniformity that marks the development of a Youth to an Ancient around age four. The Youth Acis tells his friend Strephon, whose lover has deserted him:

> I am sorry, Strephon. I am getting on for three myself; and I know what old age is. I hate to say "I told you so"; but *she was getting a little hard set and flat-chested and thin on the top, wasnt she?* (258; my emphasis)

What is remarkable here, of course, is the transition from female to male appearance in the progression to old age. The loss of female secondary sexual characteristics ("flat-chested"), combined with the advent of the evidence of male aging (hair thinning), point to a development from feminized youth to masculine maturity, a process already noteworthy in Shaw's essay "Woman Since 1860." This ultimately male appearance is confirmed in the description of the She-Ancient, who enters immediately after this exchange:

> An Ancient Woman has descended the hill path during Strephon's lament, and has heard most of it. She is like the He-Ancient, equally bald, and equally without sexual charm. . . . Her sex is discoverable only by her voice, as her breasts are manly, and her figure otherwise not very different. (258)

Shaw's vision of the last physical stage of human existence, then, is one of sexual uniformity. Since women no longer need secondary sexual characteristics to attract men or serve reproductive needs (children are now hatched fully grown from eggs), they have lost the external features that, as Shaw maintained in *Village Wooing*, "[dont] matter except on special occasions" (150). From a theatrical standpoint, the direction that the She-Ancient should retain a sexually identifiable voice no doubt serves the exigencies of casting and performance as much as it suggests the hormonal difference that would maintain the female voice's higher register, a biological distinction not in keeping with the other male features in the description of the She-Ancient.

Yet Shaw feels the need to retain some semblance of sexual difference, perhaps to reinforce the developmental stages from Youth to Ancient. The She-Ancient admits to having played with a rag doll as a Youth (290), while the He-Ancient comments on the more "masculine" artistic function of sculptor (291–92). Shaw carries over the conventions of gender roles as he points toward a time when these disparities will disappear. In the transition from Youth to Ancient, then, the memory of gender remains, while the appearance of gender vanishes—for the female, who loses her sexual markers and comes to resemble the male. This demonstrates again the sense that for Shaw, essential existence is male, that woman evolves to a better, masculine form, and, lastly, that in the progression toward the ideal time when there are "no people, only thought" (297), the masculine form is the one closer to that ideal.[20] Thus humanity seems to have evolved from the androgynous female Lilith, through separate male and female beings, to creatures who all resemble each other, appearing male. Shaw laid the groundwork for this polar view as early as 1896, when he remarked in a letter to Ellen Terry, "The ideal old person is a child, the ideal child is forty, the ideal woman is a man, though women lie low & let that secret keep itself" (*Collected Letters* 1:659).

According to Margery Morgan, "Lilith presided emblematically over nineteenth-century evolutionary theory, which regarded male organisms as later and 'higher' developments from more primitive female forms" (107), and indeed Shaw has her preside over the closing of his cycle, reinforcing the sense of historical development the plays have dramatized. Thus the androgyny suggested by the appearance and behavior of the final human form is, upon closer examination, not truly androgynous, for the feminine half of the equation somehow disappears in the projection of the unified being, the Ancient.

Although Shaw draws on his society's cultural and scientific models of androgynous appearance and behavior to inform his characters, his predominant interest in the masculine female, and relative disinterest in the feminine male, suggest that Shaw appropriated the period's concern with the androgyne to suit his own model for some women's demeanor. Shaw does not usually employ the term androgyny; rather, he utilizes some of its more tangible manifestations to create a congenial character type: the strong Shavian woman whose appeal derives from her masculine essence. This character can be seen as attractive to Shaw for several reasons: she is less foreign, threatening, and "Other" if she can be assumed to be (like a) male, and her combination of masculine traits in a feminine physical structure allow her to be an object of homo- or autoerotic attraction at the same time she is a socially acceptable heterosexual figure. The tension between these types of appeal and their social and personal consequences underlies the dramas of fathers and daughters, to which I now turn.

PART THREE

SHAW'S DAUGHTERS

7

Shaw and the Tradition of Literary Paternity

There is of course a certain irony behind this title, "Shaw's Daughters," a certain playfulness with Shavian biographical facts. Shaw had no biological daughters, or sons for that matter, although he had numerous relations with men and women notably younger than himself, such as Molly Tompkins, Harley Granville-Barker, and T. E. Lawrence, that often resembled the rapport of parent and child.[1] As with many authors, Shaw's characters and plays were his children, and he writes of their creation with the parental metaphors that contemporary critics have realized are "all-pervasive in Western literary civilization" (Gilbert and Gubar 4). In his preface to *Fanny's First Play*, to cite one example, he humorously bemoans the notoriety his works have brought him:

> If it were possible, I should put forward all my plays anonymously, or hire some less disturbing person, as Bacon is said to have hired Shakespear, to father my plays for me. (110)

Shaw's contemporary, Eunice Fuller Barnard, notes his paternal creative function as well, explaining that through the creation of his char-

157

acters he "fathered" the type of woman who came to be known as the "flapper" in the 1920s (272).

In the opening chapter of *The Madwoman in the Attic*, Sandra Gilbert and Susan Gubar discuss this metaphoric phenomenon, noting that "in patriarchal Western culture . . . the text's author is a father, a progenitor, a procreator" (6). They quote from Gerard Manley Hopkins, whom they take as "a representative male citizen" (4) of the Victorian culture they investigate. According to Hopkins, the artist's " 'most essential quality' " is " 'masterly execution, which is a kind of male gift, and especially marks off men from women, the begetting of one's thought on paper. . . . The male quality is the creative gift' " (quoted in Gilbert and Gubar 3). Jack Tanner, Shaw's "Revolutionist" who voices the opposition of the "artist-man" to the "mother-woman" in *Man and Superman* (62), certainly echoes Hopkins's belief, and, appropriately, he expresses his opinions to his friend Octavius after the latter admits literary aspirations: "I want to count for something as a poet: I want to write a great play" (60)—a play that will have his beloved Ann as the heroine.

For Octavius, as Tanner duly observes, Ann serves as a muse whom he idolizes as Dante did Beatrice (91). Implicit is the notion that Tavy's view of Ann is a poetic fiction, that she and his feelings for her are the products of his poetic imagination. This, too, corresponds to observations in Gilbert and Gubar's tracing of the traditions of Western literary culture:

> Like the metaphor of literary paternity . . . [there is a] corollary notion that the chief creature man has generated is woman. . . . From Eve, Minerva, Sophia, and Galatea onward . . . patriarchal mythology defines women as created by, from, and for men, the children of male brains, ribs, and ingenuity. (12)

Shaw makes clear his awareness of this literary tradition by creating a dialogue where Tanner exposes Tavy's unconscious adherence to this cultural history. But Shaw simultaneously embraces it, calling this same Ann his own "most gorgeous female creation" (*Collected Letters* 2:394).

Shaw also expands upon this history of literary paternalism by an appropriation of maternal metaphors to describe his creativity. Susan

Stanford Friedman, in her recent study of the use of childbirth conceits, has observed:

> The *pregnant* body is necessarily female; the *pregnant* mind is the mental province of genius, most frequently understood to be inherently masculine. . . . The male metaphor might be a covert, indeed largely unconscious, tribute to woman's special generative power. . . . This "tribute" is deceptive, however. The male comparison of creativity with woman's procreativity equates the two as if both were valued equally, whereas they are not. This elevation of procreativity seemingly idealizes woman and thereby obscures woman's real lack of authority to create art as well as babies. As an appropriation of women's (pro)creativity, the male metaphor subtly helps to perpetuate the confinement of women to procreation. . . . The male childbirth metaphor paradoxically beckons woman toward the community of creative artists by focusing on what she alone can create, but then subtly excludes her as the historically resonant associations of the metaphor reinforce the separation of creativities into mind and body, man and woman. (75, 84, 94)

In a letter to the actress Eleanor Robson, whom he envisioned as the original Major Barbara, Shaw claims,

> I swear I never thought of you until you came up a trap in the middle of the stage & got into my heroine's empty clothes and said Thank you: *I* am the mother of that play. Though I am not sure that you are not its father; for you simply danced in here & captivated me & then deserted me & left me with my unborn play to bring into existence. (*Collected Letters* 2:524)

He used a similar string of maternal images to describe a revival of his play *Misalliance*—a play that takes as its major theme the difficulties in parent/child relations:

> It [the play] immediately showed signs of life, and I have been unable to prevent him [the producer] from bringing it to a second birth in London. I trust it will not prove a miscarriage, but I cannot deny that much water, and—alas!—a good deal of

blood has flowed through the bridges since it was a more or less topical play. (*Bodley Head* 4, 264)

Shaw demonstrates the sense of both paternal and maternal creativity in his work, at the same time acknowledging the collaborative nature of dramatic production. This dual sensibility corresponds to Shaw's androgynous self-view discussed previously—the belief that he embodies both male and female essences. Yet the alternation between paternal and maternal functions displayed in the letter to Eleanor Robson shows a tension between the recognition of others' involvement with his work and the feeling that he must be totally responsible for it. He begins with the attitude that he is writing completely independently, but then, according to his narrative of the creative process, the image of the actress in the role forces itself upon his consciousness, claiming maternal responsibility for the character. Yet Shaw questions this vision, wondering if the actress's performance is not closer to that of the socially constructed image of the "bad father"—the man who seduces the woman, leaving her "in her shame" to bring forth the fruit of their union.

The multiplicity of roles Shaw envisions for himself vis à vis his plays also finds evidence in the content of the plays themselves, for as many critics have observed, Shaw frequently dramatizes familial scenarios, focusing on the parent/child dynamic. And the indeterminacy of his function—sometimes father, sometimes mother, sometimes both, with a tension between sole creativity and enforced collaboration—informs the dramas, manifesting itself in conflict between parental forces over a child.

There is also a direct relation between the initial act of creation and bringing the offspring to maturity—a relation that perpetuates the tension between male and female parental influences. Shaw shows the intersection of these roles in a comment to the actress Ellen Terry: "it is clear that I have nothing to do with the theatre of today: I must educate a new generation with my pen from childhood up—audience, actors & all" (*Collected Letters* 2:97). He brings together his didactic and creative functions, believing he must form his society with the writing he simultaneously forms, working against the other extant forces of his culture.

Scholarly views on this issue are uniform: that Shaw saw himself as an instructor in his private life, and that this self-conception manifested itself in his plays, in particular *Caesar and Cleopatra, Major Barbara,* and *Pygmalion.* Having established this pattern in the major plays, however, Shavian scholarship has not fully explored its pervasive incidence in the canon, or, more important, investigated the subtler, sometimes subtextual interpretive possibilities for this motif. Shaw's works raise questions of parental dominance, children's potential, the construction of gender, and the privileging of certain gender configurations in the familial context, elements of which I will explore in the next three chapters.

In the preface to his study *Bernard Shaw: Pygmalion to Many Players,* Vincent Wall sets forth the biographical and artistic connection in Shaw's writing:

> It was not by accident that three of Bernard Shaw's greatest plays deal with an elderly mentor's attempts to instill wisdom and understanding into a young woman. Caesar finds it to his advantage to teach a savage little Cleopatra how to be a queen; Sir Andrew Undershaft discovers that his daughter Major Barbara is a girl of great spiritual conviction who can be transformed from a Salvation Army lassie into a young woman who can "make war on war"; and in perhaps his most enduring play *Pygmalion* a crotchety, irascible professor of phonetics teaches a cockney flower girl to speak in such a manner that she can become the owner of a flower shop. Shaw was a born educator and the role of teacher to young women appealed to him. (v)

Early in his analysis, Arthur Ganz makes this related observation:

> All of the crucial Shavian characters . . . are deeply involved with those central familial relationships, including sexual relations, that more than any others define our "human nature." That many of these are symbolic does not make them any less real: Caesar's connection with Cleopatra, for example, is quite as paternal as Undershaft's with Barbara, having to do in both cases with questions of education, parental authority, and filial selfhood. (3)

The closing comment in each of these quotations is particularly of interest: why did Shaw employ the older man/younger woman relation so persistently, and what is the nature of the selfhood that these young women attain under the tutelage of their male mentors?

In another of Jack Tanner's expositions on the family—one with which Shaw most probably agreed—he maintains that "the voice of nature proclaims for the daughter a father's care and for the son a mother's" (*Man and Superman* 97). Yet paternal relations outnumber maternal ones in the plays, and there are relatively few examples of maternal characters in didactic roles, although, as noted in the last chapter, Shaw's strong, masculine women do function in that capacity, "making men of" young male characters who are in age more like their siblings than their children. The mother/son relation, whether biological or figurative, adheres to a pattern of maternal infantilization of the male. Henry Higgins, who is consistently chided about his behavior by his housekeeper and his mother, reveals that he has "never been able to feel really grown-up and tremendous, like other chaps" (*Pygmalion* 43). Shaw instructed his actresses to inform their characterizations with this overbearing quality: he told Frances Dillon, who played Ann Whitefield on tour, that she was to

> try to imagine yourself Queen Victoria every night in the 1st Act. You will notice that Queen Victoria, even when she was most infatuatedly in love with Prince Albert, always addressed him exactly as if he were a little boy of three and she his governess. (*Collected Letters* 2:817)

He gave similar direction to Mrs. Patrick Campbell for her performance as Eliza Doolittle:

> If you have ever said to Stella [her daughter] in her childhood "I'll let you see whether you will obey me or not" and then inverted her infant shape and smacked her until the Square (not to mention the round) rang with her screams, you will know how to speak the line "I'll let you see whether I'm dependent on you." (*Collected Letters* 3:224)

Lady Britomart exhibits the same attitude toward her son Stephen in *Major Barbara*, which Shaw highlights by having her say to her fully matured son, "And dont forget that you have outgrown your mother" (128). Shaw's mother/son relation never expands beyond the nurturing, maternal, domestic sphere. Mothers have only one behavioral and biological role toward their sons; it is the fathers who prepare their children for the larger social/professional sphere.

For Shaw, teaching is a masculine profession, and the lessons of the father (or father figure) always overpower those of the mother (when and if she is alive or characterized), resulting in paternal identification by the child (biological or surrogate). This identification takes on gender attributes, as the father brings up and forms the daughter in his own image, essentially imbuing her with his recognizably masculine traits. Thus the male creative impulse Shaw dramatizes in his fathers and daughters mirrors the dynamic of the potent male pen on the virginal, feminized page (Gilbert and Gubar 6), which will reflect, by the writing on it, his exertions.

The preponderance of this relation in Shaw's work also reflects the Victorian climate in which he began his writing career. As Shaw himself observed in "Women Since 1860," all young children, male and female, were feminized by clothing (*McCall's* 10), and in general were treated as feminine until school-aged. There was also growth in the publication of conduct books and domestic treatises at the time (a trend Shaw gently parodies with the *Twentieth Century* household tracts produced in great quantity by Mrs Clandon in *You Never Can Tell*). One such popular volume, first published in the 1860s, featured the title *How I Managed My Children from Infancy to Marriage*, and was written by a Mrs. Warren (!) (Gorham 116–17). These books were designed to inculcate Victorian values and morals, particularly in young women. According to Kathleen Hickok,

> Rather like Alice in Wonderland (who was only about seven years old), the typical middle-class English girl was expected to assimilate these characteristics [of "sweetness, docility, passivity and obedience"] and cultivate these abilities in childhood, long before she was old enough to put them to use. One result was the child-woman, a popular figure in children's literature . . . as well as a recurring character in the novels of Charles Dickens and others. (40)

Given Shaw's predilection for didacticism, especially toward young women,[2] it is not surprising that his "first serious literary effort" (Winsten "Editorial Note" 53), written in 1878 soon after his arrival in London, should have been a treatise on a young girl's education, the epistolary essay *My Dear Dorothea*. Comparatively little criticism on this piece exists, perhaps because it predates his self-proclaimed juvenilia, the novel *Immaturity* (1879); because Shaw does not refer to it in other writings; and possibly because it was not published until 1956, after the first tide of major Shaw criticism had already appeared.

Barbara Bellow Watson feels the work is very much of a piece with its Victorian context:

> It cannot have been mere chance that Shaw's first literary work, *My Dear Dorothea*, concerned itself with a little girl, or that its underlying theme was the spiritual management of a woman's life in a badly organized society. In addressing the Victorian little girl, Shaw was approaching society through the being who stood at the bottom of a hierarchy of dominations. (*Shavian Guide* 41)

Thus, even in this early effort, Shaw is working both with and against the prevailing literary mode. Using the familiar form of the conduct book, he subverts the tradition to impress on his female audience the need to fight against Victorian womanly conventions. His choice of subtitle for *My Dear Dorothea* echoes in tone and style numerous treatises from the genre and reflects his cognizance of the tradition he invokes:

A PRACTICAL SYSTEM OF
MORAL EDUCATION FOR FEMALES
EMBODIED IN A LETTER TO A YOUNG PERSON
OF THAT SEX

In keeping with Kathleen Hickok's parallel to the seven-year-old Alice, Shaw explains to Dorothea that, "As you have just completed your fifth year, a few words of wholesome counsel as to your conduct and feelings may not be unreasonable" (7). Shaw contrasts the suggestions he is about to convey to the "tracts" by which Aunt Tabitha "seeks to improve" the young Dorothea (7). Michael Holroyd believes Shaw modeled his pamphlet after "George Augustus Sala's rather damp squib *Lady Chesterfield's Letters to Her Daughter*, which Shaw had read the previous year" (*Search for Love* 72). Shaw may also have had in mind such volumes as Sarah Stickney Ellis's *The Daughters of England* (1842), one of the most popular of the conduct manuals for Victorian girls. *My Dear Dorothea* could be read as a virtual debate with, and explanation/modification of, the precepts of Mrs. Ellis, whose writings exemplify the genre. In *The Daughters of England*, Ellis admonishes, "the three great enemies to woman's advancement in moral excellence [are] selfishness, vanity, and artifice, as opposed to her disinterestedness, simplicity of heart, and integrity" (338). She champions womanly self-sacrifice in a fashion similar to John Ruskin, whose widely read "Of Queen's Gardens" (1865) proposed women's education "not for self-development, but for self-renunciation" (Millet 128).

In *Dorothea*, as well as in *The Quintessence*, Shaw took a stand directly against this notion of feminine sacrifice:

> Let your rule of conduct always be to do whatever is best for yourself. Be as selfish as you can. And here I feel that I must stop to explain something to you. In reading this letter, you have been surprised at finding directions quite opposite to those which you are accustomed to receive. I will perhaps surprise you still more when I tell you that what everybody says is almost sure to be wrong. The reason is, that there are far more fools in the world than wise people; and when all the fools talk, as they often do, the wise people cannot be heard. (*Dorothea* 25)

Shaw demonstrates even in this early work his technique of positioning himself in opposition to the status quo, although his advice for Dorothea does not in any way endanger her ability to mature comfortably in Victorian middle-class society. He teaches her to distinguish between pride in self and personal vanity, clarifying two often-conflated traits (39–40), and explains how certain forms of hypocrisy, such as expressing sympathy for the death of a friend's friend, are appropriate and acceptable untruths (35–37). Above all, he stresses independence of thought and individuality (43–44), precepts unusual for Victorian children, who were usually taught to do and think as they were told.[3]

These lessons appear remarkably advanced for young girls in particular, who were inculcated with all the virtues of womanly deference and subservience to their fathers and future husbands. In fact, with the exceptions of playing with dolls and wearing dresses, Shaw's Dorothea demonstrates no traits or habits that could be identified as markedly feminine, and he includes no lessons aimed at her role as a woman—only as an adult. "I know how clever you are, and I advise you just as I would an older person" (25). One can interpret this adult treatment as advanced on Shaw's part, and in keeping with his notions of common humanity and relative lack of gender difference, but the question as to why Shaw chose a young female recipient for his "System of Moral Education" remains. Watson's explanation, quoted above, that a young girl is the proverbial "low person on the Victorian social totem pole," indeed captures the social parallel of a young child in the home and a woman in society both being "at the bottom of a hierarchy of dominations." But Shaw's treatise is not revolutionary in this regard. It does not suggest that Dorothea try to change her environment; rather, she is privately to change herself to function more successfully in society as it stands. Obviously this viewpoint anticipates Shaw's Fabian beliefs in rough, incomplete form.

Stephen Winsten notes that Shaw passes on to Dorothea those realizations he had already garnered from his own youth: his "[thinking] things out for himself" and his admiration for Bunyan's *The Pilgrim's Progress* ("Editorial Note" 53–54). Indeed all the lessons Shaw presents with "the romantic affection of a parent, tempered by the rational interest of an experimental philosopher" (*Dorothea* 52), reflect his own personal growth and development. *Dorothea* certainly exemplifies the "father's care for a daughter," but it also stands as the first example of the didactic older male and young female pupil relation in his works. An early reviewer, E. J. Batson, believes that treatise "was . . . the first of [Shaw's] onslaughts on the female mind" and was "addressed more to the incipient Intelligent Woman than to the Precocious Child" (20–21).

Even more noteworthy, however, is the projection onto Dorothea, a young girl, of the pre-enlightened status of Shaw himself. Shaw has chosen to represent the uneducated form of a child like himself as female, a child with intrusive aunts and godparents like those he depicts in *Sixteen Self Sketches*, and with various portrayals of a mother figure, but virtually no mention of a father—a significant choice, given Shaw's great ambivalence toward his own father, whom he had recently left behind in Dublin.

This potential biographical link may in part account for the relative absence of conventionally feminine characteristics in Dorothea, although she is notably lacking in any recognizably traditional gendered attributes, masculine or feminine. Later in Shaw's writing, the passing on of gendered traits will become part of the education process, but in this early piece Shaw has laid the essential groundwork for the didactic frame that shapes so many of his plays and non-dramatic pieces as well. He has assumed both paternal ("the romantic affection of a parent") and scientific ("the rational interest of an experimental philosopher") stances toward his subject—those attitudes that will reappear with the fathers and father figures like Caesar and Undershaft, and scientist/creators like Pygmalion. In *Dorothea*, Shaw has established the trope of educating a young woman—a projection of his younger self—in his own image, teaching her the lessons he has learned that make up the persona he presents as G. B. S.

Soon after composing *Dorothea*, Shaw embarked on his short-lived career as a novelist. As several critics have noted, Shaw's fictional narratives also feature the didactic, parental relations that dominate the later plays. In *Cashel Byron's Profession*, the heroine Lydia Carew receives an unconventionally advanced education from her widowed father before his death; and Elsie B. Adams makes the claim that Owen Jack, in *Love Among the Artists*, is the prototype for Henry Higgins (134–35).[4] Arnold Silver, in his analysis of *An Unsocial Socialist*, makes the significant observation that the character of Agatha Wylie, whom the hero Sidney Trefusis eventually marries, "is strikingly similar to the young Shaw himself" (67). Silver and others have remarked that Shaw was "creating in Trefusis a model for himself" (57), and thus "marries his own self . . . in the person of Agatha" (68). Silver maintains that we should "regard Agatha less as a separate woman than as himself [Shaw/Trefusis] in female form" (68–69).

Silver uses his observations to draw biographical conclusions concerning Shaw's intention in writing the novel and his relationship with Alice Lockett, who was then his platonic lover. He observes another instance of Shaw's projection of himself onto a female character in his discussion of Eliza Doolittle in *Pygmalion* (185). The thrust of his argument lying elsewhere, Silver does not stress the gender alternation he charts; but clearly he has identified Shaw's continued use of a female character to represent his younger self—once again a young woman whom his reader first encounters as a schoolgirl, some years younger than his hero, and now one who enters into an emotional relation with the father/teacher figure. Other observers have noted parallels between Shaw's young female characters and himself. Dame Sybil Thorndike, who originated the role of Saint Joan in England, believed "the model for Barbara, as for Joan, whom she foreshadows, is really Shaw himself" (Albert 75).

Arthur Ganz, too, believes that Shaw's father/daughter relations are "problematic," and he concludes the young women "are extensions" of the male characters (63). Ganz suggests this Shavian motif has a Wagnerian origin, and cites several plot parallels between *The Ring* and *Major Barbara* (63). Ganz may have based this analysis on his reading of *The Perfect Wagnerite* (1898), Shaw's Marxist interpretation of *The Ring*.

Shaw opens *The Perfect Wagnerite* with an address to his imagined reader: "Let me assume for a moment that you are a young and good-looking woman" (195). He then asks this imagined audience to imagine in turn being at the Klondike during the recent gold rush. She is to see herself in a plight that thus might be within the realm of her imaginative capabilities—being the known, recent past—and she is then to associate her fantasy with the more foreign Wagnerian scenario that Shaw describes for her. Hereby Shaw frames his discussion with a didactic fantasy: he creates an imaginary female audience for whom he can serve as older male teacher, both weaving her by association into the story itself, and keeping her outside it, "waiting for the curtain to rise" (196).

After this opening, the frame device changes; Shaw maintains the "you" subject into the second scene, but then seems to join her, or expand his audience, for the address becomes "us" (218) and "we" (220).[5] At the heart of his discussion, right after he makes this pronoun transition, Shaw turns to an investigation of the key characters Wotan and Brynhild, father and Valkyrie daughter. According to Shaw, "This daughter, the Valkyrie Brynhild, is his true will, *his real self* (as he thinks): to her he may say what he must not say to anyone, *since in speaking to her he but speaks to himself*" (219: my emphasis). As he merges with his female audience, Shaw writes of the father's sense of his unity with his daughter in the opera.

Whether Shaw identified Wagner's character relations with, or imposed on those figures a communion germane to, his own (as some critics have said of his readings of Ibsen), he presents in this interpretation the essence of the father/daughter equation that appears repeatedly in his own writing. By the time he was producing *The Perfect Wagnerite*, Shaw had already dramatized an early version of this relation in *Widowers' Houses*, in the characters of Sartorius and his daughter Blanche. But Shaw's best known work of male to female instruction comes later in his career, and shows the continued importance of this dynamic to both his plays and prose pieces. *The Intelligent Woman's Guide to Socialism and Capitalism* (1928) took for its pretext the request of his sister-in-law for a short explanation of socialism for a women's study circle (*Collected Letters* 3:900). Shaw's dedication reads, "To my sister-in-law / Mary Stewart Cholmondeley / The intelligent woman / to whose question this book / is the best answer / I can make" (5). According to Dan Laurence, Shaw

> claimed [it] was the first work on economics and political science addressed specifically to women instead of to "a sort of abstract reader who is conceived as aridly and academically male as far as he is conceived of having any sex at all." (*Collected Letters* 3:900)

Most early reviews of the study ignored the device of the female addressee, but one female critic, Mrs. Le Mesurier, devoted herself to producing a lengthy rebuttal, showing Shaw's failure to understand fully woman's position in the economic structure of English society. *The Socialist Woman's Guide to Intelligence: A Reply to Mr. Shaw* (1929) features Mrs. Le Mesurier's analysis of the book: "If we must, then we have to conclude that Mr. Shaw rates his Intelligent Woman's intelligence insultingly low" (30), although she later concedes that "no woman could cordially dislike the creator of Lady Cecily Waynfleet [*sic*] and Major Barbara, for whose sake we are ready to forgive him even for Ann!" (201). During the period of its composition, Shaw's close friend and colleague Beatrice Webb remarked that he was "putting in a great deal of work on *The Intelligent Woman's Guide to Socialism*, trying to reduce each thought to its simplest and most lucid expression, 'so that any fool can understand it'" (*Diary* 4, 63). It is unclear whether Webb is quoting Shaw here, but the association of the (female) audience with "any fool" certainly raises questions about his attitude toward the proposed (female) readers.

Rebecca West takes a more balanced tone in her review of the book. She corroborates Shaw's notion that books on economics were written exclusively for men:

Behind all this lies, one perceives, the assumption that women are definitely inferior to men in their grasp of one of the most vitally important subjects that the intellect includes in its purview, so definitely inferior that they cannot understand textbooks dealing with it; and the writers of such books take it for granted that their readers will be exclusively male and limit themselves to material of interest to men and, Feminist though I am, I do not feel inclined to dispute that assumption. I freely admit its truth because I know that the inferior grasp of Economics manifested by women is not due to any intellectual inferiority. . . . If women do not concern themselves with the study of Economics as men do it is simply because they are not equally interested; and that is not to their discredit. For it is not due to lethargy. It is due to a profound scepticism concerning the value of male ratiocination concerning the fundamentals of existence which is very far from being without just cause. (515–16)

West spends the bulk of the article showing how Shaw perpetuates misconceptions about the economic position of women in English society, yet feels women should read the work, essentially to see what they are up against "in the everyday world" (520).

More recently, Barbara Bellow Watson has viewed the treatise more favorably, and given her study of Shaw's female characters the allusive title *A Shavian Guide to the Intelligent Woman* (1964). That Shaw maintained an unwavering notion of his position as women's teacher over the span of his career emerges from a letter to Ellen Terry, written more than thirty years earlier, in 1896, which included his lengthy comments on how she should handle her role of Imogen in the Irving production of *Cymbeline*. Shaw entitled these directives "The Intelligent Actress's Guide to Cymbeline" (St. John 36).

Before turning to an examination of the variations on the father/daughter motif that appear in the plays, I would like to discuss one additional prose work, the late novella *The Adventures of the Black Girl in Her Search for God* (1932). Not only does the story show the continuity of this theme and character relation into the later part of Shaw's career, but it also incorporates all the significant components of the dynamic, which can then be analyzed separately in the better known dramas.

The Adventures of the Black Girl is most often considered among Shaw's theological writings, a parable of sorts showing up the inconsistencies and hypocrisies of established religions. According to Eric Bentley,

> As a theologian Shaw is very unpretentious. What he again and again says about God is that He exists but that He is very different from the Jehovah of the Jewish-Christian tradition. . . . In his story *The Adventures of the Black Girl in Her Search for God* Shaw specifies several other phases of Deity; but the conclusion as to all of them is that they are too crude or too flattering. Shaw's God is less personal and less perfect. . . . Above all, He is not yet finished. He is an evolving God, learning, as we learn, by trial and error. (44)

Little attention has focused, however, on either the narrative structure of the story or the development of the plot, which, as Shaw readily admits, loosely follows a Voltairean schema (*Adventures* 74) to end in a place not dissimilar to Pangloss's garden.

If Shaw indeed used *Candide* as a model, then it must be immediately noted that he switched the sex of his adventurer to the (otherwise unnamed) Black Girl. Another major influence on Shaw, Bunyan's *The Pilgrim's Progress*, clearly underlies this text as well, and Shaw similarly exchanges the sex of the main character in search of salvation, and, significantly, has his heroine *end* in a scene of domesticity, rather than start with an escape therefrom as does the male pilgrim. Thus Shaw imposes on this story of religious exploration in a more primitive world the pattern of a young, unlearned female character who is to be educated to function independently in her society but also to embrace the Victorian tradition of marriage and family for women.[6]

As with *Dorothea* and *Wagnerite*, Shaw creates here an inexperienced female pupil figure. Whereas Dorothea has much to learn because of her youth (five years old), and the "young and good-looking woman" because of her unfamiliarity with art and culture beyond her era's material history (the recent goldrush fervor)—both of which are plausible scenarios within Victorian society—in the *Adventures of the Black Girl* Shaw chooses to depict a character at extreme remove from this Victorian environment in order to emphasize her relative ingenuousness. The Black Girl is an African native, uneducated in any conventional sense, yet instinctively intelligent, inquisitive, and opinionated.

One cannot help but think Shaw is exploiting a racial stereotype in this portrayal: an image of the primitive Black, intuitive and in tune with her jungle habitat. He seems to need an extreme version of his young female pupil for this story—one removed from Victorian tradition and conventions, a clean slate. Part of this narrative calculation derives from Shaw's interest in exposing those very conventions—an intention that requires such contrast and distance to be successful. And Shaw effects this by introducing a group of British tourists who voice the epitome of imperialist fears, stupidities, and prejudices, thereby deflecting the sense of exploitation away from the narrator and his heroine, who appear enlightened by comparison.

> "Are you in search of God?" said the first gentleman. "Had you not better be content with Mumbo Jumbo, or whatever you call the god of your tribe?" (34)

> "You cannot teach these people the truth about the universe" said a spectacled lady. (35)

> "Can you count forwards from one?"
> "One, two, three, four, five, do you mean?" said the black girl, helping herself by her fingers.
> "Just so" said the lady. "Now count backwards from one."
> "One, one less, two less, three less, four less."
> They all clapped their hands. "Splendid!" cried one. . . . And then altogether, "Marvelous! marvelous!" (38)

It is certainly possible that Shaw used the character of a young black female with the intention of highlighting others' prejudice, showing how the Black Girl's intelligence and individuality distinguish her from stereotype. Yet although she does refer to herself, and other characters occasionally refer to her, as a woman,[7] the titular and narrative appellation of "girl" dominates in the story and thereby becomes an evaluative term, keeping the character in a position of inferiority, whether from race, sex, or lack of education. It is also interesting to note that there are no "boys" presented in the tale, only younger and older men.

Stanley Weintraub observes that Shaw seems to have based his story on his encounter with a young English missionary, Mabel Shaw. According to Weintraub,

A year after G. B. S. wrote the following letter [to Mabel Shaw] he told Nancy Astor (12 May 1930) that he had invited to lunch "a certain Miss Mabel Shaw (no relation), a woman with a craze for self-torture, who broke off her engagement with a clergyman (he died of it) to bury herself in the wilds of Africa and lead negro children to Christ. She has a very graphic pen; and some of her letters were shewn to me. She has come home on a missionary-furlough . . ." Not long afterward G. B. S. was visiting in South Africa; and when the visit was prolonged because Charlotte was injured in an auto accident, he used his enforced leisure to write *The Black Girl*, which appears to owe much of its inspiration to Mabel Shaw. (Shaw *Portable* 632)

Miss Shaw had apparently asked the famous author if he felt she had any literary ability, and if he thought she should write of her experiences as a missionary in Africa. Shaw replied:

Now it is clear from what you have written that you are one of the would-be saviors, like Bunyan and Voltaire. Having found happiness with God (so to speak) you wish to bring others to him. Jesus, who was strongly anti-missionary, as his warning about the tares and the wheat shews, would probably tell you to mind your own business and suffer little children to find their own way to God even if it were a black way; but he certainly would not demur to your describing your own pilgrimage and testifying that you had found God in your own white way. (Shaw *Portable* 633)

Perhaps Shaw felt that his own fictional guidance of the Black Girl was "anti-missionary" (or nonmissionary), in that she chooses to abandon all conventional forms of worship, for as narrator of *The Black Girl*, Shaw clearly manipulates the Black Girl's search, despite his physical absence (in name) from the text.[8] Another reading, of course, suggests that Shaw adheres to his advice to Miss Shaw, and once again projects his own discoveries onto his young female character, "describing his own pilgrimage" by narrating his own course of religious discovery, leading to the conclusions Bentley describes above, which are like the Black Girl's, although hers are not as lucid.

Shaw opens his story with a scene of instruction between the Black Girl and the female missionary:

> "Where is God?" said the black girl to the missionary who had converted her.
> "He has said 'Seek and ye shall find Me'" said the missionary. (7)

Shaw devotes the next page of text to a lengthy description of the missionary, "a small white woman, not yet thirty" (7). The description indeed bears much resemblance to the story of Mabel Shaw, complete with the engagement to, and death of, the clergyman (7). From the amount of detail given at the opening, the reader is led to believe that this character will play an important role in the story, but on the contrary, Shaw then turns to a description of the Black Girl and the beginning of her search, and the missionary is never seen or heard from again. Shaw has taken over as the guiding force in the text.

The issue of narrative control and literary paternalism is particularly relevant here, for although Shaw chooses third-person narration for his story, unlike the direct address to the young woman in *Wagnerite* or the epistolary construct of *Dorothea*, the hand of the author and his guiding presence are very much felt despite the absence of his voice *per se*. One of the best examples of this comes near the opening of the story, after the Black Girl receives "her teacher's reply very literally" and strides "right off into the African forest in search of God," taking "the Bible with her as her guidebook" (8). She encounters on a pile of rocks the first in a series of false gods, whom she tries to smite with her knobkerry for his trickery, but who disappears in thin air.

But when she reached the top there was nothing there. This so bewildered her that she sat down and took out her Bible for guidance. But whether the ants had got at it, or being a very old book, it had perished by natural decay, all the early pages had crumbled to dust which blew away when she opened it. (10–11)

Shortly thereafter, "she resorted to her Bible again [and] the wind snatched thirty more pages out of it and scattered them in dust over the trees" (14). Nature, under the narrative supervision of Shaw, is clearly dispensing with the precepts of established religion so that the Black Girl has her way cleared to receive the new values she will garner from her search for God. And although she retains a memory of the lessons of the female missionary, she learns to replace these teachings with those she acquires subsequently. She grows out of the fictional Christianity propounded by her female teacher and comes under the narrative supervision of a male guide who ultimately enters the text in self-caricature to take a more active role in the outcome of the tale. This depiction of the abandonment of the female teacher for the male typifies one of the patterns of the parent/child, teacher/pupil works.

Shaw devotes most of the story to the titular "adventures" of his heroine, whom he clearly molded in the form of the independent Shavian woman. Like Vivie Warren, she is physically strong, with a "grip of iron," which, in this case, is "softly padded, however" (57), adding an underlying feminine quality. The Black Girl emerges as one of the descendants of the Shavian New Woman,[9] one who bucks the cultural traditions that, in the parable, appear to be as strongly enforced as the religious precepts of the English missionary. Her own beliefs emerge at odds with the teaching she has received, although Shaw depicts them as equally unexamined, even if intuitively "right."

The first point of revolt for the Black Girl involves her dress—or lack thereof, a detail highlighted by the text's frequent illustrations of the nude Black woman.

The black girl, having been taught to fear nothing, felt her heart harden against him [an older white male god figure], partly because she thought strong men ought to be black, and only missionary ladies white, partly because he had killed her friend the snake, and partly because he wore a ridiculous white nightshirt, and thereby rubbed her up on the one point on which her teacher had never been able to convert her, which was the duty of being ashamed of her person and wearing petticoats. (9)

The Black Girl expresses this opinion more vocally later in the story, in an encounter with an Arab and an idol maker:

> "I have found many gods" said the black girl. "Everyone I meet has one to offer me; and this image maker here has a whole shopful of them. But to me they are all half dead, except the ones that are half animals. . . . But even these gods who are half goats are half men. Why are they never half women?"
>
> "What about this one?" said the image maker, pointing to Venus.
>
> "Why is her lower half hidden in a sack?" said the black girl. "She is neither a goddess nor a woman: she is ashamed of half her body, and the other half of her is what the white people call a lady. . . . I have no use for her." (47)

This independent outspokenness characterizes the Black Girl throughout the tale. She is one of Shaw's free-thinking women, and she explains this attitude in opposition to blind faith in divine direction:

> "Walk humbly and God will guide you" said the Prophet. "What is it to you whither He is leading you?"
>
> "He gave me eyes to guide myself" said the black girl. "He gave me a mind and left me to use it. How can I now turn on Him and tell Him to see for me and to think for me?" (19)

Her most notable point of departure from tradition is her recognition of the patriarchal structure of society and religion, as the quotation "Why are they never half women?" reveals. She exposes the hypocrisy of Muslim polygamy, for example, in conversation with this same Arab:

> "A man needs many wives and a large household to prevent this cramping of his mind" said the Arab. "He should distribute

his affection. Until he has known many women he cannot know the value of any; for value is a matter of comparison. I did not know what an old angel I had in my first wife until I found what a young devil I had in my last."

"And your wives?" said the black girl. "Are they also to know many men in order that they may learn your value?" (50)

Similarly, the Black Girl rebels against the paternalism of Christian doctrine, having literalized the metaphoric parallel between the family and the Church:

"I am in search of God. Where is He?"
"Within you" said the conjurer. "Within me too."
"I think so" said the girl. "But what is He?"
"Our father" said the conjurer.
The black girl made a wry face and thought for a moment. "Why not our mother?" she said then. . . . "My father beat me from the time I was little until I was big enough to lay him out with my knobkerry" said the black girl; "and even after that he tried to sell me to a white baas-soldier who had left his wife across the seas. I have always refused to say 'Our father which art in heaven.' I always say 'Our grandfather.' I will not have a God who is my father." (26–28)

It is interesting that despite the feminist inclination here, Shaw chooses to hedge the patriarchal revolt—raising the issue of matriarchy, but maintaining a patriarchal liturgy with the substitution "grandfather" in the prayer. By introducing the issue of domestic violence, a theme carried over from *Dorothea*, where the brutal parent is the mother (19–21), he also deflects the political thrust of her question onto a more personal basis: the Black Girl wants a mother God perhaps as much because her experience with father figures has been negative as because she feels more affinity with a female deity.

During her encounter with the English tourists, the Black Girl thinks she has learned of the right female goddess, one she hears of by listening to the conversation of a "mathematical lady" (38) who has clearly embraced science as the religion of the future:

"It is, we now know, a mathematical universe. Ask that girl to divide a quantity by the square root of minus x, and she will not have the faintest notion what you mean. Yet division by the square root of minus x is the key to the universe." (35)

The Black Girl, totally untrained in mathematics, misunderstands this speech, and takes the "key to the universe" as "the square root of Myna's sex" (38).[10] Shaw expands on this pun in her later encounter with the image maker:

"To make a link between Godhood and Manhood, some god must become man."

"Or some woman become God" said the black girl. "That would be far better, because the god who condescends to be human degrades himself; but the woman who becomes God exalts herself." . . .

"There is a goddess of whom I have heard, and of whom I would know more" said the black girl. "She is named Myna; and I feel there is something about her that none of the other gods can give." . . . "She most surely exists" said the black girl; "for the white missy spoke of her with reverence, and said that the key to the universe was the root of her womanhood and that it was bodiless like a number, and that it was before the beginning instead of after it, just as God was before creation. It is not Myna's sex but that which multiplied by itself makes Myna's sex. Something like that must have been the beginning; and something like that it must be that endures when we return to the dust out of which it made us. . . . But now I know through Myna that one is that which is multiplied by itself and not by a married pair." (47–48)

The similarity here to Shaw's use of the Lilith myth in *Back to Methuselah* is unmistakable. Myna, like Lilith, is an image of female fecundity that holds the potential to create mankind independent of men. Calling the "means by which her [the Black Girl's] faith develops" "devious," Daniel Dervin remarks:

Shaw's pun, regardless of its scientific fallacy, is a brilliant leap of wit. It links numbers not only to sex but to the omnipotence of the Primordial Mother. Myna is the name given to that prehistoric moment of matriarchal parthenogenesis discussed by Don Juan and later in Lilith. (311–12)

Yet despite the "cleverness" of the pun and the possibility that it suggests a female source of faith, Shaw propels the Black Girl onward away from this female-oriented religion, into the Voltairean garden in which he concludes his story, showing that this last misunderstanding is only the most blatant and amusing of all the naive forms of worship she has encountered and/or embraced.

The last old gentleman the Black Girl meets tells her to "make a little garden for yourself: dig and plant and weed and prune; and be content if He jogs your elbow when you are gardening unskilfully, and blesses you when you are gardening well" (54). The Black Girl accedes to his suggestion, and gives up her search to join him in the garden. Given the argumentative nature of her other encounters in the story, it is surprising that she offers no opposition to his plan, but accepts it unquestioningly, becoming "very devoted to the old gentleman" (55). She comes to know a fellow gardener, "a redhaired Irishman" (54) who proclaims his "Socialism" (55) and voices opinions on God much like the Shavian ones summarized by Bentley: "My own belief is that He's not all that He sets up to be. He's not properly made and finished yet" (55). Together, the old gentleman and the Black Girl

> did their best to teach him nicer habits and refine his language. But nothing would ever persuade him that God was anything more solid and satisfactory than an eternal but as yet unfulfilled purpose, or that it could ever be fulfilled if the fulfilment were not made reasonably easy and hopeful by Socialism. (55)

In shortened form, Shaw again depicts a version of the *Pygmalion* story, showing the autobiographical parallels to his own adaptation from the manners and sounds of his Irish youth to the refinements of London. The Black Girl has become civilized and a civilizing force from her own exposure to the old gentleman, and despite her earlier protestations against the "terrible tyranny" of love (29), she acquiesces to the Life Force urgings of the old gentleman who tells her, "It is not right that a fine young woman like you should not have a husband and children. I am much too old for you; so you had better marry that Irishman" (55).

As in *Man and Superman,* the Irishman vociferously objects to matrimony, but the Life Force wins out over his objections. The closing image is of the Black Girl surrounded by her children and occupied completely by her domestic responsibilities:

> So they were married; and the black girl managed the Irishman and the children. . . . Between them and the garden and mending her husband's clothes . . . she was kept so busy that her search for God was crowded out of her head . . . but there were moments . . . in which her mind went back to her search; only now she saw how funny it was. (57)

Shaw concludes his narrative with the confirmation of the Black Girl's "strengthened mind," which was now "far beyond the stage" of her youthful search for God and her idol-smashing adventures (58).

As in some of the New Woman plays of his early career, Shaw here follows the pattern of reinscribing an independent woman in a domestic environment. Perhaps even more than in those works, he shows the abandonment of the feminist inclinations associated with that independence—inclinations that give way to a conformity with convention that regards those youthful feelings as naive, self-centered, and ill-advised. As the literary father of the narrative, Shaw shapes the maturation of the Black Girl, pointing to her "strengthened mind" as the result of his guidance of her to the Voltairean garden where she realizes the follies of her search. She embraces the paternal precepts and makes them her own life philosophy, having already abandoned the teaching of the female figures of the missionary and the mathematician, whose views have been depicted as flawed. These structural principles inform a number of Shaw's best known works as well, and it is to issues of fathers and daughters in the dramas that I now turn.

8

My Daughter, My Self(?)

Shaw's first major commercial suc-
cess came in 1911, with the production of *Fanny's First Play*, a piece
that the playwright labeled "a potboiler" (109), but that audiences
found delightful for its spoof of theatrical criticism and contemporary
social concerns (Henderson 605). Although Shavian scholars treat the
play rather lightly, it stands out in the canon for several reasons. It
is his only drama to feature the play-within-a-play construction (Morgan 4), and the only one to deal with the actual writing of plays. It is
also one of only two works that depict a woman as a writer (*You Never
Can Tell* is the other). Yet, as with Shakespeare's metatheatrical comedy *A Midsummer Night's Dream* and Shaw's story *The Adventures of
the Black Girl in Her Search for God*, the audience is very conscious here
of the controlling hand of the author over the text. Ironically, with
this play, Shaw initially chose to mask his identity as playwright
(*Bodley Head* 4:343) (advertisements referred only to Xxxxxxx Xxxx
[*Bodley Head* 4:449]), and in it he depicts a young female dramatist
who herself does not wish to be identified by the critics as the author
of the play they attend.

As with the prose pieces already analyzed, Shaw here portrays the
novice character as a young woman—a figure who acknowledges his
literary paternity as a significant influence on her own professional

development at the same time that he projects a version of his younger, less mature self onto her. Significantly, Shaw sets the frame action on Fanny's birthday. At the same time that we become conscious of the festivities, we hear of the creation of her first play; both are being celebrated on the evening of its premiere. The audience can thus associate its own first viewing of Shaw's latest piece with the nested images of birthing and creativity in Fanny and her play—all generated by Shaw, all metaphorically related.

Shaw makes the connections between himself and Fanny quite obvious in the prologue spoken by the actress/playwright, written for productions "when the Play alone is performed":

In childhood's sunny days, I, by an aunt of mine,
Was taken—prematurely—to the pantomime.
From that time forth, each evening I would be at her:
"Take me again, dear Auntie, to the theatre":
Twas thus I first on Shakespear's golden page struck.
The natural result was, I got stage struck.
(Bodley Head 4:347–48)

Shaw's biographer, Archibald Henderson, includes this description of the young Shaw's "introduction to the theater":

Thanks to Shaw's remarkable memory and microscopic precision, we are enabled to catch a revealing glimpse of his introduction to the theater and the drama in Dublin. "The first play I ever saw . . . was Tom Taylor's *Plot and Passion*. It was followed by *Puss and Boots*, a full-length Christmas pantomime. . . . I had to be removed forcibly from the theatre at the end because after the falls of the curtain three times in *Plot and Passion* I could not be persuaded that it would not presently go up again." (39)

The induction to *Fanny's First Play*, which establishes the frame for the ensuing action, explains expositionally that Fanny's play is being performed privately, which was "done often enough" (115) at the time, especially by Shaw, who had to secure copyrights for plays the censor would not allow to be produced publicly. Fanny's father, who knows nothing of the play's content, naively assumes the drama will be like a harlequinade from the commedia tradition or the pantomime:

The heroine will be an exquisite Columbine, her lover a dainty Harlequin, her father a picturesque Pantaloon, and the valet who hoodwinks the father and brings about the happiness of the lovers a grotesque but perfectly tasteful Punchinello or Mascarille or Sganarelle. (114)

But Fanny's play eschews such traditionally innocuous entertainment in favor of the "modern" dramaturgy her father abhors—a style she has acquired from theatrical contact during her Cambridge education. Fanny, whose mother is never mentioned in the play, has been sent to Cambridge by her father, who has resided for many years in Venice,[1] and is thus unaware of the changes in education brought about by the appearance of socialism and other revolutionary influences at the university. Fanny has adopted Fabianism as her guiding force at Cambridge, thereby substituting the doctrine shaped by Shaw (and the Webbs) for any familial precepts introduced in her sequestered childhood.

Without revealing her identity as playwright, Fanny asks the critic Trotter (Shaw's pseudonym for his friend A. B. Walkley, to whom he had previously dedicated *Man and Superman*) to cover for the play if her father seemed upset, by telling him that "its style and construction . . . are considered the very highest art nowadays; that the author wrote it in the proper way for repertory theatres of the most superior kind" (122). Trotter, however, resists, and through his doing so Shaw has a chance to poke fun at contemporary criticism of his plays and establish the clear association of Fanny's new form of dramaturgy with his own:

I am aware that one author, who is, I blush to say, a personal friend of mine, resorts freely to the dastardly subterfuge of calling them conversations, discussions, and so forth, with the express object of evading criticism. But I'm not to be disarmed by such tricks. I say they are not plays. Dialogues, if you will. Exhibitions of character, perhaps: especially the character of the author. Fiction, possibly, though a little decent reticence as to introducing actual persons, and thus violating the sanctity of private life, might not be amiss. But plays, no. I say NO. Not plays. (122)

Trotter, who resembles "the leading representative of manly senti-ment in London," *The Philanderer*'s theater critic Jo Cuthbertson (122), shares the latter's discomfort with the younger generation and its advanced views. When Fanny starts discussing the attitudes toward the modern stage she shares with her fellow Cambridge University Fabians, Trotter exclaims,

> And now let me warn you. If youre going to be a charming healthy young English girl, you may coax me. If youre going to be an unsexed Cambridge Fabian virago, I'll treat you as my intellectual equal, as I would treat a man. (121)

Shaw highlights the irony of Trotter's conventional views of women here, that only when they are "unsexed"—no longer women—can he converse with them on an equal level, which Trotter perceives as a threat to Fanny, but which is actually a threat to his masculine security. The tension between them echoes the conflict presented in *The Philanderer*, where the issue of gender identity, depicted by the characterizations of the extremely womanly Julia Craven, her carica-tured masculine sister Sylvia, and the more moderately male-identi-fied New Woman Grace Tranfield, puts in question Shaw's stance on the potential for combinations of female intellect and femininity.

After viewing the play, Trotter deprecates it to some extent, re-marking with dramatic irony, "Any clever modern girl could turn out that kind of thing by the yard" (177), while his fellow critics speculate on whether Shaw might be the author. And after the truth of Fanny's authorship comes out, she demurs at their comparisons: "Oh, of course it would be a little like Bernard Shaw. The Fabian touch, you know" (181).

The play-within-the-play indeed sparkles with typically Shavian wit and concern for such issues as cross-class marriage and the forc-ible feeding of suffragettes.[2] Thus Shaw "fathers" (110) both his young, female protégée and the play she ostensibly creates. He spawns a literary daughter who grows up to be just like her father figure and writes a play remarkably similar to his own, thereby actu-ally becoming her father through the literary paternalism that gener-ated both the frame and the interior play. Shaw projects a female persona growing into, and fusing with, his own maturing capabilities as a playwright, encapsulating the motif of the father's bringing up the daughter not only to be male/father-identified, but actually to become the father himself.

Shaw was nowhere nearly as popularly successful with his first dramatic effort, *Widowers' Houses*, produced by the Independent Theatre Society in 1892.[3] But his fascination with the father/daughter relation was present even then, and *Widowers' Houses* illustrates it in paradigmatic fashion. The opening exposition of act 1 alerts the audience to the yet unnamed father and daughter, who, in typically well-made-play fashion, arrive on the scene immediately after their description. Blanche Sartorius and her father are imposing characters. Just before their entrance, Cokane remarks to his traveling companion Dr Trench, "I am sure they were persons of consequence: you were struck with the distinguished appearance of the father yourself" (32). Shaw tells his actors and readers in the stage directions,

> They are *apparently* father and daughter. The gentleman is 50. . . . His incisive, domineering utterance and imposing style . . . give him an air of importance. . . . His daughter is a well-dressed . . . strongminded young woman, presentably ladylike, but still *her father's daughter*. *Nevertheless* fresh and attractive, and *none the worse for being vital and energetic rather than delicate and refined.* (33; my emphasis)

Shaw clearly wants the actors in these roles to convey a dispositional similarity (the physical resemblance being unlikely without extremely fortuitous casting) that should be obvious at first sight. He establishes their bond by the phrase "her father's daughter"—a description that will recur throughout the plays under examination. Shaw feels he must also emphasize that despite Blanche's paternal resemblance— "nevertheless"—she has a personal appeal, the appeal of the Shavian vital, Life Force woman, who does not fit the image of the conventional, reserved Victorian heroine, and is a relatively new English type on the Victorian stage, having been appropriated and "naturalized" after the appearance of Ibsen's heroines.

Sartorius and his daughter are vacationing on the Rhine at the play's opening, a resort setting similar to the one Shaw later uses in *You Never Can Tell*. Their travels, we learn, are an integral part of Blanche's "education and her breeding" (44), tasks Sartorius has undertaken with great dedication. "Her education has been of the most expensive and complete kind obtainable" (50), Sartorius explains, and it is clear that although she may not be enchanted with her formal learning (38), she has obviously absorbed a great deal from her father's influence. As Sartorius's former assistant Lickcheese notes late in the play, "she has her father's eye for business" (92), and Blanche herself observes that they share personality traits, even those Sartorius may not have intended her to acquire or inherit:

Sartorius. . . . Need you be so inflexible, Blanche?
Blanche. I thought you admired inflexibility: you have always prided yourself on it.

(79)

One of their most noticeable shared characteristics is a bad temper, a distinction Sartorius identifies not only with Blanche's vitality, but also with conventional masculinity. He addresses her fiancé, Harry Trench:

Dr Trench: I will be plain with you. I know that Blanche has a quick temper. It is part of her strong character and her physical courage, which is greater than that of most men, I can assure you. (68)

Shaw highlights the accuracy of Trench's observation by dramatizing parallel scenes between Blanche and her maid and Sartorius and his assistant Lickcheese. Early in act 2, in the Surbiton villa of Sartorius, the man of property dismisses his rent collector Lickcheese, who complains of his "hardness" (56). Later in the same act, Blanche has a "fierce" exchange with her maid, one that repeats earlier, violent encounters between them (75).[4] Sartorius implies a similar pattern with regard to his own history of verbal run-ins with Lickcheese (56), run-ins that may demonstrate the control over his temper of Sartorius's advanced years, but that stem from the same basic disposition as Blanche's.

When Tanner speaks of "the voice of nature proclaim[ing] for a daughter a father's care and for the son a mother's" (*Man and Superman* 97), Shaw adds no commentary on the acquisition of parental traits across sexual lines. Yet he gives numerous instances of parental identification by children, and shared characteristics between them. The majority of examples are of father/daughter parallels, although in both *Mrs Warren's Profession* and *Major Barbara*, the audience realizes the daughter's similarity to her mother. Interestingly, we never hear the line "I am my mother's son" in Shaw, despite the affectional preference Mrs Tarleton and Lady Britomart, for example, share for their boys. And the masculine qualities of the father-identified daughters have no corollaries with the sons—even those like Henry Higgins or the Doctor in *The Millionairess* who have "mother fixations." Shaw does not feminize Stephen Undershaft or Johnny Tarleton, although the former may share his mother's moral views of right and wrong and the latter his mother's lack of mental acuity (Crane 487). In the Shavian familial context, a daughter's resemblance to her father is regularly considered worthy of praise, while virtually nothing is made of mother/son likeness.

In Blanche's case, Shaw portrays neither a brother nor a mother with whom to compare this father/daughter dynamic. Like Fanny O'Dowda and other Shavian daughters, Blanche has received only her father's care, the mother figure being totally absent. Sartorius remarks on how he must take on both parental roles as "the father of a motherless girl" (43), and Blanche, an independent, quite mature young woman, capitalizes ironically on the Victorian, womanly need for a mother's care, in essence demonstrating just how unnecessary this figure is for her in an early coquettish exchange with Trench:

> Blanche (impatiently) Everybody is afraid of papa: I'm sure I
> dont know why. . . .
> Trench (tenderly) However, it's all right now: isnt it? . . .
> Blanche (sharply) I dont know. How should I? You had no right
> to speak to me that day on board the steamer. You thought I
> was alone, because (with false pathos) I had no mother with
> me.
> Trench (protesting) Oh, I say! Come! It was you who spoke to
> me.
>
> (38–39)

Arthur Ganz observes that in *Widowers' Houses* Blanche functions as both mistress and mother figure in the Sartorius household (88), but he makes no mention of the significant absence of, and lack of necessity for, any other female. This gap in the familial structure corresponds to the other weak maternal characters and mothers who lose or have little influence over their children in Shaw's works.

Ganz associates these roles for Blanche with her strong emotional attachment to her father, a bond he reads psychoanalytically as "erotic" "wish-fulfillment" in the parent/child dynamic (87). *Widowers' Houses* dramatizes the first of the father/daughter relations that incorporate romantic with didactic elements, as the daughter expresses her attachment to the paternal figure who has stressed his educational relation to her:

> (She throws her arms hysterically about his neck) Papa: I dont want to marry: I only want to stay with you and be happy as we have always been. I hate the thought of being married: I dont care for him: I dont want to leave you. (77)

In rather programmatic fashion, however, Shaw makes clear that Sartorius has not been a good teacher, as he has kept his daughter in ignorance of his livelihood, in keeping with Victorian conventions of the "woman's sphere" being the home and not the financial concerns of the patriarchally controlled world at large. Sartorius commends Trench for not saying anything about their financial dealings to Blanche: "I thank you for refraining from explaining the nature of your scruples to Blanche. . . . Perhaps it will be as well to leave her in ignorance" (73). When Blanche accidentally learns of her father's slum landlordism, she rejects him: "Oh, if only a girl could have no father, no family, just as I have no mother!" (85). But he shows her she is implicated in his profession, as its profits have educated and provided for her. Her disdain for the poor tenants of Sartorius's dwellings makes her father realize what effect his education of her has had. "I see I have made a real lady of you, Blanche" (86). Anticipating Higgins and other molders of Shavian women, Sartorius sees Blanche develop into the image he has created for her, one that both reflects a womanly ideal and mirrors its maker.[5]

Much later in Shaw's career, he once again portrayed a woman who inherits business acumen from her father, "the millionairess" Epifania Ognisanti di Parerga. *The Millionairess* (1936) follows the Shavian tradition of strong heroines, and Eppy most certainly holds center stage throughout. Despite its late composition date, *The Millionairess* has much in common with the earlier *Widowers' Houses*, in terms of both character and theme. Although Shaw deems it Jonsonian (7), in its socioeconomic content it more closely resembles Dickens's works such as *Hard Times*, in that it exposes capitalist exploitation of labor, here in the bleak depiction of a garment sweatshop. Furthermore, Shaw highlights the late nineteenth-century milieu of the piece through character description and literary allusion. Adrian Blenderbland, one of Epifania's conquests, appears "bearded in the Victorian literary fashion" (59), while her estranged husband, Alastair Fitzfassenden, comes from the same lower class pugilist stock as Cashel Byron. Epifania, a livelier and more entertaining version of Lydia Carew, shares with her novelistic predecessor strong paternal identification, but Shaw diverges from his earlier romance plot in giving Alastair a lover as well, the "pleasant quiet little woman" Patricia Smith (52), who is as colorless as her name. Polly Seedystockings, as Epifania has renamed her (53), is the perfect domestic wife, a self-proclaimed "angel in the house" (58). The allusion to the Coventry Patmore poem that characterized the ideal Victorian woman also helps connect the play thematically with earlier Shavian works.[6]

Polly understands that she is a foil for Epifania, who, as an example of the Shavian "vital" woman, shares her author's distaste for domestic "doormats."

> Patricia. . . . I should say that you are the Sunday wife, Mrs Fitzfassenden. It's I that have to look after his clothes and make him get his hair cut. . . . You dont understand men: they get interested in other things and neglect themselves unless they have a woman to look after them. . . . There are two sorts of people in the world: the people anyone can live with and the people that no one can live with. The people that no one can live with may be very goodlooking and vital and splendid and temperamental and romantic and all that . . . but if you try to live with them they just eat up your whole life. . . .
>
> Epifania. So I am the Sunday wife. (To Patricia, scornfully) And what are you, pray?
>
> Patricia. Well, I am the angel in the house, if you follow me.
>
> Alastair (blubbering) You are, dear: you are.
>
> Epifania (to Patricia) You are his doormat: thats what you are.
>
> Patricia. Doormats are very useful things if you want the house kept tidy, dear.
>
> (57–58)

Epifania, who has inherited "thirty millions" from her deceased father (43), can afford to hire someone to keep her house tidy, and has no use for Polly, whose modest self-sufficiency does not preclude her asking Alastair for gifts of hosiery.

Despite Epifania's father's physical absence from the play, he is very much there in spirit, through the constant references to and comparisons with him of his daughter Epifania. She calls him "the greatest man in the world" (43) and reveals that he has educated her for the contingencies of her wealth and position. He held to the advanced belief "that women should be able to defend themselves. He made me study Judo" (50). Interestingly, this seemingly masculine training was initially conceived differently by Shaw. He told Lawrence Langner, "In the original version I made the woman a boxer;[7] but, on the stage, that was unconvincing and unladylike. So I have made her a Judo expert" (*Collected Letters* 4:551). The external grace of action of the martial art, which masks the strength and violence underneath, thus becomes a perfect metaphor for the convention of the female exterior with a male core. In addition, Eppy explains, "My father instructed me most carefully in the law of libel" (47). The elder di Parerga clearly fits the father/teacher mold, apparently educating all around him, a trait inherited by his daughter. In a conversation with her solicitor, Epifania informs him of the details of his profession:

> I instruct you that it is the law. My father always had to instruct his lawyers in the law whenever he did anything except what everybody was doing every day. . . . My father was a great man: every day of his life he did things that nobody else ever dreamt of doing. I am not, perhaps, a great woman; but I am his daughter; and as such I am an unusual woman. You will take the law from me and do exactly what I tell you to do. (47)

Perhaps her father's most important lesson concerned finance:

> Nobody is anybody without money, Seedystockings. My dear old father taught me that. "Stick to your money" he said "and all the other things shall be added unto you." He said it was in the Bible. I have never verified the quotation; but I have never forgotten it. I have stuck to my money; and I shall continue to stick to it. (70)

Shaw's relatively thin plot for *The Millionairess*, which owes something to the parental injunction of the casket test in *The Merchant of
Venice* (Morgan 329), simultaneously privileges the parent/child
relation and satirizes the psychological attention it has received
since the advent of Freud.[8] Shaw moves the epilogic discussion of
Higgins's maternal attachment in *Pygmalion* (112–13) into the text
here, poking fun at his heroine at the same time he makes the
audience realize Eppy's paternal devotion and likeness have made
her such a vital character. Her lover Adrian (of the Victorian beard)
remarks,

> My dear Epifania, if we are to remain friends, I may as well be
> quite frank with you. Everything you have told me about your
> father convinces me that though he was no doubt an affection-
> ate parent and amiable enough to explain your rather tiresome
> father fixation, as Dr Freud would call it, he must have been
> quite the most appalling bore that ever devastated even a Rotary
> club. (78–79)

The plot denouement revolves around the identification of the
psychological condition Adrian finds in Epifania and, in maternal
form, in the Egyptian doctor with a "mother fixation" (88) whom she
realizes is her ideal mate. This neat symptomological parallel works
only as a comic device, however, for neither the Doctor's condition
nor his character is as fully developed as Epifania's. *The Millionairess*
demonstrates how much more interesting Shaw finds the "father
fixation," and, furthermore, how imbalanced the gender attributes
are for children displaying this complex. As noted earlier, Shavian
sons attached to their mothers do not carry over their feminine traits.
The following speech by the Doctor demonstrates how the creative
maternal force in Shaw cannot function independently of a male
counterpart—unless, as with Lina, the female creator who "makes a
man" is a masculine, androgynous woman—whereas the paternal
creator can "make a woman" all by himself. Significantly, there are
no references to a mother for Epifania in the play, an omission that
underscores the relative insignificance of a maternal force in her life.
In response to his revelation of a maternal test that parallels her
father's, she inquires,

Epifania. What was your mother?

The Doctor. A washerwoman. A widow. She brought up eleven children. I was the youngest, the Benjamin. The other ten are honest working folk. With their *help* she made me a man of learning. It was her ambition to have a son who could read and write. *She prayed to Allah; and he endowed me with the necessary talent.*

(88; my emphasis)

In the scene in the sweatshop in act 3, where Epifania has gone to prove she can live on "two hundred piastres" (87 ["thirtyfive shillings" 89]) for six months in accordance with the Doctor's mother's test, Shaw provides another example of the weak womanly woman incapable of "making a man" of her husband. When Epifania tries to take over the operation of the sweatshop to make it workable in Undershaftian fashion, the wife of the cowed manager exclaims,

Go up and stop her, Joe. Dont let her talk: just put her out. *Be a man, darling: dont be afraid of her.* Dont break my heart and ruin yourself. Oh, dont sit there dithering: you dont know what she may be doing. Oh! oh! oh! (she can say no more for sobbing).

(99; my emphasis)

Epifania's success with men and money clearly stems from her masculine behavior and mindset, the physical strength and business acumen that derive from her father's influence and teaching. Inadvertently forgetting her own powers for a moment, she breaks a chair in her lawyer's office simply by "flouncing" into it (48), and when Polly inquires what has "happened to the chair," Eppy retorts, "*I* have happened to the chair. Let it be a warning to you" (53).[9] Upon meeting her, the Doctor identifies her among the "unwomanly" women Shaw frequently portrays:

The Doctor. . . . Enormous self-confidence. . . . Insane egotism. *Apparently sexless.*

Epifania. Sexless! Who told you that I am sexless?

The Doctor. You talk to me *as if you were a man.* There is no mystery, no separateness, no sacredness about men to you. A man to you is only a male of your species.

Epifania. My species indeed! Men are a different and very inferior species. Five minutes conversation with my husband will
convince you that he and I do not belong to the same species.
But there are some great men, like my father. And there are
some good doctors, like you.

(85; my emphasis)

Shaw conflates here his philosophy of the vital geniuses—Life Force
characters of both sexes—with that of common humanity. Here as
elsewhere, this gender resemblance manifests itself dramatically in
the female character's masculine likeness. Although it is certainly
important for men—the source of gender conventions as Hypatia
Tarleton makes clear in *Misalliance* (167)—to recognize the likeness
of women to themselves, one wonders why Shaw never finds it necessary for that recognition to work in the other direction. In other
words, men never recognize that they are like women.[10] The male-
identified daughters gravitate toward vital men, as with Epifania's
recognition of the resemblance of the Doctor to her father. When, as
in *Misalliance*, the father figure fuses with the love object, the relationship takes on other resonances, however.

Although all the daughters under examination identify strongly
with their fathers, and demonstrate paternal traits, they do not usually exhibit the androgynous behavior associated with the Shavian
women relatively more autonomous of their families, such as Joan
or Lina. The Polish acrobat actually serves as a foil for Hypatia Tarleton, throwing into relief the significant impact the father has had
over his more traditionally feminine, vital daughter. Hypatia is "a
conventional woman" (Crane 480), very much a reflection of her Edwardian environment. Frederick P. W. McDowell observes that
Hypatia's Life Force energy emerges side by side with her astrin-
gency, suggesting "her environment—and her father—have been
largely responsible." He continues his explanation with an analysis
of her domestic training ground, the "girl's prison" identified in "The
Revolutionist's Handbook" (*Man and Superman* 262):

Her father has kept her at home, sealed off from the social
realities with which he himself has had to contend; and if she
is brutal to him, he has deserved her harshness by virtue of his
inability to see what her needs really are. He cannot see that

her bourgeois home, replete with comfort and fostering a sheltered existence for women, could never be a suitable place in which Hypatia's nature might expand. (McDowell 67)

Hypatia's forthright criticism of her sequestered home life, including her father's refusal to let her work for his company while her brother Johnny learns the family business, has a socially progressive ring to it:

> Hypatia. . . . You see what living with one's parents means, Joey. It means living in a house where you can be ordered to leave the room. Ive got to obey: it's his house, not mine.
> Tarleton. Who pays for it? Go and support yourself as I did if you want to be independent.
> Hypatia. I wanted to and you wouldnt let me. How can I support myself when I'm a prisoner?
>
> (199)

Hypatia's earlier explanation of her wish to work places the conflict in a different but related sphere. She wants the personal freedom and excitement that women are denied in her society: "They tell me that the girls there [in the shop] have adventures sometimes" (148). She also echoes Shaw's concerns with womanly self-sacrifice as a result of this domestic enslavement. She explains to Lord Summerhays that she wants "to be an active verb" (145) instead of a passive woman and challenges him to observe firsthand the boredom and waste that domestic lassitude fosters:

> Stay down here with us for a week; and I'll shew you what it means: shew it to you going on day after day, year after year, lifetime after lifetime. . . . Girls withering into ladies. Ladies withering into old maids. Nursing old women. Running errands for old men. Good for nothing else at last. Oh, you cant imagine the fiendish selfishness of the old people and the maudlin sacrifice of the young. It's more unbearable than any poverty: more horrible than any regular-right-down wickedness. (145–46)

Thus Shaw introduces the daughter's frustration with her home and desire for extrafamilial sources of experience, interjecting tension in the paternal relation that the woman thinks will be resolved with an escape to marriage—even one with a husband reminiscent of the father.

The title of Shaw's preface to the play, "Parents and Children," underscores the importance of this relation to the disquisitory drama, and although the main title, *Misalliance,* suggests the problems with romantic entanglements that occupy the characters, the notion that children can somehow grow up with the wrong parents serves as a thematic misalliance as well. Shaw demonstrates the affinity for an alternative parental figure in the rapport of Frank Gardner and Praed in *Mrs Warren's Profession,* and in *Misalliance* Johnny Tarleton and Bentley Summerhays both feel a more natural bond with each other's fathers than with their own. Daughters, however, never gravitate toward alternative parent figures of either sex if their own are still in place, although they may express a desire for an emotional and/or sexual relation with a male that shares paternal qualities. John Tarleton has educated his daughter in a fashion similar to that of Blanche Sartorius in *Widowers' Houses.* He has sent Hypatia to a school not attended by children of the upper class: "a school that was so expensive that they [the upper class] couldnt afford to send their daughters there; so that all the girls belonged to big business families like ourselves" (125). He tells his friend Lord Summerhays, "I think my idea of bringing up a young girl has been rather a success" (147), although he realizes Patsy is "not satisfied" (147) with his techniques. He remarks that "she's active, like me" and reveals with a tone of incredulity, "She actually wanted me to put her into the shop" (148). Gladys Crane believes Shaw wanted to emphasize this resemblance structurally as well:

> It is clear, for example, where Hypatia developed her desire for amorous adventures. She has taken secret delight in her father's "amours" and has longed to imitate him, much to his embarrassment. It is no coincidence that when the two strangers, Lina and Joey, appear on the scene after their plane crashes into the greenhouse, Tarleton immediately tries to seduce Lina and Hypatia Joey. To make his point Shaw has placed these two seduction scenes back to back. (486)

Hypatia better recognizes the affinity between them than her father, who cannot see that, beyond his conventional views of gender, her likeness to him would lend itself to success outside the home. It is this paternal resemblance, perhaps even more than the larger social issue of women's domestic entrapment, that Shaw stresses in the dramatization of father/daughter rapport. Shaw gives the understanding of this likeness to the daughter, moreover, so that it is the woman who learns of her paternal correspondence—an insight not shared by the sons of Shaw's mothers. Like other young Shavian women, Hypatia delivers the key line "I'm my father's daughter" (166), and tells her mother that she wants to marry Bentley because of his mental abilities like her father's. She explains that "living with father, Ive got accustomed to cleverness" (128),[11] and wants to find that quality in a mate.

Anticipating the relation of Ellie Dunn and Captain Shotover in *Heartbreak House,* Shaw presents in *Misalliance* an earlier dramatic version of the emotional attachment of a young woman to a significantly older man, here, the flirtation of Hypatia with Bentley's father, Lord Summerhays. In a variation on the scenario already dramatized in *Man and Superman* between Violet and her father-in-law, Bentley has Hypatia meet with his father before he announces their engagement to prove she's "a ripping girl" (144). Not knowing of her relations with his son, Lord Summerhays falls in love with her himself, and proposes. But the relation he envisions as much resembles that of a parent for a child as a husband for a wife—perhaps because of his Victorian background, which assumed the convention of the child-wife.

> I'll put it as bluntly as I can. When, as you say, I made an utter fool of myself, believe me, I made a poetic fool of myself. I was seduced, not by appetites which, thank Heaven, Ive long outlived: not even by the desire of second childhood for a child companion, but by the innocent impulse to place the delicacy and wisdom and spirituality of my age at the affectionate service of your youth for a few years, at the end of which you would be a grown, strong, formed—widow. (143)

Hypatia cements the connection between husband and father figures by telling him, "You can never imagine how delighted I was to find that instead of being the correct sort of big panjandrum you were supposed to be, you were really an old rip like papa."

Lord Summerhays. No, no: not about your father: I really cant
   bear it. And if you must say these terrible things . . . at least
   find something prettier to call me than an old rip.
Hypatia. Well, what *would* you call a man proposing to a girl
   who might be—
Lord Summerhays. His daughter: yes, I know.
Hypatia. I was going to say his granddaughter.

(146)

Summerhays's view of their life together echoes the position of the
narrative voice in *Dorothea*, with its paternal and philosophic interest
in the "formation" of the young lady with "wisdom" and experience.

Summerhays also becomes a second father for Hypatia in a play
full of multiple parent figures. As already noted, Johnny and Bentley
each have alternative paternal models, and as Bentley explains before
his schoolmate's unexpected arrival, Joey Percival has three fathers,
a phenomenon Shaw explains autobiographically (*Collected Letters*
3:368; *Sixteen Self Sketches* 31). Bentley points out the advantages of
having these multiple paternal influences, a Shavian motif that applies to both the male and female characters so enriched. He concludes his description of Joey's family with a tantalizing quotation:
"He [Joey] said if he could only have had three mothers as well, he'd
have backed himself against Napoleon" (132–33).

Extending the biographical connection for a moment, Shaw, of
course, claims to have had only one mother, although he gravitated
toward many maternal women in his life. He appears to have felt
considerable ambivalence about her, and the conclusion to this
speech may simply be a projection of his own wish for as much
maternal influence over his own life as he had paternal—which included the input of his father, his mother's companion and music
teacher Vandeleur Lee, and his Uncle Walter. Perhaps this accounts
for both the frequency of multiple father figures in the plays and the
absence of dominant, let alone multiple mothers.[12] The effects of the
dramatization of this maternal abundance must remain only hypo-
thetical; Shaw never chose to portray or even allude to any mother(s)
with "Napoleonic" impact.

Certainly within the Tarleton household, Mrs Tarleton, familiarly
known as "The Chickabiddy" (153), may rule the roost. Yet Shaw

exposes her conventionality and prejudices to such comic effect that she becomes little more than a stereotype of the uneducated middle-class matriarch, both victim and product of her circumscribed environment. She follows a code of moral absolutes: "With really nice good women a thing is either decent or indecent; and if it's indecent, we just dont mention it or pretend to know about it; and theres an end of it" (127)—even when "it" concerns such critical health matters as indoor sanitation ("drainage" [126]). When "Gunner" breaks into their home to seek revenge for the poor treatment he believes his mother received at Tarleton's hand, he exclaims, "If people only knew what goes on in this so-called respectable house it would be put a stop to. These are the morals of our pious capitalist class! This is your rotten bourgeoisie! This—"

> Mrs Tarleton. Dont you dare use such language in company. I wont allow it.
> Tarleton. All right, Chickabiddy: it's not bad language: it's only Socialism.
>
> (176)

Endearing, if domineering, Mrs Tarleton exemplifies the well-meaning but narrow-minded maternal force that helps shape English youth. Through parody, Shaw may well be trying to educate the maternal segment of his audience as well as expose the serious limitations engendered in them by social convention. Yet the subtextual thrust of such characters is ultimately their inconsequentiality, their lack of significant impact, certainly on their society, and even within their homes.

In *Heartbreak House*, Shaw gives Ellie Dunn one tantalizing series of speeches about her mother, a character who never appears in the play and is rarely mentioned. In her thoughtful comment to Boss Mangan, who has just revealed the truth about his intentional financial destruction of her father, Ellie remarks,

> How strange! that my mother, who knew nothing at all about business, should have been quite right about you! She always said—not before papa, of course, but to us children—that you were just that sort of man. (95)

Mangan wonders why, knowing this, Ellie's mother nevertheless encouraged their wedding plans.

> Well, you see, Mr Mangan, my mother married a very good man—for whatever you may think of my father as a man of business, he is the soul of goodness—and she is not at all keen on my doing the same. (95)

Thus Ellie calculatedly intends to follow her mother's advice, and marry a man old enough to be—yet decidedly unlike—her father. It would seem that this offstage mother might prove an exception to the established pattern of the displacement of the maternal figure. She certainly has the perceptiveness of Mrs Clandon, for example, who similarly sees through Gloria's suitor Valentine. But the daughters Gloria and Ellie, central to *You Never Can Tell* and *Heartbreak House*, each ultimately gravitate toward a man much more closely identified with their fathers, rejecting the maternal lessons on husband selection. Gloria, in choosing Valentine over her mother's concerns, accepts the man structurally and attitudinally linked to her father.[13] Ellie, rejecting Mangan, her mother's choice, instead finds a second father in Shotover, a virtual grandfather in age and worldly experience.

Instruction of daughters emerges as a dominant theme in *Heartbreak House*, however, which could almost be subtitled "Educating Ellie." References to teaching abound, including Shotover's accusation of Nurse Guinness's inadequacy toward his own children "whom you have brought up in ignorance of the commonest decencies of social intercourse" (52), and Hesione's observation that education works in two directions, she having "picked up so much slang from the children" (64). Ariadne and Hesione, the fully grown daughters, have of course had no real mother to bring them up and have matured under Shotover's influence. The younger daughter Ariadne, now Lady Utterword, comments, "Almost before we could speak we were filled with notions that might have been all very well for pagan philosophers of fifty, but were certainly quite unfit for respectable people of any age" (57).

Captain Shotover introduces the issue of Ellie's education at the play's opening, as he (jokingly) expresses concern that the young visitor has not been properly taught about his daughter Hesione.

Nurse Guinness. She says Miss Hessy invited her, sir.
The Captain. And had she no friend, no parents, to warn her
against my daughter's invitations?

(51)

Ellie herself reveals the impact of her father's education of her: "My
father taught me to love Shakespear" (66). The inadequacy of that
teaching becomes clear, however, when we see how Ellie's naively
romantic interpretation of *Othello* has allowed her to fall in love with
Hesione's husband in the guise of Marcus Darnley, adventurer *ex-
traordinaire*. Significantly, as Ellie comes to grips with her disappointment through her conversation with the older woman Hesione,
Shaw gives no indications of the latter's evolving into a mother figure. He has Hesione represent the outcome of their discussion as
"life" educating Ellie, not herself (72). Rather, Shaw presents Hesione
in a similarly seductive capacity to that with which she "bewitches"
(70) the men, and stresses in several letters the contrast between
Ellie's "virginal" status and initial "girlish[ness]" and the older
woman's "irresistible[ness]" (*Collected Letters* 3:553, 735, 744, 749).
He provocatively gives Hesione a series of stage directions that suggest a lesbian attraction: "She snatches at Ellie's waist, and makes
her sit down on the sofa beside her" (63), "catching her dress" (70),
"caressing her" (70), "laying Ellie down at the end of the sofa" (71),
and finally "fondling her" (72), a gesture from which Ellie "disen-
gag[es] herself with an expression of distaste" (72). The dialogue
throughout this scene, however, revolves solely around Ellie's various heterosexual involvements with Mangan and Hector Hushabye,
and the exchange that prompts Ellie's final "disengagement" is a
reference to the "distasteful" Mangan.

The tension here between verbal and physical texts exemplifies the
inability of the dominant heterosexual culture to incorporate scenes
of lesbian representation. Jill Dolan, drawing on the writing of Teresa
de Lauretis, theorizes this problem:

The lesbian subject is "the elsewhere of discourse . . . the
blind spots . . . of its representations." The lesbian subject is in
a position to denaturalize dominant codes by signifying an existence that belies the entire structure of heterosexual culture and
its representations. The lesbian signifies "a blockage in the sys-

tem of representation" by expressing forbidden contents in forbidden forms. The forbidden content is active female desire independent of men, and the forbidden form is a self-representation that separates gender from a strict correlation with biological sex and compulsory sexuality. (116)

Shaw's inability to fully dramatize such relations suggests his profound discomfort with this form of expression, as well as its ongoing fascination for him. Another lesbian scene in *Pygmalion,* closer in its suggestion of physical violence to that between Blanche and her maid in *Widowers' Houses,* will be discussed in chapter 9.

These scenes with lesbian subtext always occur in strongly heterosexual contexts. In the Blanche/maid sequence discussed earlier in this chapter, Blanche's hostility results ostensibly from her frustration over her fiancé Trench. Here, the issue is Ellie's fiancé Mangan. Interestingly, there are no parallel scenes (even similarly subtextual) in Shaw of male homoeroticism. This may reflect Shaw's relatively intimate acquaintance with the lesbian Kate Salt—a closer relation than he acknowledges with any male homosexual—as well as the greater cultural sensitivity about male homoeroticism. These scenes also reflect Victorian concepts of female interaction, which posit a continuum of friendship with physical contact from acquaintance through sexual love interest. Male friends and acquaintances, of course, shared no such physical intimacy, only having close contact in aberrant homosexual contexts.[14]

As the audience observes Ellie's interactions with the older male characters, Shotover, Mangan, and her father, it becomes clear that she is one of Shaw's daughters with three fathers,[15] each balancing the others' instruction, as do the fathers in Joey Percival's household. Act 1 has featured Mazzini Dunn's incomplete but well-intentioned romantic instruction of Ellie with Shakespeare. Early in act 2, Mangan undertakes Ellie's training in the ways of capitalism. "Of course you dont understand: what do *you* know about business? You just listen and learn" (94). And later in the same act, and continuing on to the final curtain, Shotover begins to share the wisdom of his age with the enraptured young woman (124–31). The progression of age and experience of these father figures, each older and wiser than the one before, points toward the association of masculine wisdom with the figure of the Ancients in *Back to Methuselah,* Shaw's next play. And

the movement toward a platonic union in *Heartbreak House* also anticipates the ensuing work's ideal form of human interaction—the communion of minds.

Shotover becomes one of a series of male teacher/lover figures, one
that Ellie also identifies as her "spiritual husband and second father"
(149). Arthur Ganz sees this as

> the culmination of a line of impassioned father-daughter rela-
> tionships (real or symbolic) extending from Blanche Sartorius
> and her father through Cleopatra and Caesar, Barbara and Un-
> dershaft, Eliza and Higgins. (193–94)

Ganz's sense that the platonic consummation of the father/daughter
pairing in the union of Ellie and Shotover resolves this Shavian motif
accounts only for the more obvious romantic thrust of this relation,
however; the complexities of these three intertwined male roles of
father, teacher, and lover cannot be summarized and dismissed so
easily. For although the father/daughter dynamic has an essentially
similar structure throughout Shaw's works, the ramifications for the
central daughter character, particularly in terms of her instruction in
gender roles and their impact on the plot resolution, merit closer
study. Before moving on to a consideration of the three last plays
mentioned by Ganz, I will turn to a discussion of *Man and Superman*,
a play other critics do not group with these paternally didactic dramas.

No Shavian mother demonstrates the process by which older matriarchs lose force in the world of the plays better than *Man and
Superman*'s Mrs Whitefield, whom Tanner describes as "nonenti-
tized" (60). Initially calling her "an eyesore" (54), Shaw continues
with a fuller portrait in his stage directions:

> Mrs Whitefield, *by the way*, is a little woman, whose faded
> flaxen hair looks like straw on an egg. She has an expression of
> muddled shrewdness, a squeak of protest in her voice, and an
> odd air of continually elbowing away some larger person who
> is crushing her into a corner. One guesses her as *one of those*
> *women who are conscious of being treated as silly and negligible, and*
> *who, without having strength enough to assert themselves effectually,*
> at any rate never submit to their fate. (55; my emphasis)

Shaw's own introduction to the character, his treatment of her as an aside with his "by the way," establishes the "negligibility" and marginality that define her. The responsibility for her ineffectualness goes two ways, however; it is not only others' treatment of her that renders her impotent, but her abdication of parental responsibility after the recent death of her husband, who in his will leaves the possibility for two male guardians for Ann. Her mother claims such issues fall within the males' purview, and maintains she cannot decide who is the proper guardian:

> Mrs Whitefield (hastily) Now, Ann, I do beg you not to put it on me. I have no opinion on the subject; and if I had, it would probably not be attended to. I am quite content with whatever you three [Ramsden, Tanner, and Ann] think best.
>
> Ann (. . . ignoring her mother's bad taste) Mamma knows that she is not strong enough to bear the whole responsibility for me and Rhoda without some help and advice. Rhoda must have a guardian; and though I am older, I do not think any young unmarried woman should be left quite to her own guidance. . . . I feel I am too young, too inexperienced, to decide. My father's wishes are sacred to me.
>
> Mrs Whitefield. If you two men wont carry them out I must say it is rather hard that you should put the responsibility on Ann. It seems to me that people are always putting things on other people in this world.
>
> (56, 58)

Ishrat Lindblad feels "Mrs. Whitefield is an extreme case of a woman who has been completely dominated by others because she believes in the ideal of self-sacrifice" (68), a portrait, perhaps, of what ultimately happens to the "womanly woman" of *The Quintessence*. But with a certain selfishness, which may be the reality behind her abnegation, Ann's mother clearly will take none of the burden on herself, hypocritically accusing the men of refusing to carry their share. Ann, meanwhile, obviously sees her mother as incapable of any real impact on her, as she claims without the men she would be "left to her own guidance." She capitalizes on her new status as "an orphan" (49)—a designation technically accurate for a child with only one living parent, but more commonly used for children with no parents—to minimize her mother's role even further.

Of course, Ann is in part merely recapitulating Victorian conventions of maternal and paternal functions, including that of the mother having little to do with the larger concepts of moral supervision that Ann implies by "guidance": "You know how timid mother is. All timid women are conventional" (96). Yet as numerous critics of the play have observed, Ann makes only a pretense of taking anyone's advice, manipulating the excuse of filial duty to do anything she chooses. Ramsden's blindness to this makes him a satirized figure, for shortly after his opening quotation of and remarks about Ann, we meet her and realize how she handles these very lines of Ramsden's: "It's always 'Father wishes me to,' or 'Mother wouldnt like it.' It's really almost a fault in her. I have often told her she must learn to think for herself " (44).

In generating the dramatic conflict inherent in the device of the execution of the will, Shaw creates a parent/child dynamic that fuses with and is ultimately overshadowed by the mating ritual of the duel of sex between Ann and Jack Tanner. By the conditions of the late Mr Whitefield's will, Roebuck Ramsden and Tanner are to share the guardianship of Ann, and Shaw gets much comic mileage from Ann's superficial insistence that she needs both father surrogates despite her obvious independence and single-minded determination. Equally entertaining is the seriousness with which the men take their paternal responsibility, thinking they must exert the proper influence over the fully formed Ann. What emerges from an examination of this comic tension is the realization that despite the particular comic spin Shaw gives the parent/child dynamic in this play, the underlying structures and even vocabulary of parenting remain constant.

Although Shaw gives Ann two living male advisors, Tanner obviously has the more dominant role, given his dual function as guardian and antagonist in the duel of sex. Shaw establishes this connection early in the play, during Tanner's opening conversation with Ramsden about the will. Tanner, who, unlike Ramsden, can already see through Ann, objects to the latter's admonishments "to stand by" the "orphan" Ann:

Stand by her! What danger is she in? . . . All she wants with me is to load up all her moral responsibilities on me, and do as she likes at the expense of my character. I cant control her; and she can compromise me as much as she likes. I might as well be her husband. (49)

Mr Whitefield's leaving Tanner "the charge of Ann's morals" (50) resonates with the Victorian consciousness and attitudes toward the education of daughters that the play's 1903 publication has not quite left behind. Equally indicative of the era is the assumption that Tanner is equipped to carry out this responsibility. As we learn by the middle of act 1, Jack and Ann have grown up together, making them roughly the same age. Yet somehow Jack has amassed in the same period of time sufficient worldly wisdom to become Ann's moral superior, able to take on the duty of overseeing her conduct. Despite the numerous ironies exposed in the play, this is not one of them. Integral to the humor of Jack's uncomfortable position as teacher and lover is the assumption of the similarity of these roles with respect to the care for a woman's morality. Jack's attempt to stave off Ann with the excuse of his advisory function reveals his resistance to the similarity of these roles, but not a recognition of their inherent patriarchal structure: "Your father's will appointed me your guardian, not your suitor. I shall be faithful to my trust" (205). That Ann requested Tanner as guardian (205) knowing full well her own intentions to have him ultimately as a mate only reinforces her acceptance of the convention of a woman's movement from a father's care to a husband's.

Tanner believes "it is my duty to improve your [Ann's] mind" (75), a responsibility he later discusses with Tavy (94), who tells him that all Ann's "duty to her father is now transferred to you" (90). Thinking he will break Ann's "vile abjection of youth to age" (96)—the hypocrisy of young women's devotion to their mothers—he tells Ann that he wants to provide her with an experience (a high-speed ride in his automobile) that will "make a woman of you," to which Ann agrees as she reminds him, "you stand in my father's place, by his own wish" (98).

Tanner explains his belief in his superiority to Ann on both moral and educational grounds, drawing on evidence from their culture specifically, and generally from the more timeless struggle between the womanly woman and the independent man:

Tanner. . . . You fought harder than anybody against my emancipation.

Ann (earnestly) Oh, how wrong you are! I would have done
anything for you.

Tanner. Anything except let me get loose from you. Even then
you had acquired by instinct that damnable woman's trick of
heaping   obligations   on   a   man,   of   placing   yourself . . . entirely . . . at his mercy. . . .

Ann. But, Jack, you cannot get through life without considering
other people a little.

Tanner. Ay; but what other people? It is this consideration of
other people—or rather this cowardly fear of them which we
call consideration—that makes us the sentimental slaves we
are. To consider you, as you call it, is to substitute your will
for my own. How if it be baser than mine? Are women taught
better than men or worse? Are mobs of voters taught better
than statesmen or worse? Worse, of course, in both cases.

(76)

Ann's rejoinder that she "would have done anything for" Jack
strongly resembles the cry of the self-sacrificing woman that is so
often the object of Shaw's didacticism. The prevalence of this kind
of woman in the society Shaw depicts may well lie behind the critically controversial designation of Ann as "Everywoman" (28). One
female contemporary of Shaw, in her study *The Truth About Woman*,
corroborates the aptness of Ann's characterization, showing how
women of the time embraced this new doctrine created for them by
a man:

It would seem but a small step from the female spider, so ruth-
lessly eating up her lover, to the type of woman celebrated by
Mr. Bernard Shaw's immortal Ann. I recall a woman friend
saying to me once, "We may not like it, and, of course, we
refuse to own to it, but there is something of Ann in every
woman." . . . You believe, perhaps, the fiction, still brought forward by many who ought to know better, that in love woman
is passive and waits for man to woo her. I think no woman in
her heart believes this. She knows, by instinct, that Nature has
unmistakably made her the predominant partner in all that re-

lates to the perpetuation of the race; she knows this in spite of all fictions set up by men. (Hartley 65–66)

Ann's ready admission of her own conventionality (96), as well as Tanner's understanding that she "has nothing" (91) to occupy her professionally except the pursuit of a husband, position her amid women in the mainstream of her culture. Thus inherent in Jack's commitment to "improve Ann's mind" is the belief that he needs to make hers more like his, to change the female's will and make it more closely resemble the male's.

Running up against this is Tanner's sense of the adversarial nature of male/female relations, and the distinctive life roles they fill. One of *Man and Superman*'s most noted lines is Jack's explanation to Tavy of "the struggle between the artist man and the mother woman" (62), a concept he expands upon in his dream role of Don Juan in act 3. According to Don Juan, Woman thinks of "Man as a separate sex" (147), unlike Shaw's own often repeated notions of the sexes' essential similarity. Don Juan invokes the Lilith myth of mankind's originally androgynous ancestry, and then explains that the primal matriarch intentionally created man "in order to produce something better than the single-sexed process can produce" (147). But he then recounts how short-sighted this decision was, given the subsequent evolution of the sexes:

But how rash and dangerous it was to invent a separate creature whose sole function was her own impregnation! For mark what has happened. First Man has multiplied on her hands until there are as many men as women; [so] that she has been unable to employ for her purposes more than a fraction of the immense energy she has left at his disposal by saving him the exhausting labor of gestation. This superfluous energy has gone to his brain and to his muscle. He has become too strong to be controlled by her bodily, and too imaginative and mentally vigorous to be content with mere self-reproduction. He has created civilization without consulting her, taking her domestic labor for granted as the foundation of it. (148)

Doña Ana, the dream version of Ann, acquiesces, "That is true, at all events" (148), ambiguously confirming some unspecified portion of

Don Juan's history. Her famous exit cry, "A father! a father for the Superman!" (173) suggests a willingness to perpetuate the gender roles and social history Don Juan propounds.

In 1904, Beatrice Ethel Kidd reviewed the first edition of the play, and pointedly isolated the problems for feminist readers with Shaw's new work. Her article merits quoting at length for its acute sense of the assumptions about women and the inequalities between women and men in Shaw's outline of the future:

"Superman" is the author's conception of the ultimate development (or at any rate an approaching development) of the male human being. The drama deals with the struggle of man (represented by the hero, John Tanner) to become Superman, and the efforts of his evil genius, woman (under the guise of a charming syren called Anne [sic] Whitefield) to prevent him. . . .

Taking for granted that the author speaks through his hero, as much in the dedication leads one to suppose, it will be seen from all this that the Superwoman is not admitted at all, even as an ideal. Woman, so far as he has observed her, has no other object in life than to entrap men. . . .

We ask, amazed, where is the writer's sometimes almost uncanny perspicacity, that he has failed to observe the modern woman's increasing independence of marriage, and the fact that she, too, is apt to regard it as something of a hindrance to *her* "dreams, follies, ideals, heroisms, and the like?" Can it be that Mr. Bernard Shaw is ignorant of women? . . . The fact is, women are quite as anxious for superhumanity as men, and are probably nearer its attainment; and if marriage be a hindrance to the man, what must it be to them? Not that they wish to disobey the Life-Force, and deliberately shirk the sacred duty of maternity which Mr. Shaw (ignoring the surplus and childless women) regards as their main purpose in life, but they will not go out of their way to seek it. As a notable food-reformer, he may, perhaps, have forgotten that to most women marriage means chiefly the eternal thinking about a man's dinner. . . . It is necessary to protest against the assumption that the ideal is less attractive to the woman than to the man. . . .

Instead of vanishing into the void, according to Mr. Shaw's tableau, crying to the Universe, "A father! A father for the Superman!" She is more likely to emerge into the broad light of day demanding (with a little gentle assistance to the supposed "prey," who is making himself ridiculous by his frantic efforts to get out of her way) "Room—room for the Superwoman!" (67–71)

As Kidd points out, Shaw leads his audience to associate his views with those of Tanner, a hypothesis perhaps also initially based on costuming in the first production, where Harley Granville-Barker (Tanner) was made up to resemble the author. Subsequently, critics have perceived similarities between Tannerian and Shavian philosophy, particularly the concept of the Life Force, which finds its clearest elucidation in this play. Shaw leaves the door open for this reading by admitting in the preface that all the characters express his views in some fashion:

> I not only tell you that my hero wrote a revolutionists' handbook: I give you the handbook at full length for your edification if you care to read it. And in that handbook you will find the politics of the sex question as I conceive Don Juan's descendant to understand them. Not that I disclaim the fullest responsibility for his opinions and for those of all my characters, pleasant and unpleasant. They are all right from their several points of view; and their points of view are, for the dramatic moment, mine also. (26)

Since Shaw gives no voice in the play to refute Don Juan's reading of the history of civilization and the roles of men and women, however, there is a certain absolutism here about woman's purely biological versus man's progenitive and cultural functions. As Michael Holroyd observes, "The Shavian theatre treats [a woman's body] as an instrument for the manufacture of babies" (*Search For Love* 387–88).

In the preface to *Man and Superman*, Shaw chooses not to mention that his sole example of a woman of genius, the artist George Sand, was an androgynous figure who cross-dressed, a point he makes clear when it serves his purpose in the preface to *Saint Joan*. Instead, he here characterizes Sand as a woman who "gobbles up men of genius" in order to "become a mother" and "gain experience for the novelist" (20), thereby restricting her image to fit his mold.

Shaw's prefatory comments to *Man and Superman* motivated another female contemporary, the American poet and dramatist Josephine Preston Peabody, to write to Shaw in 1904 concerning his separation of maternal and artistic functions. Shaw's response indicates how clearly he sees the impossibility of the conjunction of these roles. As in his debate with Lady Rhondda, discussed in chapter 1, he here relies on the specific instance of one character—Ann Whitefield—to avoid dealing with the implication of generalizations about women's potential to combine social and maternal functions. Ironically, Shaw sidesteps his own remark about Ann as "Everywoman" (28), as it would complicate his argument:

> You do not seem to have quite taken in the very important passage in my preface in which you yourself, as what you call (rightly) an Artist Woman, are put out of court in this matter. The ordinary woman lets you write about her, and laughs at you, having quite another purpose in life than yours. . . . You talk of the Mother Woman as if she could be bracketed with the Artist Woman. You might as well bracket her with the mere pleasure fancier. Ann is the Mother Woman. She is not an artist . . . she is a breeder of men, specialized by Nature to that end and endowed with enormous fascination for it. (*Collected Letters* 2:474–75)

Don Juan's version of humanity's sexual history stands out as one of the more objectionable, least progressive of Shavian lessons. As one of the most famous and highly regarded works in the canon, *Man and Superman* exemplifies and reinforces interpretations of the depiction of gender roles in Shaw that conflict with the relatively recent critical trend to see him as an advanced feminist. As Ishrat Lindblad observes,

> The way in which the significance of woman's role as mother is diminished in the last play of the *Methuselah* cycle; the lack of convincing portrayal of a mother; the many unhappy mother-child relationships, and the general vagueness of the idea of a superman within the plays, are all indications that Shaw did not ultimately give woman the primary role as the agent of evolution. (82–83)

Lindblad contrasts Shaw's maternal figures with the New Woman characters whom, because they are "unusual" and "have achieved equality with men," Shaw accepts as "the equivalent of his male genius" (83). The historical accuracy of this statement aside—the notion of equality being decidedly arguable—Lindblad's analysis points to the polarization of gender in Shaw, a tension between the lauding of male-identification or masculine qualities in female characters, and the ultimate indeterminacy of those who come under male influence but cannot achieve the same privileged status because of their role as Life Force women, potential mothers and conventional wives.

The eugenic fervor of Doña Ana's cry for a "father for the Superman" further complicates the positioning of Shaw within the matrix of arguments surrounding women's roles and the future of the English population. In *Misalliance,* the character Gunner expresses increasing consternation over the conflict he feels between his progressive socialist views and his background in Victorian conventions of strict gender roles and social propriety. After he observes Hypatia's open pursuit of Joey Percival, he exclaims:

> After all, why shouldnt she do it? The Russian students do it. Women should be as free as men. I'm a fool. I'm so full of your bourgeois morality that I let myself be shocked by the application of my own revolutionary principles. If she likes the man why shouldnt she tell him so? (178)

Shaw had claimed in a letter, "Gunner is ME" (*Collected Letters* 3:233), and certainly in his plays' tension between the expressions of women's biological role and her other potential capacities and place in society he resembles the young clerk. Shaw's commitment to eugenics, which skewed his view of women toward essentialism and the primacy of their maternal function, ironically gave him strange bedfellows in the proponents of the Victorian womanly ideal, who also supported the eugenics movement:

> The self-sacrifice commended by Sarah Ellis, Ruskin, Coventry Patmore and the rest as quintessentially womanly could now be held to have a biological, functional basis: women sacrificed themselves, and it was essential that they *should* sacrifice themselves, in the interests of social evolution and "the progress of the race." (Dyhouse 153–54)

Barbara Bellow Watson tries to clarify the notion of selfishness that Shaw propounds in *Dorothea, The Quintessence,* and elsewhere:

> The grand selfishness Shaw recommends is not self-serving, but self-respecting; it does not result in petty self-seeking, but in a rehabilitation of the idea of the self. Selfishness is the opposite of meekness, humility and self-sacrifice (the womanly virtues), not the opposite of generosity and altruism (the virtues of strength). (*Shavian Guide* 44)

Thus it appears Watson would read the child-bearing inclinations of Ana/Ann as "altruistic," which indeed seems in keeping with the juxtaposition of men's military to women's maternal duties in *The Quintessence,* for example (60). Although Shaw readily acknowledges here the conventional extrapolation of women's biological capacities to "the idealist illusion that a vocation for domestic management and the care of children is natural to women" (60), he does not dramatize the distinction between a woman's desire altruistically to fulfill a social responsibility and her interest in finding a mate and establishing herself professionally within the domestic sphere. The process of male maturation and individuation described by Tanner (*Man and Superman* 73–77) shows how moral and intellectual differentiation pulls the sexes apart as they reach adulthood. The feeling of superiority conveyed by Tanner over Ann's conventionality may coincide with the Shavian interest in educating young women to be more male-identified. But the irreconcilable conflict between Shaw's belief in the demands of eugenics and the impetus to "improve female minds" ultimately leaves the women characters dangling between his goals for them. They cannot achieve the masculine stature of their teachers, and thus appear to recede into the less ideal but inevitable role of future wife and/or mother.

9

The Daughter in Her Place

The three Shaw plays best known
for their dramatization of the father/daughter relation, *Caesar and
Cleopatra, Major Barbara,* and *Pygmalion,* share with the works already
discussed the complexity of this character mapping, replete with
emotional and subtle sexual tension as well as the energy of the
didactic framework, the motif of maternal marginalization, and the
issue of gender programming for the young female heroine. The
essential thematic similarity of an instructional frame and the character resemblances of the fathers and daughters in these three works
have been well established by such critics as Eric Bentley, Margery
Morgan, and Arthur Ganz, among others, and there is no need to
repeat their observations here. Instead, I wish to examine the implications of the relation for the maternal figures in the plays, for the
depiction of gendered attributes, and for the tonal nuance of the
instructional rapport.

In *Caesar and Cleopatra* (1900), one of the *Plays for Puritans* that
followed the collection of *Plays Pleasant and Unpleasant,* Shaw establishes a link to many of his earlier dramas' heroines by (anachronisti-
cally) associating Cleopatra with the figure of the New Woman, the
sometimes masculine, sexually unconventional young woman who
was notorious for opposing the Victorian image of the feminine ideal.

Shaw gives the speech that accuses her of this affinity to Ftatateeta, Cleopatra's mysterious, violent female nurse/advisor, who feels it is inappropriate to leave the young queen alone with Pothinus, the older male guardian of her brother Ptolemy.

> Ftatateeta. It is not meet that the Queen remain alone with—
> Cleopatra (interrupting her) Ftatateeta: must I sacrifice you to your father's gods to teach you that *I* am Queen of Egypt, and not you?
> Ftatateeta (indignantly) You are like the rest of them. You want to be what these Romans call a New Woman.
>
> (92)

Shaw introduces this designation at a critical point in the play, the period early in act 4 when Cleopatra begins to put Caesar's precepts into effect. The first two acts have established the didactic tone, first between Caesar and Cleopatra, then in a parallel sequence in her rival brother's court.[1] Caesar's sexual attraction to Cleopatra emerges clearly, as Caesar wishes he were a young lover that the Egyptian could desire. We know that the nubile queen "already troubles men's wisdom" (20), and Caesar asks her to "dream that I am young" (28) so that she can reciprocate his attraction, instead of regarding him as "a funny old gentleman" whom she likes (28). Toward the end of act 1, during Caesar's first lesson with Cleopatra, he begins to teach her how to handle her servants and assert herself as a queen. This lesson, directed at Ftatateeta, sets the tone for the instruction to follow: Ftatateeta represents the primitive Egyptian force that Cleopatra must learn to balance with Roman wisdom.

> Cleopatra (cajoling) Ftatateeta, dear: you must go away—just for a little.
> Caesar. You are not commanding her to go away: you are begging her. You are no Queen. You will be eaten. Farewell.
>
> (33)

Capitalizing on her childish fears of Caesar (who she does not yet know is one and the same as her teacher, and who she believes will eat her [26]), the Roman uses the same ploy of outlandish threats that Higgins uses with Eliza (*Pygmalion* 36–37). By imitating Caesar's

Fig. 7. Gertrude Elliott and Forbes Robertson toured to New York in 1906 with *Caesar and Cleopatra*. This production photo captures the authoritative posture of Caesar toward the Egyptian queen, and her suppliant position echoes that of Gloria Clandon with her father in *You Never Can Tell*.

commanding voice, Cleopatra soon learns how to control her slave, a success she wants to crown with the more primitive exercise of physical violence, a gesture reminiscent of the relation of Blanche Sartorius and her maid.

> Cleopatra (blazing with excitement) Go. Begone. Go away. (Fta-
> tateeta rises . . . and moves backwards towards the door . . .)
> Give me something to beat her with. . . .
> Caesar. You scratch, kitten, do you?
> Cleopatra (breaking from him) I *will* beat somebody. I will beat
> *him.* (She attacks the slave) . . . I am a real Queen at last—a
> real, real Queen! Cleopatra the Queen! (Caesar shakes his
> head dubiously. . . .)
>
> (33–34)

Arthur Ganz calls Ftatateeta's relation to Cleopatra "maternal de-votion" (130), and indeed she represents the mother figure that Caesar battles in the instruction of the queen. In *Misalliance,* Shaw establishes the connection between imperialism and education (150), and *Caesar and Cleopatra* can certainly be read as the playwright's dramatic study of the colonial enterprise.[2] In the act 4 line associating Cleopatra with the New Woman, the conflicts between Egypt and Rome, Britain and the colonies, and Victorian conventions and more modern social and personal behavioral trends all begin to resonate. Ftatateeta, the mother figure, becomes associated with colonial primitivism, which father Caesar hopes to overpower. At the same time, her feminine "nursing," which includes the pattern of physical violence demonstrated by Cleopatra in act 1 and the stigma of Victorian images of female propriety, loses hold to the masculine lessons that associate the queen with Rome and the new Britain of the (often masculine) New Woman and more modern views.

Cleopatra aligns herself at this moment with her male instructor/ model Caesar by announcing she must "teach" her nurse, thus appropriating the masculine function of educating. This exchange immediately follows the establishment of Cleopatra's growing resemblance to Caesar, a likeness that becomes apparent through the queen's use of language. In the scene with her slaves Iras and Charmian, she announces,

Cleopatra. . . . Do you know why I allow you all to chatter im-
pertinently just as you please, instead of treating you as Ftatateeta would treat you if she were Queen?

Charmian. Because you try to imitate Caesar in everything; and
he lets everybody say what they please to him.

Cleopatra. No; but because I asked him one day why he did so;
and he said "Let your women talk; and you will learn something from them." What have I to learn from them? I said.
"What they *are*," said he. . . .

Iras. . . . Heighho! I wish Caesar were back in Rome.

Cleopatra. . . . Why do you wish him away?

Charmian. He makes you so terribly prosy and serious and
learned and philosophical. . . . (The ladies laugh).

Cleopatra. Cease that endless cackling, will you. Hold your
tongues.

Charmian (with mock resignation) Well, well: we must try to
live up to Caesar.

(90–91)

As in *Pygmalion*, Shaw here associates power to command (politically
or socially) with language, and language—literary/textual as well as
spoken—comes from the father. Thus Cleopatra becomes a better
queen by turning from her nurse/mother Ftatateeta, by assuming a
male voice, and by demonstrating her growing resemblance to her
teacher and surrogate father, Caesar. She explains "neither mother,
father, nor nurse have ever taken so much care for me, or thrown
open their thoughts to me so freely" (93).[3]

Shaw uses the "matricide"—the "silencing" of the mother by slit-
ting her throat—which colors the closing scenes of the play to show
that Cleopatra has not totally abandoned all feeling for the nurse of
her youth. Arthur Ganz maintains that the Queen "remains Ftatateeta's violent, passionate nursling" (132), but it would be more
accurate to say that she is left, instead, in a transitional moment,
clearly not a perfect image of Caesar and his teaching, but not the
same young woman of sixteen we meet at the play's opening. One
critic of a 1925 revival of the play—a date well after the establishment
of Shaw's debt to Nietzsche in *Man and Superman*—remarks, "Against
this super-man, superbly as well as wittily created, is set Cleopatra,
a sub-woman in character as in age" ("Super-Man and Sub-Woman"

434). Expressing petulance over the murder of Ftatateeta, Cleopatra refuses to forgive Caesar as he prepares to depart for Rome. He rebukes her gently, delivering the line of male creation integrally connected with all the plays of this section: "What! As much a child as ever, Cleopatra! Have I not made a woman of you after all?" (124). The "child" Cleopatra, that part of her associated with the maternal influence of Ftatateeta, is antithetical to the "woman" who would ideally have mastered all the teachings and would reflect the paternal, masculine precepts of Caesar—those that comprise his notion of what distinguishes the two phases of female existence.

Suspended in this adolescent female limbo, Cleopatra is left feeling at odds with both her evolving identity and her departing teacher. Caesar attempts to resolve their conflict with the promise of a mate for Cleopatra, the Roman Mark Antony, whom he will soon send to Egypt. Sensing Caesar's disappointment in his pupil, we are made to wish she could see beyond the physical desirability of Antony. But the young woman, who preferably would have evolved into a mature ruler like her teacher, must instead remain an imperfect blend of her woman/child nature. Within the parallel worlds of ancient Egypt and modern-day England constructed by Shaw, little seems to have changed in the developmental process wherein a woman comes to fulfill a conventionally gendered role. Over the span of hundreds of years, the immutability of this vision of woman's life course appears remarkable.

In *Major Barbara*, the theme of education occurs in the form of efforts at salvation and conversion, as Shaw sets the instructional power of the daughter against that of the father. As in *Caesar and Cleopatra*, paternal resemblance emerges through the recognition that the child shares the parent's didactic strain, and here the link is even stronger, as it is inherited, rather than learned, behavior. In the preface, Shaw asserts Undershaft's "perfect comprehension of his daughter" (22), an understanding that would not be possible without an inherent similarity between them.

The first half of the play, however, stresses Barbara's maternal resemblance, which Shaw notes in several stage directions (87, 92) as well as in a wonderfully comic speech by her mother, from whom, it is patently clear, Barbara has inherited her bossiness:

Ever since they made her a major in the Salvation Army she has developed a propensity to have her own way and order people about which quite cows me sometimes. It's not ladylike: I'm sure I dont know where she picked it up. (61)

During the first act, set in Lady Britomart's home, we learn that her estranged husband, Andrew Undershaft, will be arriving shortly to meet his children after many years' absence. As Barbara Bellow Watson has observed, the plot here echoes that of *You Never Can Tell* ("Sainthood" 234), but there are also notable structural similarities underlying the two plays. Essential to both dramas, as well as to *Caesar and Cleopatra*, is the tension between maternal and paternal dominance over a child. Barbara, like Gloria, has both a brother and a sister, but is the child most like her mother. Both daughters come to know their fathers during the course of the action and recognize their deeper moral and intellectual connections to the paternal figures—as opposed to more superficial personality traits and cultural tastes shared with their mothers. Shaw even repeats the stage directions central to this recognition: in both instances, the daughters seize their fathers' hands to express their fervent realizations (*You Never Can Tell* 295; *Major Barbara* 128). And this new-found understanding of paternal likeness influences the outcome of both plays, with the daughters' impending marriages indicating the triumph of the fathers.

In certain ways, Shaw chose in the later play structurally to underline this movement from maternal to paternal affiliation. The settings in particular mirror the transition, but Lady Britomart foreshadows it verbally as well (although she presents the phenomenon in her own subjective fashion, which gives a narrower view of the events than emerges from the ensuing action and debate):

That is the injustice of a woman's lot. A woman has to bring up her children; and that means to restrain them, to deny them things they want, to set them tasks, to punish them when they do wrong, to do all the unpleasant things. And then the father, who has nothing to do but pet them and spoil them, comes in when all her work is done and steals their affection from her. (74)

She makes her observation in the library of her home in Wilton Crescent (51), the setting for the first act of the play and the space she controls. By the end of the act, however, the other characters, under the influence of Undershaft, begin to leave Lady Britomart's environment. The second act, set at the Salvation Army shelter in West Ham (75), represents a cross between a maternal and a paternal realm, as the Army's essential function is more "feminine": nurturing and concerned with the personal, while its structure is "masculine": an army with hierarchies of power and financial concerns. The last act moves into the paternalistic world (Morgan 138) of Perivale St Andrews (*Major Barbara* 128), a movement reinforced by the initial return to the maternal setting followed abruptly by the transition to Undershaft's domain, with no intermediate sphere. And Shaw retrospectively makes the West Ham shelter seem less of a middle ground than it might have before: he strews straw dummies around the stage to parallel the appearance of the destitute shelter dwellers sitting about at the opening of act 2. Thus the physical movement from the first scene to the last mirrors the transition from maternal to paternal dominance in the play.[4]

Arthur Ganz and Barbara Bellow Watson have both noticed the thematic similarity among Shaw's three early dramatizations of capitalist practices, *Widowers' Houses*, *Mrs Warren's Profession*, and *Major Barbara* (Ganz 155; Watson "Sainthood" 230–31). But neither notes the strategic difference in the parent/child relations in the three plays, the second of which features a capitalist mother, as opposed to the fathers of the other two works. All three include a recognition scene, where the daughter learns of her involvement with capitalist exploitation. But in both *Widowers' Houses* and *Major Barbara*, the daughters come to grips with the revelation and initial dismay, and discover how to accept their fathers and transform their disillusionment into personal triumph. Only in *Mrs Warren's Profession* does the daughter reject the parent—the capitalist *mother*—and decide to function independently of her support. It would seem that the trope of rejecting the mother runs deeper than thematic concerns with capitalism, leadership, or religion.

As noted above, Barbara's alignment with Undershaft begins as early as act 1, when she makes a wager with him concerning the ability of each to convert the other. But it is in act 2 that Shaw begins to establish the stronger ties between father and daughter, ties of the emotional sort seen in *Caesar and Cleopatra,* for example, as well as those of male-identification. Left alone while Barbara is at work inside the shelter, Undershaft and Cusins plot how to secure her for themselves:

> Undershaft. Religion is our business at present, because it is through religion alone that we can win Barbara.
> Cusins. Have you, too, fallen in love with Barbara?
> Undershaft. Yes, with a father's love.
> Cusins. A father's love for a grown-up daughter is the most dangerous of all infatuations. I apologize for mentioning my own pale, coy, mistrustful fancy in the same breath with it.
>
> (96)

Immediately after this expression of paternal love, Undershaft recognizes the connection between his daughter and himself.

> Cusins. . . . Barbara is quite original in her religion.
> Undershaft (triumphantly) Aha! Barbara Undershaft would be. Her inspiration comes from within herself.
> Cusins. How do you suppose it got there?
> Undershaft (in towering excitement) It is the Undershaft inheritance. I shall hand on my torch to my daughter. She shall make my converts and preach my gospel—
>
> (96)

It is interesting that Shaw gives the vocalization of this discovery to the paternal figure, as it is often the daughter who senses the likeness. But as part of Undershaft's conversion of Barbara is showing her her similarity to himself, this dialogue is perfectly in keeping with the overall momentum of the play. The father sees in the daughter an image of himself, and intends to develop her capacity to carry on his public functions, as well as convert her to a form of Undershaft philosophy.

Shaw also constructs a network of resemblance, not only to Undershaft, but to the other central male character, Barbara's husband-to-be Cusins. The young Greek scholar determines from his future father-in-law that "Barbara is as mad as we are" (97), and later he determines that like them, she is filled with the spirit of Dionysos

(134), making them "three of a kind, a Bacchic triumvirate" (M. Goldman 104).[5] By this association, Shaw builds on the motif of conflating the father and lover figures: here, two separate characters that nevertheless resemble each other and will similarly influence the daughter. In the final moments of the play, Barbara seizes Cusins's hands, as she has grabbed her father's, and announces that "he [Cusins] has found me my place and my work" (152–53), an accomplishment made possible by Cusins's affiliation and identification with Undershaft.[6] Barbara wants to join the Undershaft enterprise: "I want to make power for the world too; but it must be spiritual power" (149).

Many critics have observed the relative unimportance of Barbara in the last act—how the dialogue is dominated by Cusins's negotiations with Undershaft, and particularly by the latter's lengthy philosophical discourse. There is clearly a connection between Cusins's and Undershaft's scene in act 2, discussed above, and the final exchanges between them as Cusins debates taking on the Undershaft empire. Shaw also alludes to an extradramatic encounter between them, a Bacchic revel of sorts, that followed the Salvation Army procession in act 2 (115). The emerging structure of their relationship, with Barbara as the apex of a triangular pull, not only mirrors other triangular relations in Shaw, such as that of Marchbanks, Morell, and Candida, but also echoes a similar dynamic in the novelist Shaw himself identified as so influential on his own writing, Charles Dickens. Eve Kosofsky Sedgwick, in her analysis of this pattern in the later novels *Great Expectations, Our Mutual Friend,* and *Edwin Drood,* makes the following observation, which seems peculiarly relevant to Shaw's work as well:

> Specifically, each of these novels sites an important plot in triangular, heterosexual romance . . . and then changes its focus as if by compulsion from the heterosexual bonds of the triangle to the male-homosocial one, here called "erotic rivalry." In these male homosocial bonds are concentrated the fantasy energies of compulsion, prohibition, and explosive violence. . . . At the same time, however, these fantasy energies are mapped along the axes of social and political power; so that the revelation of intrapsychic structures is inextricable from the revelation of the mechanisms of class domination. (162)

This homosocial identification between the older and younger men, which revolves primarily around issues of the male social sphere, excludes Barbara because her work will predominantly involve more "feminine" concerns.

> There is nothing at the conclusion of *Major Barbara* to indicate that she will take over leadership and much in the play to indicate that she will not. It is hard to see her as the dynamic visionary who will lead the way to a better future. In keeping with Shaw's general male-female principles, Barbara is biological vitality, relentless producer of the next generation of life, but dependent on the male principle to make a better life for that next generation. (Noel 140–41)

In addition to being structurally similar to Dickens, *Major Barbara* also resembles late versions of the New Woman novels.

> Fiction of the pre–First World War period . . . take[s] the emancipated woman as a representative figure of the age, and . . . show[s] time after time how she may be led back to an appreciation of the softer charms of love and home. Freedom is now the starting point; the social world in which these heroines move seems entirely different from the one occupied by the New Woman of the nineties. (Cunningham 153)

Barbara, who starts the play as an independent working woman, during the course of the drama gives up her external employment and agrees to marry. Her closing lines in the play reflect her new domestic focus; she asks her mother to help her choose a house in the village to live in with her husband (153). As the quotation from Thomas Noel implies, there is nothing concrete in the drama to suggest a specific, active professional function for Barbara once she marries, unlike her husband-to-be, who will report to the office promptly at six the next morning (153). Her soaring speech on salvation and the elimination of the bribe of bread, despite the distinction she makes in it between her mother's domestic concerns and her religious ones, does not focus her energies in any tangible way (152).

And the turn toward her mother, clutching "like a baby at her mother's skirts" (153) and running to her for advice, conflicts with the immediately preceding image of strength and independence. Thus like the final glimpse of Cleopatra, the last image of Barbara is confused, part strong woman, part helpless child. The pattern of these endings suggests one interpretive possibility: these Life Force women, unable to match the moral, intellectual, and philosophical heights of their male mentors because of the necessity of their biological duty, must also be reinscribed within the feminine realm to rationalize or confirm their final status. As Victorian culture associated the child with the feminine, a display of childish behavior affirms the gender of the daughter, and fuses sexual and gender roles at the critical moment of separation from the father (through departure or marriage). Cleopatra's petulance, Barbara's babyishness, Ann's fainting (certainly a feminine, if not a childish, act for Victorians), and Eliza's sticking out her tongue at the mirror image of herself—formed in Higgins's house—as she leaves it to marry Freddy are all of a piece. Shaw reinforces the femininity of his daughters, keeping at bay the threat of woman's assumption of paternal ability and power.

In the late extravaganza *Too True to Be Good* (1932), Shaw explicitly addresses and condemns the type of mother/daughter relation characterized at the end of *Major Barbara*. The daughter here tries to escape the clutches of her over-protective, infantilizing mother, exclaiming,

> No woman can shake off her mother. There should be no mothers: there should be only women, strong women able to stand by themselves, not clingers.... Mothers cling: daughters cling: we are all like drunken women clinging to lamp posts: none of us stands upright.... If only I had had a father to stand between me and my mother's care. (509)

Shortly thereafter, she presents her goals for the future:

> I have the instincts of a good housekeeper: I want to clean up this filthy world and keep it clean. There must be other women who want it too. Florence Nightingale had the same instinct when she went to clean up the Crimean war. She wanted a sisterhood; but there wasnt one.... I want a sisterhood. Since I came here I have been wanting to join the army, like Joan of Arc. It's a brotherhood, of a sort. (511–12)

Although we are to see the narrowness of the young woman's interests—particularly as she wants those who do not join her "strangled" (511)—her remarks merit attention for their complex fusion of themes. She rejects her mother and longs for a father figure to intercede and support her. She relies on a feminine, domestic metaphor ("housekeeper") to ground herself and describe her larger social inclinations. She expresses interest in a "sisterhood," a communion of women in which there is no place for the older women, the mothers (and for which there is no model anywhere in Shaw, who avoids any female bond more compelling than the luncheon date between Grace and Sylvia in *The Philanderer*). And the only image she can find for the sisterhood she desires is male: the army. Compressed in these speeches is Shaw's division of female experience, the gulf that separates younger from older women and strips any sense of continuity or purpose from the matriarchs. Through "The Patient" (as Shaw designates her throughout), Shaw reinforces an essentially domestic role for women, although they may be motivated to bring their domestic experience into the larger social sphere. That larger world exhibits its own patriarchal structure clearly, yet the young woman cannot conceive of entering it without emulating men and male institutions; she has no idea what a female structure in the larger sphere could be.

The fusion of the domestic with a (re)movement for a woman into a professional domain similarly characterizes the epilogue to *Pygmalion*, although Shaw does not portray the transition with as much revolutionary fervor as he does in *Too True*. This may in part be because Eliza's separation is from a paternal, rather than maternal, figure, and Shaw clearly presents this division as negligible—the Colonel still oversees Eliza's and Freddy's business, while Eliza continues "to meddle in the housekeeping at Wimpole Street" (123–24).

Different critics organize the progress of Shaw's writing in various ways. Arthur Ganz, for example, sees the marriage of Ellie Dunn and Captain Shotover as "the culmination of a line of impassioned father-daughter relationships" (193), while Eric Bentley seems to suggest that the character named Pygmalion in *Back to Methuselah* demonstrates the ultimate result of attempts at human creation (83). Bentley also depicts "the 'education of Eliza'" as "a caricature of the true process" (86), although he does not explain, or give examples of, what that "true process" might be like. But Bentley's remark suggests why *Pygmalion* strikes me as the logical end point for this study, in that the play both exposes and exploits the subgenre Shaw has been creating: that which revolves around the intricacies of the father/daughter, teacher/pupil/lover relation. In *Pygmalion* the playwright demonstrates a better balance between the central male and female characters, calling into question the extent of Higgins's impact on Eliza and the relative power each brings to their relationship.

Pygmalion is a favorite target for Shavian and drama critics generally, and it has particularly attracted biographical and psychoanalytic readings. Arthur Ganz groups the romance with other works in which Shaw projects himself as a young female: "When he wrote a play about a flower girl who in acquiring a new speech acquires a new soul, Shaw was dramatising a central action of his life" (6). Arnold Silver expresses a similar theory: "Shaw could sympathetically speed her on this journey [to selfhood] because in certain important respects Eliza's fairy-tale career paralleled his own" (185). Maurice Valency feels "Shaw himself had learned upper-class English ways in somewhat the same manner as Eliza" (323). Philip Weissman constructs a more elaborate interpretation, seeing in Shaw's difficult childhood and subsequent need of a mother figure the impetus for the creation of Eliza. Shaw's rapport with Mrs. Patrick Campbell informed the drama, for he served as a teacher/director for her, while she mothered him. Weissman maintains that the idea for *Pygmalion* was a logical outgrowth of Shaw's work on *Caesar and Cleopatra*: "In his 'unconscious drama' he was recasting Caesar as the West End gentleman, Henry Higgins. . . . Similarly, he transformed Cleopatra into Pat Campbell as the East End donna, Eliza Doolittle" (163).

These various interpretations, each of which strikes me as plausible and ingenious, represent attempts to contain and explain the sustained power struggles and complex nexus of pseudofamilial relations in the play. What intrigues me, however, is not what lies behind Shaw's portrayals, but the implications and (subtextual) thrust of the action of these characters. Clearly he uses established dramatic structures to spin out variations on his theme. *Pygmalion* follows patterns of paternal pedagogy, maternal marginalization, and emotional complication found elsewhere. But Shaw introduces key distinctions in this drama found in none of the related pieces. One singular difference is Eliza's active entrance into the teacher/pupil situation. Unlike Cleopatra, who learns from Caesar during his colonial invasion of her land, or Barbara, whose growth is integrally connected to her biological tie to her father, or Dorothea, who as a child has no control over the behavior of adults who take her education as their personal responsibility, Eliza independently chooses to seek out Higgins's tutelage.

By invoking the Pygmalion myth in his title, Shaw clearly asks his audience to be aware of the idea of human creation and formation and to think about the problems inherent in the drive to mold an ideal being. Yet as with the depiction of Undershaft in *Major Barbara*, the attractiveness and power of a character or situation may conflict with the authorial desire to expose that very magnetism. Shaw's work does not distance his audience with the methods of alienation later developed by Brecht to avoid this problem. Rather, he seems to rely on an informed, thoughtful audience's "self-alienation." It must subsequently disengage itself from the seductive quality of the characters by realizing how and why Shaw's work evolved the way it did, and ideally engage in a Fabian-like attempt to resolve similar struggles in the real world differently. Yet equally possible is the sense that this is a critical rationalization for the conflicts the audience may face between the immediate impact of the work and its later feeling that Shaw's intention must have been different, given his sociopolitical position. This speculative spiral is irresolvable, however; surely it is too much to expect complete coherence, particularly if *Pygmalion* emerged from the depths of psychological and emotional conflict so many critics suggest.

It is intriguing that Shaw conflates two seemingly separate myths in the play, the Pygmalion story and a fairy-tale plot that overtly resembles *Cinderella* in its transformation of ragged young woman to "princess," but also more subtly invokes *Snow White*. The French feminist critic Hélène Cixous shows the connection between these male-authored myths—a connection that fits the Shavian rendition peculiarly well.

One cannot yet say of the following history "it's just a story." It's a tale still true today. Most women who have awakened remember having slept, *having been put to sleep.*

Once upon a time . . . once . . . and once again.

Beauties slept in their woods, waiting for princes to come and wake them up. In their beds, in their glass coffins, in their childhood forests like dead women. Beautiful, but passive; hence desirable: all mystery emanates from them. It is men who like to play dolls. As we have known since Pygmalion. Their old dream: to be god the mother. The best mother, the second mother, the one who gives the second birth. (66)

Through Mrs Higgins's censure of Pickering and her son, Shaw expresses his understanding, parallel to Cixous's analysis, of the "artist-men": "You certainly are a pretty pair of babies, playing with your live doll" (68). Shaw's fairy-tale allusions make the connection even more apt. Shaw also includes strategic references to the Snow White tale, which features in many versions the famous glass coffin, and, more important, the queen's magic mirror and her poisoned apple.

In the well-known Grimm version of the tale, the evil queen, stepmother to Snow White, disguises herself as an old peddler to seek out the young princess, who is hiding from her in the forest at the home of the dwarfs. She brings with her an apple, half of which has been poisoned. She tricks Snow White into sharing the apple with her, by breaking it in two and safely eating the unadulterated portion. The poisoned bite that Snow White takes becomes lodged in her throat as she falls into a deathlike sleep. In *Pygmalion*, Shaw casts Higgins in the stepmother role, as he tries to seduce Eliza into staying to learn to talk like a duchess:

> Higgins (snatching a chocolate cream from the piano, his eyes suddenly beginning to twinkle with mischief) Have some chocolates, Eliza.
>
> Liza (halting, tempted) How do I know what might be in them? Ive heard of girls being drugged by the like of you. (Higgins whips out his penknife; cuts a chocolate in two; puts one half into his mouth and bolts it; and offers her the other half.)
>
> Higgins. Pledge of good faith, Eliza. I eat one half: you eat the other. (Liza opens her mouth to retort: he pops the half chocolate into it). You shall have boxes of them, every day. You shall live on them. Eh?
>
> Liza (who has disposed of the chocolate after being nearly choked by it) I wouldnt have ate it, only I'm too ladylike to take it out of my mouth.
>
> (35)

Eliza's room in Higgins's house also contains a full-length mirror, the first one she has ever encountered. In the Snow White tale, the stepmother learns from the magic mirror of Snow White's whereabouts as well as of her own loss of superior beauty. Although Shaw does not use this prop as exactly, he does imbue it with the evil connotations of the fairy-tale (from Eliza's viewpoint), and it does become a vehicle for self-appraisal and self-recognition. After Eliza's bath in act 2, she sees an unrecognizable self in the mirror for the first time. Reflecting her puritanical upbringing, she feels the vision of her naked body is indecent, and she covers it with a towel (52).[7] Yet it also reveals her physical beauty, and thus the mirror "tells" the same news as in the fairy-tale. The mirror reappears in the last scene of act 4, moreover, to demonstrate Eliza's disenchantment with the image of herself created by Higgins. Dressed in the clothes Pickering has provided, surrounded by the furnishings Higgins has procured, Eliza rejects her reflection as she severs the tie with Wimpole Street, sticking her tongue out at the mirror princess who has achieved Higgins's ideal as she exits her room for the last time, leaving fairy land behind (85).

Shaw's association of Higgins with the evil stepmother adds a dark tone to *Pygmalion*—one that contrasts with the fairy godmother transformation of the slavey Cinderella. This shading in the play finds its strongest evidence in the repeated threats to Eliza's sexual and physical safety. Martin Meisel centers this action in "the seduction scene of the second act," where "everyone suspects Higgins' designs" (175–76). But the theme is introduced much earlier, in the opening scene of the play, with her first "terrified" and "hysterical" insistence of her respectability and the fear of losing her "character" (15). Eliza's concerns operate on two levels here: not only does she fear a loss of reputation (meaning actually the acquisition of one as a loose woman) and legal livelihood, but her speech also foreshadows the larger issue of Eliza's loss of self—the transformation into a new identity and "character" created by Higgins.

From her act 1 protestation that "I'm a good girl, I am" (17) through her act 5 taunt to Henry, "Wring away. What do I care? I knew youd strike me some day" (108), Eliza consistently expresses concern for her physical and moral well-being at the hands of her teacher and surrogate father Higgins. Both Higgins and the bystanders at Covent Garden identify the former with teaching (19–20), and

Shaw establishes the didactic nature of the drama in its brief preface (9). But he explicitly fuses paternal and pedagogical roles with the threat of physical violence early in act 2:

> Mrs Pearce. Dont cry, you silly girl. Sit down. Nobody is going to touch your money.
> Higgins. Somebody is going to touch *you*, with a broomstick, if you dont stop snivelling. Sit down.
> Liza (obeying slowly) Ah-ah-ah-ow-oo-o! One would think you was my father.
> Higgins. If I decide to teach you, I'll be worse than two fathers to you.
>
> (30)

Higgins, of course, is actually one of three fathers for Eliza, the other two being Colonel Pickering—another teacher from whom she "learnt really nice manners" (97)—and "the regulation natural chap," Alfred Doolittle. These three men represent the social spectrum of patriarchy, each with his own mode of keeping Eliza "in her place." Doolittle, who knows nothing of the didactic arrangement under which Eliza will stay at Wimpole Street, arrives at the house to arrange the "sale" of his daughter for five pounds, acting out the exchange of women in patriarchal culture. He makes the Victorian assumption that Higgins's job, as the prospective husband in this burlesqued exchange, will be to "improve Eliza's mind" and suggests that the most efficacious method will be "with a strap" (52).

Unbeknownst to Doolittle, of course, Higgins manipulates their conversation so that the member of "the undeserving poor" (48) will reveal his class differences and prejudices. Eliza, from the same class origins, is a victim of both class and sex discrimination, and Shaw draws parallels between these two forms of injustice in the play. Although Eliza repeatedly asserts her essential similarity to the upper classes, with whom she shares self-respect and human feelings, Higgins maintains a stance in opposition to her beliefs.

> Pickering (in good-humored remonstrance) Does it occur to you, Higgins, that the girl has some feelings?
> Higgins (looking critically at her) Oh no, I dont think so. Not

any feelings that we need bother about. (Cheerily) Have you,
  Eliza?
Liza. I got my feelings same as anyone else.

(34)

Through Higgins's infantilization of Eliza, treating her as a child and
talking about her as if she weren't present or able to understand,
Shaw creates a parallel between issues of class and sex: discrimination toward the poor and toward women (who are tantamount to
children) appear very similar. By erasing detectable class difference
in Eliza through speech education, Higgins believes he will be en-
dowing her with the humanity she lacks. The issue of Eliza's sex,
however, does not enter into Higgins's equation in any considered
way. Speech training and gender programming go hand in hand with
Higgins's method, and thus as Eliza learns Henry's speech, she also
absorbs the masculine context from which it evolved.

Late in the play, Henry delivers the first of his "creation" speeches,
fulfilling his Pygmalion image: "I have created this thing out of the
squashed cabbage leaves of Covent Garden" (97). Eliza clarifies this
creative, educational process, highlighting the masculine nature of
his precepts: "I was brought up to be just like him, unable to control
myself, and using bad language on the slightest provocation" (97).
In other words, Higgins has reared Eliza in his own image, a male
image. Significantly, language, the instrument of male paternity, is
the medium through which Eliza assumes her resemblance to Higgins. As Mrs Higgins observes:

Mrs Higgins. You silly boy, of course she's not presentable.
  She's a triumph of your art and of her dress maker's; but if
  you suppose for a moment that she doesnt give herself away
  in every sentence she utters, you must be perfectly cracked
  about her.
Pickering. But dont you think something might be done? I mean
  something to eliminate the sanguinary element from her conversation?
Mrs Higgins. Not as long as she is in Henry's hands.
Higgins (aggrieved) Do you mean that *my* language is im-
  proper?
Mrs Higgins. No, dearest: it would be quite proper—say on a

canal barge; but it would not be proper for her at a garden party.

(67)

Mrs Higgins opposes the masculine realm of the canal barge to the more feminine location, the garden party, and shows that Eliza speaks her teacher's masculine language. Eliza confirms this, speaking of both the class and sexual nature of language:

> You told me, you know, that when a child is brought to a foreign country, it picks up the language in a few weeks, and forgets its own. Well, I am a child in your country. I have forgotten my own language, and can speak nothing but yours. Thats the real break-off with the corner of Tottenham Court Road. (99)

In act 4, after Eliza's triumph, when she expresses anger and frustration over the men's insensitivity to her dominant role in the success, Higgins remarks, "Youre not bad-looking: it's quite a pleasure to look at you sometimes—not now, of course, because youre crying and looking as ugly as the very devil; but when youre all right and quite yourself" (82). The subtext of his comment, "when you behave in a feminine fashion—that is, crying or being temperamental—you are 'not yourself,' not the creature I made," comes through clearly. When in act 5 Eliza asserts her independence Higgins exclaims triumphantly—in the same manner in which Shaw's avuncular persona instructed "his" Dorothea—"By George, Eliza, I said I'd make a woman of you; and I have. I like you like this" (108–9). Her attainment of Higgins's sense of "womanhood" allows her access to male identity: "Now youre a tower of strength: a consort battleship. You and I and Pickering will be three old bachelors instead of only two men and a silly girl" (109).

In shorter form, Shaw reinforces the paternal education of Eliza by creating a parallel scenario for Clara Eynsford-Hill in his "sequel" (5), the prose epilogue that follows the play. Clara becomes Eliza's legal sister through the latter's marriage to her brother Freddy Eynsford-Hill, and spiritual sister through her education into moral, socially conscious humanity. Clara, "who appeared to Higgins and his mother as a disagreeable and ridiculous person, and to her own mother as in some inexplicable way a social failure, had never seen herself in either light" (118), not, at least, until she read H. G. Wells and Galsworthy. Clara, Shaw tells us, formed "a gushing desire to take her [Eliza] for a model" (119), but experienced quite a shock when she learned "that this exquisite apparition had graduated from the gutter in a few months time" (119).

> It shook her so violently, that when Mr H. G. Wells lifted her on the point of his puissant pen, and placed her at the angle of view from which the life she was leading and the society to which she clung appeared in its true relation to real human needs and worthy social structure, he effected a conversion and a conviction of sin comparable to the most sensational feats of General Booth. (119)

Thus Clara, through male literary paternity, similarly achieves a laudable social stature, having taken the authors' precepts to heart and having substituted them as her models. In the process, of course, Clara leaves her mother's conventional views and her circle at Largelady Park.

> It exasperated her to think that the dungeon in which she had languished for so many unhappy years had been unlocked all the time, and that the impulses she had so carefully struggled with and stifled for the sake of keeping well with society, were precisely those by which alone she could have come into any sort of sincere human contact. (120)

Clara, another princess locked away, learns from Galsworthy of the potential that lay within her all the time. By negative association with her mother and her mother's circle, these unspecified "impulses" take on masculine qualities.

The maternal rejection presented in this sequel also continues a matriarchal theme from the main drama. Eliza is another of Shaw's orphan characters, having been brought up in a motherless home: "I aint got no mother. Her that turned me out was my sixth stepmother. But I done without them" (34). Higgins offers his housekeeper, Mrs Pearce, as a maternal substitute for the girl: "You can adopt her, Mrs Pearce: I'm sure a daughter would be a great amusement to you" (34), and indeed entrusts this older woman with all domestic matters relating to Eliza's stay, including those feminine matters of hygiene inappropriate for him to supervise. Shaw establishes Mrs Pearce as a parallel character to Higgins's mother (Morgan 172), a domineering, scolding, condescending woman, who is the object of Henry's continual rebellion. As such, the mothers are both ineffectual teacher figures; their "boy" Henry never carries out their instructions, particularly with regard to his pupil, Eliza:

> Then might I ask you not to come down to breakfast in your dressing-gown, or at any rate not to use it as a napkin to the extent you do, sir. And if you would be so good as not to eat everything off the same plate, and to remember not to put the porridge saucepan out of your hand on the clean tablecloth, it would be a better example to the girl. You know you nearly choked yourself with a fishbone in the jam only last week. (42–43)

The women's failure as teachers corresponds to Higgins's patriarchal belief in pedagogy as a masculine occupation. This also accounts for his surprising reaction to Eliza's notion of being an elocution instructor. As the "assistant to that hairyfaced Hungarian" (108), Eliza would place herself in the traditionally feminine position of inferiority, appropriating male privilege while maintaining a feminine identity. This prompts Higgins's threat to "wring your neck" (108). But when Eliza realizes her ability to perform independently, to mirror her teacher/father instead of compete with him via feminine affiliation with another male, his response is altogether different. Eliza cries,

> Aha! Now I know how to deal with you. What a fool I was not to think of it before! You cant take away the knowledge you gave me. You said I had a finer ear than you. . . . I'll advertize it in the papers that your duchess is only a flower girl that you taught, and that she'll teach anybody to be a duchess just the same in six months for a thousand guineas. (108)

Her discovery elicits his above-quoted exclamation of pleasure with the woman he has "made," a woman who to his eyes resembles a man like himself. This characterological mirroring corresponds to the physical mirror emblem that runs through the play. Higgins's mirror reflects Higgins in Eliza, a correlation he confirms at the end of act 4, after the passage quoted earlier about her not being "herself" when she, essentially, does not project his image of her. He tells her, "You go to bed and have a good nice rest; and then get up and look at yourself in the glass; and you wont feel so cheap" (82).

The disparagement of Eliza, calling her "cheap" and a "dirty slut" (38) again has class connotations, with a heavily sexual undertone. Mrs Pearce echoes Higgins's defamation of Eliza, and as his minion she enters into the darker mythic subplot discussed earlier. Higgins informs Eliza in act 2, "If youre naughty and idle you will sleep in the back kitchen among the black beetles, and be walloped by Mrs Pearce with a broomstick" (36). Despite Higgins's numerous threats of physical violence, he never actually hurts Eliza, mental and emotional cruelty notwithstanding. Instead, Shaw projects onto Mrs Pearce the physical, sexual violation of Eliza that Henry suppresses throughout, in a lesbian "rape" scene added to the original script at the time it was filmed (1938).[8]

Higgins insists that Mrs Pearce "bundle her off to the bath-room" (37) to clean her as a first step toward respectability. This action fits neatly with the mythic "rebirth" of Eliza, for bathing has always been symbolically associated with the remission of sin and rebirth in the Western Christian tradition.[9] Mrs Pearce conducts Eliza to "a spare bedroom" on "the third floor." Eliza had "expected to be taken down to the scullery" (38), but she begins her transformation by a physical elevation that metaphorically parallels her expected rise in social stature. She is told "to make [herself] as clean as the room: then [she] wont be afraid of it" (38)—a simile that counters the previous elevation metaphor with its continuation of the girl's dehumanization. Eliza associates cleanliness with death; however, the metaphoric, sexual sense of death remains perhaps subtextual:

> Liza. You expect me to get into that and wet myself all over! Not me. I should catch my death. I knew a woman did it every Saturday night; and she died of it. . . . (weeping) . . . Its not natural: it would kill me. Ive never had a bath in my life.
>
> (38)

Mrs Pearce counters with inducements and slurs: "Well, dont you want to be clean and sweet and decent, like a lady? You know you cant be a nice girl inside if youre a dirty slut outside" (38). The reasoning is the twisted logic of upper-class male seducers of lower-class women in eighteenth and nineteenth century romance: submit, succumb, and receive the outer embellishments of higher social status. The ambiguity of the term *slut*, which can mean either a physically dirty or morally questionable woman, stands out strongly; Eliza's claims of being a "good girl" are thrown into question by the alternative, sexual connotation of the label. This indeterminacy resonates with the link between physical cleanliness and sexual purity that is inverted by the scene's subtext into physical cleanliness and sexual defloration.

Despite Eliza's cries of protest, she is ordered to "take off all [her] clothes" (39).

> Mrs Pearce puts on a pair of white rubber sleeves . . . then takes a formidable looking long handled scrubbing brush and soaps it profusely with a ball of scented soap. Eliza comes back with nothing on but the bath gown . . . a piteous spectacle of abject terror. . . . Deftly snatching the gown away and throwing Eliza down on her back . . . she sets to work with the scrubbing brush. Eliza's screams are heartrending. (39–40)

The blatancy of these stage directions implies Shaw's cognizance of their implications. The phallic brush and cleansing ball are applied with the clinical coldness of the bath/laboratory's rubber gloves. That Eliza should be thrown on her back to be "cleaned," which in a bathtub would literally lead to drowning, cements the rape imagery, highlighting for the reader the symbolic interpretation over the literal. Using a female surrogate for the male rapist, Shaw again conceives of this lesbian encounter in a heterosexual context, in keeping with the late Victorian/Edwardian medical paradigm for a lesbian relation. But perhaps more important, he transfers the onus of sexual violence onto a woman, thereby safeguarding the gruff geniality of Higgins and insuring his respectability at the same time that he fulfills the dark threat to Eliza that the play's opening dialogue foreshadows.

The film version, which facilitated the inclusion of this scene, graphically follows the outline of Shaw's directions, and creates a profoundly disturbing atmosphere on screen. At the start of the bath

Fig. 8. Wilfrid Lawson (Mrs Pearce) drags Wendy Hiller (Eliza) toward the bathtub in the 1938 film version of *Pygmalion*. Note Eliza's look of horror and her clutching of her dress as if to protect her soon-to-be-exposed breasts.

scene, Mrs Pearce wraps herself in a sheet/apron (instead of the printed "sleeves") and promptly corners Eliza in the bathroom, trying to talk her into removing her clothes. She finally pushes Eliza out into the adjacent bedroom to change into a robe, leaving Mrs Pearce alone. At this point, ominous music begins quietly, and almost like the witch whose broomstick has been alluded to earlier, she begins to mix bath salts in a tub that quickly foams with the appearance of a bubbling cauldron. Mrs Pearce looks toward the bedroom door with a determined glint in her eye and picks up the scrubbing brush and soap. After another brief tangle getting Eliza to remove the robe—the camera having cut to Mrs Pearce draping the bathroom mirror with a towel—Eliza is seen in the tub, screaming and struggling with Mrs Pearce, who, like Blanche before her, has the other woman by the hair, grabbing hold of it to keep Eliza submerged in the bathwater. Interspersed with her genuinely "heartrending" screams, Eliza cries, "I've never done this kind of thing before, really I haven't . . . No, Mrs Pearce, no, don't . . . stop it . . . this has never happened to me before . . . oh help, help . . . I've never been . . . stop it . . . help."[10] Amid her screams, the camera cuts to a shot of Higgins and Pickering at the foot of the stairs below. They are staring up at the sound of the cries, and they exchange a bemused look. Higgins shrugs and turns back into his study, while Pickering remains, smirking. The camera cuts back to Eliza, still screaming, eyes shut (to keep out soap), hand groping along the tile wall of the tub. Her hand grasps hold of a handle, and suddenly the shower head above explodes with a cascade of shooting water. This ejaculatory conclusion to the scene clearly literalizes the subtextually heterosexual paradigm controlling the attack on Eliza.

Although the actors, screenwriters, and directors[11] must be credited for the overall production, Shaw's close involvement with the film implicates him in its creation and impact as well.[12] The thrust of this scene in particular is patently clear; the "innocuous" bath barely masks the reality of female violation conveyed by the dialogue and action.

When Eliza reenters Higgins's study, Shaw provides a description for her as he would for a new, as yet unnamed character: "a dainty and exquisitely clean young Japanese lady in a simple blue cotton kimono" (50–51), and indeed she is unrecognized by the other characters, with the exception of Mrs Pearce, who has conducted the transformation. Significantly, Eliza cannot "see" herself in the mirror after the bath; she cannot confront the new self that has been robbed of all vestiges of her old identity, including a symbolic virginity.

When she finally comes into her own at the end of the play, Higgins observes that she has "had a bit of [her] own back" (102), meaning a little revenge on him, but also suggesting another interpretation. She has chosen to return to a life independent of Higgins and Pickering, thus reasserting some of the original identity she had lost while at Wimpole Street. She declines Higgins's offer to "adopt [her] as [his] daughter and settle money on [her]" (105), his attempt to formalize the structure that has defined their relationship to date. Needless to say, his earlier suggestion that Mrs Pearce adopt Eliza has long been forgotten, and Eliza expresses no indebtedness to the housekeeper for any of her learning. Ultimately, Mrs Pearce emerges as an alter image for Eliza: what she might become were she to stay in Higgins's household, for the older woman has never been able to break free of the hold Higgins has over her (104).

Eliza's announcement, "I'll marry Freddy, I will, as soon as I'm able to support him" (107), seems a refreshingly feminist twist on the usual pattern of young female pupils' marrying men inferior in some way to their paternal teacher. But Shaw's "sequel" undermines this assertiveness, by showing Eliza's financial dependence on Pickering and emotional involvement with Higgins for years to come. Thus in the narrative resolving the conflicts of the play, Shaw reasserts literary control over the more balanced voices of the drama and removes the power Eliza seems to gain in her fight for independence. Eliza may not "like" her father-figures all that much (124), but Shaw makes it clear in his closing sentence that for her, they will always be "godlike" (124).

Epilogue

The writing of the first chapters of this book coincided with my rehearsal for and performance in a summer-stock production of *Arms and the Man*. Leading a dual life as critic and actress was both complicated and provocative. The nature of that particular production process necessitated my leaving my scholar self at home when I had to be at the theater, but as a critic I embraced the opportunity to reflect on that other interpretive environment where my Shavian insights had no place. Our production (by all critical accounts a solid success of the light comic variety) eschewed "concept"; the director relied on Shaw's set descriptions and stage directions for guidance, emphasizing the physical and verbal humor of the piece. Unquestionably an enjoyable experience, it nevertheless reminded me of Shaw's own thoughts on the theatrical life of Ibsen after the turn of the century: "Now that Ibsen is . . . safe in the Pantheon, his message is in worse danger of being forgotten or ignored than when he was in the pillory" (*Quintessence* 27–28).

Recently, in *Sexual Anarchy*, Elaine Showalter has written of the links between the fin de siècle and the present moment, and these cultural parallels may help account for the successful resurgence of Shaw productions in the theater over the last decade. Yet as Caryl Churchill demonstrates in her play *Cloud 9*, we can also see that comparatively little has changed in the intervening century (at least with respect to such issues as race, class, and gender), which suggests other reasons for the theatrical vitality of Shaw's work. Certainly with respect to his female characters, there is passive familiarity, enjoyment, and comfort, on the part of the audience, with the best-known types, especially the broadly termed "Life Force woman," who has become virtually a generic character in the intervening decades.

In recent commentary on Caryl Churchill's work, Austin Quigley remarks that many of her female characters are "suspended between stereotypes they failed to follow and prototypes they failed to initiate" (40). Although none of Shaw's early female critics phrased it so succinctly, I believe Quigley's evaluation turns into a dramaturgical strength what appeared to these other critics as Shaw's failure to create new role models for women. The strong response we now have to the ambivalence of Churchill's female portraits, like the sense of betrayal Shaw's female contemporaries demonstrated in their criticism of his women characters, speaks to the power of the stage to provoke us and make us think. Current productions of Shaw, on the whole, seem to have lost their provocative impact, however, relying on their comic value or historical importance to the theater in a fashion often antithetical to Shaw's original intent.

Although many of us may no longer look to the stage for our images of ideal characters, we do still anticipate that drama may have the power to tell us something about ourselves and our world, regardless of the moment of its composition. And surely by trying to understand earlier times, we can have a better grasp of the genesis of our own. Certain forms of contemporary literary criticism, among them new historicist and feminist, strike me as extremely viable for theatrical application to this end. Productions that incorporate—in whatever subtle or overt form they choose—new comprehension of the past may well speak to their audiences in an increasingly compelling fashion. And texts like Shaw's that have already proven their stageworthiness may elicit new, unexpected response through reconceptualization.

One of the reasons we re-mount older drama is, of course, that we see in it reflections of current interests or issues. Shaw's concern with such perennial debates as the relation of the sexes, as well as moral, social, and political dilemmas, gives his drama a distinctive contemporary resonance that invites this kind of theatrical investigation. As we continue to engage in discussions of such issues as the evolving role of women in society and our sense of gender identity—and these debates' sociopolitical applications to such phenomena as violence toward women and lingering sexual discrimination in a patriarchal culture—our knowledge of history in all its varied forms may help us work toward change. Shaw exemplifies for me some of the contradictions inherent in attitudes toward women expressed over the last century; although the surface sense or initial impact of these presentations might appear progressive and supportive, deeper analysis and more thorough investigation reveals latent prejudice, regressive values, and even hostility. Full understanding of this range of views can aid the effort to confront and challenge the more difficult elements of women's cultural and historical past.

Dramatic criticism that can be of no value or use in the theater—that treats the text solely as a work of literature without a cognizance of its stage life and origins—is misguided. Although I have talked little of productions of Shaw in the course of this study, I have, throughout its composition, remained acutely aware of theater artists' reliance on historical and critical material to aid their work. If I have had an overarching agenda, it has been not only to bring Shaw criticism into a dialogue with other forms of current scholarly discourse, but also to provide artists with information, opinions, and historical insights that may, in some way, inform their work. If Shaw is to have an ongoing life in both the academy and the theater, then our work with his writing must prevent his dramas from becoming museum pieces, by connecting them strongly with current thoughts, cultural interests, and concerns. I hope in some measure *Shaw's Daughters* will contribute to this goal.

Notes

Introduction

1. For an excellent discussion of current trends in feminist thought as they apply to the theater, see Dolan 1–18.

2. Shaw's response to these articles can be found in the fourth volume of his *Collected Letters* (179–84). He objects to Rhondda's criticism of his avoidance of female friendships, claiming he dramatizes no male ones either. But *Widowers' Houses, The Philanderer, Mrs Warren's Profession,* and *Man and Superman,* to name just a few, have clearly defined male friendships, contrary to Shaw's contention. He also universalizes the concept of the "Conduit Pipe" that Rhondda raises in a specifically feminist context—focused on women and childbearing—thereby diluting her argument and also appropriating it in this exchange to fit his own theory of Creative Evolution.

Chapter 1

1. See, for example, Aveling and Aveling; Caird; "Dies Dominae"; Linton, "Wild Women"; Linton, "Wild Women as Social Insurgents"; Linton, "Partisans"; Schreiner; Sheldon; and Stutfield.

2. See, for example, Allen; Gissing; Grand; Hardy; and Meredith.

3. Jordan's dating of 1894 may indeed be the first published instance, but as the 1893 draft of *The Philanderer* shows, Shaw used the phrase in his first version of the play, indicating that the expression was already in use at least a year earlier than Jordan suggests (*The Philanderer: Facsimile* 102).

4. Susan Gorsky notes that this periodical, first published in 1971, "is directed towards the modern career woman, the frustrated housewife, the divorcee, or any woman who is exploring one of the many new roles available to her" (85).

5. Ibsen's Nora and Hedda clearly have other concerns, as do the similar, if satirized, figures in Sydney Grundy's *The New Woman* (1894).

6. For a complete discussion of New Woman fiction, see Cunningham; Stubbs; Fernando; and Showalter, *Literature*.

7. Four of the five novels were serialized between 1884 and 1888, but the first, *Immaturity*, did not appear in print until 1930 in the *Collected Works* (Dietrich 4–5).

8. Shaw started to compose a sixth novel in May 1887, but never finished it (*An Unfinished Novel* 13–14). Only two central female characters seem to be emerging in the extant opening chapters, and neither seems to fit the profile of a New Woman. It is of course impossible to know whether Shaw might have created another such character, and whether he would have perpetuated the narrative patterns of New Woman fiction, had he continued with this work.

9. Even if discussion were to expand through the Edwardian era—as some scholars claim the New Woman figure survived until the outbreak of the Great War—this paradigm would still hold for Shaw's plays of these years. Despite unconventional tactics, Ann and Violet Whitefield (*Man and Superman* [1903]) "get their men," and Barbara Undershaft (*Major Barbara* [1907]) is reduced from an independent, professional woman to a child crying for her mother to help her select a house for herself and her husband-to-be. Lady Cicely (*Captain Brassbound's Conversion* [1901]), like Mrs Clandon (*You Never Can Tell* [1898]), belongs to the previous generation, while Lesbia Grantham (*Getting Married* [1911]) is mired in her attempts to escape the marriage proposals of General Bridgenorth. However, unlike other Shaw critics, I am not trying to apply these parameters to a series of characters across the canon. Later figures such as Saint Joan clearly must be discussed from other perspectives that correspond more closely to the historical milieu of the time of their composition.

10. See, for example, the preface to *Pygmalion:* "[The play] is so intensely and deliberately didactic . . . that I delight in throwing it at the heads of the wiseacres who repeat the parrot cry that art should never be didactic. It goes to prove my contention that great art can never be anything else" (9).

11. A good example of this comes in the preface to *Mrs Warren's Profession*, where Shaw states: "I hope Mrs Warren's Profession will be played everywhere . . . until Mrs Warren has bitten that fact [that you cannot cheapen women in the market for industrial purposes without cheapening them for other purposes as well] into the public conscience . . ." (207). It appears to me that Mrs Warren stands here not as an individual, but as a character serving a larger social function for Shaw. It could be argued that Shaw's Saint Joan is an exception to this rule from a later stage in his career.

12. Vivie the college graduate and actuary-to-be *(Mrs Warren's Profession),* Louka the maid *(Arms and the Man),* and Proserpine the secretary *(Candida).*

13. Shaw's "Life Force," which he referred to often throughout his career and which is integral to many of the character relations in his plays, can be summarized as an inescapable force in nature that draws men and women together for the purpose of procreation. In Shaw's work, this force is most often acted upon by women, such as Ann Whitefield in *Man and Superman,* who actively seek a mate despite male objections to marriage—Shaw's requisite, accompanying social institution. Thus a number of Shaw's female characters have been critically designated "Life Force women" for their pursuit of men, as they oppose lingering Victorian conventions that preclude the admission of female sexual desire or any active role in the process of mating.

Chapter 2

1. The fungus Candida (Stedman 237) and the specific organism Candida albicans (Schmidt 76) had been identified by 1839. I am grateful to Dr. Charles Gainor for his research assistance in this area.

2. Other dramas with symbolic rape content will be discussed in part 3.

3. In her recent study *Women in Modern Drama,* Gail Finney identifies Candida as the New Woman in the play. Although we use many of the same sources to provide background for our discussions, I cannot agree with Finney's conclusions. She calls Candida "a hybrid type" of the New Woman and maintains, "Candida seems more realistic than such figures as Vivie and Lina. Being a New Woman did not always exclude motherhood, and while Candida clearly does not manifest all the qualities of the New Woman, she does possess some of them" (197). From Shaw's own use of the term, I believe others of his characters bear a much closer resemblance to the historical composite than does Candida, whom Finney must continually qualify to fit the designation. Finney also seems oblivious to the "Candidamaniac" phenomenon, which is antithetical to public response to the New Woman. Lastly, she ignores the one structural detail that would have lent more credibility to her argument for New Woman characters in *Candida:* Shaw's careful, geometric construction of the drama to contrast the figures of Proserpine and Candida. By realizing that Shaw had made each woman a foil for the other, Finney could have identified Prossy as another variant on her "hybrid" categorization and perhaps noticed that this character fits the type of the New Woman she details much more closely than the character she tries to contain in an inappropriate category.

4. See *Man and Superman* 62.

5. Charles A. Berst and other scholars have identified Arabella Susan Lawrence, a young woman educated at Cambridge and sharing many of Vivie's traits, as a likely source for the character (Berst 7). Their theory strikes me as eminently reasonable, but since the notion of the academic competition is so central to the details of the opening scene, and Fawcett's well publicized

victory in 1890 was still considered a distinct triumph when Shaw wrote the play four years later, I believe the links between Vivie and Fawcett are equally compelling and worth establishing in Shaw scholarship.

6. For example Letitia Cairns, from his early novel *Love Among the Artists*, as discussed above.

7. For a fuller discussion of Grace Tranfield and *The Philanderer*, see chapter 3.

8. By this, I mean a play whose main topic is directly connected with issues historically linked primarily to women, such as prostitution and women's suffrage. I believe these subjects can be categorized separately from those general human concerns affecting both men and women, such as poor housing, religious persecution, and legal imbalances, found in other Shaw dramas that feature strong female characters.

9. Shaw doesn't even mention the suffrage content of the play in his letter to Siegfried Trebitsch of 28 July 1915; he discusses only the "British Commander in Chief" (*Collected Letters* 3:304).

10. Note the similarity of this speech to that of Gloria Clandon to Valentine (*You Never Can Tell* 266), discussed in the next chapter. Each presents a similar, prototypical attitude of the New Woman toward marriage in her day.

11. Shaw makes this point explicit in the closing of another "Pleasant" play, *Arms and the Man*. The ingenue, Raina, informs her parents she is "not here to be sold to the highest bidder" (88).

12. According to information provided by Ann Sutcliff, librarian of the Institute of Actuaries in London (founded 1848), Shaw's choice of an actuarial career for Vivie may have been uninformed. The first application by a woman for admission as an actuarial student came in 1894, but was apparently not accepted (Simmonds 150). Actuaries had to study and pass qualifying examinations in order to practice. Furthermore, Reginald Simmonds's history of the Institute of Actuaries indicates that they initially worked for companies, rather than on a freelance basis, as Shaw proposes for Vivie. However, salary records indicate that actuaries were paid quite well at that time. The clerk in an insurance office might have received £50 per annum, whereas the company's top-ranking actuary commanded a salary of £2000 per year. Ms. Sutcliff had no information on what the starting salary of an actuary might have been at that time, but one of her sources, who was connected with the London firm R. Watson & Sons, Consulting Actuaries, hypothesized that a young professional from the prewar era could expect an income of approximately £350 per year, a salary that would certainly make Vivie more financially comfortable than her mother suggests. I am extremely grateful for Ms. Sutcliff's efforts on my behalf.

13. George Gissing makes a similar connection in his novel *The Odd Women* through his New Woman character, Rhoda Nunn. Monica Widdowson mentally associates a former acquaintance, now a prostitute, with this other "odd," New Woman: "Rhoda Nunn would have classed her and mused about her [the prostitute]: a not unimportant type of the odd woman" (343).

Chapter 3

1. Archibald Henderson calls Mrs Clandon a "new woman" (*George Bernard Shaw* xiv), but this seems a misapplication backward of the term, which was most often applied to young women in the 1890s. (See the first chapter of this section.)

2. As opposed to the other major type of New Woman, who is extremely open about her sexuality and observes no social constraints on her sexual behavior.

3. The notion of parental "rights" is a motif for Shaw, occurring also in *Mrs Warren's Profession* and *Pygmalion*. The parents *in absentia* (Mrs Warren, Alfred Doolittle) always claim rights to filial respect and affection, despite the fact that they have done nothing to earn them through direct contact and personal influence on their children.

4. She becomes the aggressor toward Valentine shortly after the resolution of her emotional/intellectual conflict, precipitating their decision to marry (311–13).

5. The issue of Shaw's mother's marriage to a man who turned out to be an alcoholic may have significant bearing on his preoccupation with this theme throughout his writing. See Rosset.

6. Charteris is approximately 35 (99), and although Julia's age is not given, we know her younger sister Sylvia is 18 (124). It seems reasonable to assume Julia is probably no less than ten years Charteris's junior, particularly since Grace, age 32 (99), has already been married and widowed, which Julia has not.

7. In his creation of the Ibsen Club, Shaw is no doubt parodying the male social club phenomenon at the fin de siècle. For an examination of "Clubland," see Showalter, *Sexual Anarchy* 11–14.

8. Similarly, in *Pygmalion*, Shaw has Eliza distinguish between Pickering's treating every woman as a lady and Higgins's treating every woman as a flower girl (102).

9. It is extremely interesting that Shaw's admiration for Bashkirtseff seems to have had no bearing on his creation of female characters, in that his opposition of the artist-man, mother-woman virtually precludes the existence of a figure modeled on this woman.

10. A similar matrimonial possibility arises with Ann Whitefield in *Man and Superman*. If she cannot marry Jack, she will settle for Tavy or another man so that she can avoid spinsterhood.

Chapter 4

1. For various discussions of the literary and dramatic significance of female transvestism, see Ackroyd; Gubar; Herr; and Senelick.

2. For commentary on female modernists, see Gubar; Newton; and Senelick.

3. Or, at least, in the injunction to do so immediately after the plot resolution.

4. Ellis and Symonds allude to a book called *Woman Adventurers* edited by Mrs. Norman. I believe Dowie's *Women Adventurers* is most probably the same text. In a review of Dowie's novel *Gallia* in the *Saturday Review*, the unnamed writer notes, "Miss Ménie Muriel Dowie . . . prefers this title to that of Mrs. Norman" ("Gallia" 383), and I suspect Ellis and Symonds (or their typesetters) simply confused the *e* and *a* in *Women* in Dowie's title.

5. Holroyd dances around the reality of Kate's sexual orientation. Although he straightforwardly acknowledges Carpenter "was homosexual," he demurs that Kate just "fell in love with other women" (*Search For Love* 222)—perhaps trying to make a (specious) distinction between the psychological/emotional and physical realizations of sexuality, or perhaps simply paraphrasing Shaw (*Collected Letters* 4:529).

6. For a fuller discussion of the terms Urning and Uranian and their relation to the discourses of androgyny and homosexuality, see Carpenter 190–91.

7. See part 3 for a discussion of scenes with lesbian subtext.

8. Shaw may have gotten this idea from John Stuart Mill's *The Subjection of Women*, a tract influential to his concept of sexual equality and referred to specifically in his play *You Never Can Tell*. The *Edinburgh Review* article on Mill's book states "we altogether reject [Mill's] hypothesis that woman is man in petticoats" ("Subjection" 306).

9. This same article appeared in slightly different form in two American publications. "Woman Since 1860" was published in *McCall's* in October 1920, while "Woman as I Have Seen Her" appeared in two installments in the *New York American* the next month. Unless otherwise noted, citations will be from *McCall's*.

10. The section in brackets is not contained in the *McCall's* text. This passage can be found in "Woman as I Have Seen Her" 5.

11. It is also possible that buried in this statement is Shaw's sense that the death of his mother precluded further personal understanding of women, in the way that children learn about humanity and sexual difference initially from their parents.

12. This concept has Wordsworthian echoes that resonate with the sense of Coleridgean androgyny Shaw may have adopted. Like the infant "trailing clouds of glory," who, as he grows, loses a child's special grasp of the world, so the young Shaw loses the balanced sensitivity to both sexes as he grows.

Chapter 5

1. In the early "Unpleasant" play *Mrs Warren's Profession*, Frank and Vivie talk about their "babes in the wood" game (267), a possible reference to the popular pantomime of that title.

2. Shaw's critique of the play, contained in his review of the 1896 produc-

tion, clearly provides some of the foundation for his 1945 revision. See "Blaming the Bard" in *Dramatic Opinions and Essays* 2:51–60.

3. The composition of *Cymbeline Refinished* corresponds neatly with the end of the Second World War, a moment when many women who had taken over vital male occupations during the war effort were forcibly returned to exclusively domestic duties. Shaw may have intended this new conclusion to reflect not only a generally modern ambience, but also a very specific timeliness for its intended audience, or his revision may coincidentally echo the tenor of the times.

4. The same issue is voiced more openly in contemporary plays of gender identity, for example Caryl Churchill's *Cloud 9* and David Henry Hwang's *M. Butterfly*.

5. The adoration of Varinka for Catherine has no sexual component in speech or action and cannot be construed as lesbian.

6. These descriptions of strength and devilry link this character to the quintessential Shavian heroine Ann Whitefield, a role McCarthy had also originated in 1905.

7. Shaw expanded upon the characterization of such twins in *You Never Can Tell*.

Chapter 6

1. Although outside the scope of this study, the remarkable suggestion of sexually related violence in this exchange surfaces elsewhere in Shaw. Other examples include the striking of Jenny Hill in *Major Barbara*, the continual threat of violence to Eliza in *Pygmalion*, and the invitation to the pleasures of beating offered by Napoleon to the Strange Lady in *The Man of Destiny*.

2. Watson's reading parallels Shaw's characterization in its ambiguity. It is unclear whether she is rejecting the consideration of Lesbia's sexual orientation in favor of other aspects of Lesbia's life or suggesting that Shaw does not want us to make any assumptions about an individual's sexual lifestyle based on an observation of that person's other behaviors. Her later assertion that "Shaw's androgynous beings are neither undersexed nor are they members of an intermediate sex" (*Shavian Guide* 141) seems designed to ward off any consideration of the potential for inversion or homosexuality in his plays, however.

3. For an in-depth analysis of Shaw's Joan in comparison to those of Twain and France, see Searle, *The Saint & The Skeptics*.

4. Shaw says nothing about woman authors who took up Saint Joan as a subject, particularly Cicely Hamilton, whose extremely popular depiction of her in *A Pageant of Great Women* (1909) was directed by Edy Craig for the Actresses' Franchise League in the same year the league produced Shaw's *Press Cuttings*. Nina Auerbach claims "Shaw watched with interest ordinary women as well as professional actresses battling to play the sort of disruptive, cross-dressing woman Henry Irving and his fellow actor-managers had

barred from the respectable stage" (422), but she does not imply any connection between Shaw's watching and his dramatization of cross-dressing. Hamilton's drama was motivated by Gladstone's orders to forcibly feed imprisoned suffragette hunger strikers (Holledge 68–69), and Shaw also associates his Joan with the suffrage movement.

5. This connection in particular is stressed in a radio talk Shaw gave on the play for the BBC, reprinted in the collection *Platform and Pulpit* (208–16).

6. This passage, added to the third revised and enlarged edition of *Sexual Inversion*, first appeared in 1915.

7. Morgan also points out the connection between Joan as a Christ figure and the tradition of interpreting Christ as an androgyne (255).

8. This sense of femininity associated with not swearing appears more straightforwardly later in the play, after Joan has crowned the Dauphin and tells the court she has decided to return home:

> Bluebeard. You will find the petticoats tripping you up after leaving them off for so long. . . .
> La Hire. Well, I shall be able to swear when I want to. But I shall miss you at times. (104)

The juxtaposition of the resumption of her feminine dress, the petticoats, with the resumption of the men's ability to swear, seems to indicate they refrain from swearing because she is a woman, not because of her divine association.

9. Shaw represents Sand differently, but equally strategically, in his preface to *Man and Superman*, where he stresses her authorial role in the service of her maternal function (20).

10. The use of the phrase "wild women" echoes the titles of E. Lynn Linton's series of articles (1891–92) on women's rejection of proper Victorian behavior, widely read and quoted in discussions of the "Woman Question."

11. Yet Shaw has her enter in scene 1 "respectably dressed in red" (52), an ambiguous, gender-neutral description that could indicate her initial costuming in a woman's dress—which would indeed be "respectable" in a way male attire might not. If this is indeed what Shaw intends, then she has spent two days with the soldiers dressed as a woman, although, as Poulengey attests, they have not thought of her in this way. A 1951–52 production by the Theatre Guild starring Uta Hagen indeed initially dressed Joan in a woman's peasant costume (Hill 40). Margery Morgan confirms this initial appearance "in woman's clothing" (254). This issue, like that of the swearing discussed earlier, makes Shaw's handling of gender identity somewhat problematic, with a few loose ends that complicate the predominantly clear thrust of the play. At stake is the initial image we are to have of Joan. Is she a woman who seeks more male identification through dress and action, and whose religious fervor keeps male sexual advance at bay, or is she closer to a sexually neutral, masculine character whose biological sex is female, and who may have little appeal because she is not feminine? Joan maintains dress prevents sexual consideration of her as a woman (131–32); Shaw does not

account for how she would view the soldiers' deference to her in the female attire she initially wears.

12. Shaw may be mixing historical accuracy with anachronism here, as the bobbed hair Joan sports indeed fits the masculine look and body type popular in the 1920s, while a few pages earlier he describes the androgynous hairstyle popular at court in the medieval period: "the current fashion of shaving closely, and hiding every scrap of hair under the headcovering or headdress, both by women and men" (65). The Duchess's aside, "My dear! Her hair!" (72) could just as easily be uttered by any society matron frozen in the Edwardian era as in the fifteenth century.

13. The denial by Joan here of the potential for her marriage contradicts the possibility Shaw notes in his preface (11), continuing the tension between his characterization—based on historical documents—and the image he wants to convey to the audience.

14. This juxtaposition of maternity and soldiering echoes the similar parallel Shaw drew in his essay "The Womanly Woman" in *The Quintessence:*

> The domestic career is no more natural to all women than the military career is natural to all men; and . . . in a population emergency it might become necessary for every able-bodied woman to risk her life in childbed just as it might become necessary in a military emergency for every man to risk his life in the battlefield. (60)

It is also like the opposition of the "artist-man, mother-woman" in *Man and Superman,* in that male professional capacities are always contrasted to female biological function, which is synonymous with her domestic profession under the pressure of the Life Force. This force controls most Shavian women, with the possible exception of some of the androgynes.

15. For a series of thoughtful and enlightening interpretations of Joan with respect to feminism, see in particular comments by Zoe Caldwell (94), Eileen Atkins (199–200), and Roberta Maxwell (201–2) in Holly Hill's *Playing Joan.* Each actress has isolated important issues in Shaw's characterization, including Joan's absent sexuality, Shaw's use of historical documents, and the appearance versus the reality of a feminist consciousness for Joan.

16. Harry M. Geduld attributes Shaw's use of this alternate Creation story to the work of Charles Bradlaugh, whose *Genesis* (1882) describes a biblical parallel in the story of Lilith's splitting to make Adam and Eve (58n).

17. Read in conjunction with Don Juan's account of human history in act 3 of *Man and Superman,* the Shavian version of the Lilith myth portrays her as a culpable figure, responsible for the struggles between the sexes as well as man's difficulties in trying to make the world a civilized place (*Man and Superman* 147–48).

18. The Domestic Minister in part 3 is the future incarnation of the woman who was the Barnabases' housekeeper in part 2. Although she appears on the surface to be a woman who has attained political prominence in a future era, she is still concerned with the domestic sphere as a glorified chambermaid. Her colleague, the Minister of Health, is little more than the object of

the President's sexual interest. As visions of political, professional women in years to come, these characters show no advance over the circumscribed roles for women in Victorian/Edwardian England.

19. Given the pointed presence of a "negress" as the Minister of Health and object of the President's sexual interest, the racial implications of this line are disturbing. Here, as in *The Adventures of the Black Girl in Her Search for God*, Shaw figures black women in childish capacities, and in *The Simpleton of the Unexpected Isles* he uses the derogatory term "nigger" to denote people of color. A thorough investigation of Shaw's position with regard to issues of race and ethnicity is outside the scope of this study, but merits pursuit.

20. Shaw echoes the connection between androgynous development and the evolution of human form in the fifth of his *Farfetched Fables*. In this episode, two men, one woman, and a hermaphrodite discuss the state of human knowledge and existence. The Hermaphrodite remarks, "I dont want to be a body: I want to be a mind and nothing but a mind" (510). Interestingly, Shaw is vague on the physical description of this character. Although the costuming details suggest a blend of male and female—a harlequin pattern of the colors used for the other two sex's garments—he includes no information on other aspects of this character's appearance, although he notes that, "The men are close-cropped and clean-shaven: the woman's hair is dressed like that of the Milo Venus" (507).

Chapter 7

1. In a review of Harley Granville-Barker's play *The Voysey Inheritance*, Max Beerbohm casts the playwright in the role of student to Shaw's teacher. After calling one scene "masterly," he quips, "the master is still, to some extent, a pupil—a member of Mr. Shaw's academy for young gentlemen" (621).

2. His early letters to his first platonic love, Alice Lockett, alternate amatory and didactic tones. (See *Collected Letters* vol. 1.)

3. *Dorothea's* editor, Stephen Winsten, has observed the contemporary relevance of Shaw's advice for the training and domestic circumstances of children in our era ("Editorial Note" 54).

4. It should be noted that Shaw does not share Adams's view and proffers Henry Sweet, an Oxford phonetician, as his model for Higgins in the preface to the play (*Pygmalion* 5–6).

5. He uses a similar device at the opening of *The Man of Destiny*, when he has a "girl of bad character . . . peep in at the . . . window" (166) of the set. It is through her eyes that the reader receives the first glimpse of the set and the characters on it, but the girl then disappears, having served this voyeuristic, introductory purpose.

6. Mark Bennett corroborates this notion in his early review of *Dorothea*, which he analyzes as "the germ of that complementary sermon to this one on morality, *The Adventures of the Black Girl in Her Search for God*" (18).

7. Shaw first published the story with a series of woodcut illustrations by John Farleigh that depict the Black Girl as a physically mature, nude woman. The pictures merit close examination on their own and in the context of an analysis of the overall impact of the work. For Farleigh's discussion of the genesis of the images, see his *Graven Image*. Dan Laurence has also included many letters between Shaw and Farleigh about these illustrations in the fourth volume of the *Collected Letters*.

8. Two of the Farleigh woodcut illustrations feature images remarkably like Shaw, and a character introduced at the end of the story also resembles Shaw in many ways.

9. It is important to remember the temporal specificity inherent in the earlier discussion of Shaw's New Woman, however. Although the Black Girl may share some traits with her, this later characterization appears well after the close of the New Woman era, and she cannot be considered one as such. Rather, she exemplifies Shaw's ongoing use of certain typed behaviors, which must be considered in their own cultural and historical contexts.

10. According to Stanley Weintraub, Shaw was "charged with inaccuracy in his use of Einstein's Relativity theory" here, and he subsequently changed the pun to the square root of minus one/Myna's one. The Shaw Estate, however, chose to give "art . . . precedence over mathematics and the original pun [was] preserved" in later editions (Shaw, *Portable* 636n).

Chapter 8

1. It is fitting that Shaw should have placed Count O'Dowda in Italy, the home of the commedia. His dramatic sensibilities reflect the popularity of this traditional theatrical form.

2. See, for example, *Pygmalion* for a depiction of the difficulties of cross-class relationships and Shaw's "Torture by Forcible Feeding Is Illegal" in R. Weintraub, *Fabian Feminist* 228–35.

3. For a sample of reviews see Evans 41ff.

4. Those familiar with the work of Jean Genet will recognize a situation reminiscent of that in *The Maids* (1947) here, although Shaw's characters are played by females. Nevertheless, the homoerotic content of Genet's piece may have influenced Arthur Ganz's reading of this scene, which he feels dramatizes a "sado-masochistic relationship with overtones of barely repressed lesbianism" (86). Regardless of the Genet parallel, this scene introduces the possibility for a lesbian motif in Shaw, one that emerges in the already discussed character of Lesbia in *Getting Married* and occurs again in *Heartbreak House* and *Pygmalion*.

5. As noted in the discussion of *Mrs Warren's Profession* in part 1, there are many similarities between that play and *Widowers' Houses*, particularly in the financial plots involving parents and children. An interesting distinction is the final relation of these characters. While in *Mrs Warren's Profession* Vivie

makes a final gesture of maternal rejection, Blanche's paternal rejection is later mitigated by the resolution of the love plot, which allows for a comprehension, but not final rejection, of the economic status quo.

6. Shaw alludes to the Patmore work twice in *Man and Superman* (157, 208) to establish a domestic context that serves as a foil for the events and characters of the play.

7. This of course resonates not only with Shaw's own interest in the sport, but also with his depiction of it—associated exclusively with male characters—from his early novel *Cashel Byron's Profession* forward.

8. Diane Elizabeth Dreher, in her study *Domination and Defiance*, has traced father/daughter relations in Shakespeare and finds patterns of didacticism, as well as the incest motif and a link between father and husband figures, throughout the Shakespearean canon similar to those I trace here. Although these motifs appear widely in literature, given the strong connection Shaw felt with Shakespeare, it is significant that he used the same relations so extensively in his own plays. Shaw mentions the similarity between his and Shakespeare's female characters in the preface to *Man and Superman:* "I find in my own plays that Woman, projecting herself dramatically by my hands . . . behaves just as Woman did in the plays of Shakespear" (18).

9. The echo of the unwomanly Vivie Warren's physical strength, demonstrated by her throwing of chairs and killer handshake, is unmistakable here.

10. Shaw's one exception to this, Caesar, identifies himself as "part brute, part woman, and part god" (*Caesar and Cleopatra* 26). It may well be the integration of these qualities that has led to the interpretation of Caesar as Shaw's closest approximation of the superman figure.

11. Rodelle Weintraub accounts for Hypatia's desire for Bentley slightly differently in her psychoanalytic reading of the play ("Johnny's Dream" 183).

12. The sole exception may be *Pygmalion,* as Mrs Higgins, Mrs Pearce, and Eliza could be seen as multiple maternal figures for Henry. However, the familial dynamics are so contorted in that play, and the paternal role of Henry for Eliza so strong, that this seems to fall into some other interpretive category than the corollary to the more straightforward multiplicity of father figures.

13. See the discussion of *You Never Can Tell* in part 1.

14. For a discussion of historical constructions of female friendship and eroticism, see Faderman.

15. As Hector only seems to interact with Ellie in a romantic capacity, it does not appear that he should be considered a fourth father/lover/teacher figure, although his age and paternal status do make him another of the father figures with whom young Shavian women have romantic relations.

Chapter 9

1. The second act neatly illustrates how relatively less interesting the father/son relation is for Shaw. After this one short sequence, where Caesar lectures the young Ptolemy, the young king disappears from the play, having conveniently drowned sometime during the ensuing action.

2. In 1900, the same year that *Caesar and Cleopatra* was published, Shaw also served as editor for the Fabian publication *Fabianism and the Empire*.

3. This is one of the few references in the play to Cleopatra's biological parents, who never appear. In a note to Gilbert Murray, who had apparently criticized Shaw's characterization of the Egyptian queen, Shaw remarks,

> I am not quite convinced that I have overdone Cleopatra's ferocity. If she had been an educated lady of the time I should have made her quite respectable & civilized; but what I was able to gather about her father, the convivial Flute Blower, and other members of the household, joined with considerations of the petulance of royalty, led me to draw her as I did. (*Collected Letters* 2:180)

Shaw thus envisions Cleopatra as another child with multiple fathers, and here as in *Pygmalion*, it is the surrogate father who has the greater educational role, although the natural father may be more responsible for inherent characteristics. This, of course, parallels Shaw's autobiographical depiction of his relations to his own father and to Vandeleur Lee.

4. Catherine Schuler provides an insightful reading of the gender and power struggles in *Major Barbara* in her study of Shaw and Brecht (195–200).

5. For a reading of the larger significance of Dionysos to the play, see M. Goldman.

6. Cusins essentially becomes Undershaft's son at the end of the play, but the adoptive nature of their relation mitigates any incestuous connection in the marriage with his daughter.

7. The analysis here draws on Shaw's final, definitive edition of the play, published after his work on the film version, and incorporating several scenes (including the bath and mirror sequences) not in the original edition.

8. Arnold Silver also reads this sequence as a rape scene, but he makes no mention of the lesbian content (270–72).

9. Note the parallel context of sin from which Clara emerges in the epilogue.

10. All dialogue comes from the soundtrack to the film version, readily available on videocassette.

11. The film was directed by Anthony Asquith and Leslie Howard, who also played Higgins.

12. For a detailed discussion of Shaw's involvement in the making of the film, see Costello 50–82. The film was a tremendous box office success, and Shaw claimed major responsibility for this.

Bibliography

Works Cited

Ackroyd, Peter. *Dressing Up: Transvestism and Drag: The History of an Obsession*. New York: Simon and Schuster, 1979.

Adams, Elsie B. *Bernard Shaw and the Aesthetes*. Columbus: Ohio State University Press, 1971.

Albert, Sidney P. "More Shaw Advice to the Players of *Major Barbara*." *Theatre Survey* 11 (1970): 66–85.

Allen, Grant. *The Woman Who Did*. Boston: Roberts, 1895.

Archer, William. *The Theatrical "World" of 1894*. London: Walter Scott, 1895.

Auerbach, Nina. *Ellen Terry: Player in Her Time*. New York: Norton, 1987.

Aveling, Eleanor Marx, and Edward Aveling. "The Woman Question: From a Socialist Point of View." *Westminster Review* 125 (1886): 207–22.

Barnard, Eunice Fuller. "G. B. S.: The Father of the Flapper." *New Republic*, 28 July 1926, 272–73.

Barnicoat, Constance. "Mr. Bernard Shaw's Counterfeit Presentment of Women." *Fortnightly Review*, 1 March 1906, 516–27.

B[atson], E[ric] J. "Shaw's First Book." *Shavian* 1, no.8 (Feb. 1957): 20–21.

Beerbohm, Max. "*The Voysey Inheritance*." *Saturday Review*, 11 Nov. 1905, 620–21.

Bennett, Mark. "G. B. S.'s Advice to Children of All Ages." *Shaw Bulletin* 2, no.2 (May 1957): 17–18.

Bentley, Eric. *Bernard Shaw*. 1947. Reprint. New York: Limelight Editions, 1985.

Berst, Charles A. *Bernard Shaw and the Art of Drama*. Urbana: University of Illinois Press, 1973.

Block, Toni. "Shaw's Women." *Modern Drama* 2 (1959): 133–38.

Booth, Michael. Introduction to *Pantomimes, Extravaganzas and Burlesques*, ed. Michael Booth, 1–63. Vol. 5 of *English Plays of the Nineteenth Century*. Oxford: Clarendon, 1976.

Busst, A. J. L. "The Image of the Androgyne in the Nineteenth Century." In *Romantic Mythologies*, ed. Ian Fletcher, 1–96. New York: Barnes and Noble, 1967.

Caird, Mona. "A Defense of the So-Called 'Wild Women.'" *Nineteenth Century* 31 (May 1892): 811–29.

Carlson, Harry G. Introduction to *The Social Significance of Modern Drama* by Emma Goldman, v–xii.

Carpenter, Edward. "The Intermediate Sex" (1906). In *Edward Carpenter, Selected Writings*, vol. 1: *Sex*, ed. Noël Greig, 185–244. London: Gay Men's Press, 1984.

Case, Sue-Ellen. *Feminism and Theatre*. New York: Methuen, 1988.

Chauncey, George, Jr. "From Sexual Inversion to Homosexuality: Medicine and the Changing Conceptualization of Female Deviance." *Salmagundi* 58–59 (1982–83): 114–46.

Cheshire, David. "Male Impersonators." *Saturday Book* 29 (1969): 244–53.

Churchill, Caryl. *Cloud 9*. New York: Methuen, 1985.

Cixous, Hélène. "Sorties." In *The Newly Born Woman* (1975), by Hélène Cixous and Catherine Clément, trans. Betsy Wing, 61–132. Minneapolis: University of Minnesota Press, 1986.

Costello, Donald P. *The Serpent's Eye: Shaw and the Cinema*. Notre Dame: Notre Dame University Press, 1965.

Crane, Gladys. "Shaw's *Misalliance*: The Comic Journey From Rebellious Daughter to Conventional Womanhood." *Educational Theatre Journal* 25 (1973): 480–89.

Cruse, Amy. "The Feminists." In her *After the Victorians*, 126–37. London: George Allen and Unwin, 1938.

Cunningham, Gail. *The New Woman and the Victorian Novel*. London: Macmillan, 1978.

Dervin, Daniel. *Bernard Shaw: A Psychological Study*. Lewisburg, Penna.: Bucknell University Press, 1975.

"Dies Dominae." *Saturday Review*, 18 May–22 June 1895, 646–47, 687–89, 721–22, 760, 785–86, 824–25, 832.

Dietrich, R. F. *Portrait of the Artist as a Young Superman: A Study of Shaw's Novels*. Gainesville: University of Florida Press, 1969.

Dijkstra, Bram. *Idols of Perversity: Fantasies of Feminine Evil in Fin-De-Siècle Culture*. New York: Oxford University Press, 1986.

Dolan, Jill. *The Feminist Spectator as Critic*. Ann Arbor: UMI Research Press, 1988. Reprint. Ann Arbor: University of Michigan Press, 1991.

Dowie, Ménie Muriel, ed. *Women Adventurers*. London: T. Fisher Unwin, 1893.

Dowling, Linda. "The Decadent and the New Woman in the 1890's." *Nineteenth Century Fiction* 33 (March 1979): 434–53.

Dreher, Diane Elizabeth. *Domination and Defiance: Fathers and Daughters in Shakespeare.* Lexington: University Press of Kentucky, 1986.

Dyhouse, Carol. *Girls Growing Up in Late Victorian and Edwardian England.* London: Routledge and Kegan Paul, 1981.

Ellis, Havelock. *Sexual Inversion.* Vol. 2 of *Studies in the Psychology of Sex*, 3d ed. Philadelphia: F. A. Davis, 1924.

Ellis, Havelock, and John Addington Symonds. *Sexual Inversion.* 1897. Reprint. New York: Arno, 1975.

Ellis, Sarah Stickney. *The Daughters of England.* London: Fisher, Son, and Company, n.d.

Euripides. *The Bacchae.* Trans. William Arrowsmith. Vol. 4 of *The Complete Greek Tragedies*, eds. David Grene and Richmond Lattimore. Chicago: University of Chicago Press, 1960.

Evans, T. F., ed. *Shaw: The Critical Heritage.* London: Routledge and Kegan Paul, 1976.

Faderman, Lillian. *Surpassing the Love of Men: Romantic Friendship and Love Between Women from the Renaissance to the Present.* New York: William Morrow, 1981.

Farleigh, John. *Graven Image: An Autobiographical Textbook.* New York: Macmillan, 1940.

Felman, Shoshana. "Rereading Femininity." *Yale French Studies* 62 (1981): 19–44.

Fernando, Lloyd. *"New Women" in the Late Victorian Novel.* University Park: Pennsylvania State University Press, 1977.

Finney, Gail. *Women in Modern Drama: Freud, Feminism, and European Theater at the Turn of the Century.* Ithaca, N.Y.: Cornell University Press, 1989.

Fletcher, Kathy. "Planché, Vestris, and the Transvestite Role: Sexuality and Gender in Victorian Popular Theatre." *Nineteenth Century Theatre* 15 (1987): 9–33.

Friedman, Susan Stanford. "Creativity and the Childbirth Metaphor: Gender Difference in Literary Discourse." In *Speaking of Gender*, ed. Elaine Showalter, 73–100. New York: Routledge, 1989.

"Gallia." *Saturday Review*, 23 Mar. 1895, 383–84.

Ganz, Arthur. *George Bernard Shaw.* New York: Grove, 1983.

Geduld, Harry M. "The Lineage of Lilith." *Shaw Review* 7 (1964): 58–61.

Gilbert, Sandra M. "Costumes of the Mind: Transvestism as Metaphor in Modern Literature." In *Writing and Sexual Difference*, ed. Elizabeth Abel, 193–219. Chicago: University of Chicago Press, 1982.

Gilbert, Sandra M., and Susan Gubar. *The Madwoman in the Attic: The Woman Writer and the Nineteenth-Century Literary Imagination.* New Haven: Yale University Press, 1979.

Gissing, George. *The Odd Women*, 1893. Reprint. Intro. Elaine Showalter. New York: New American Library, 1983.

Goldman, Emma. *The Social Significance of Modern Drama*, 1914. Reprint. Intro. Harry G. Carlson, preface Erika Munk. New York: Applause, 1987.

Goldman, Michael. "Shaw and the Marriage in Dionysus." In *The Play and Its Critic: Essays for Eric Bentley*, ed. Michael Bertin, 97–111. Lanham, Md.: University Press of America, 1986.

Gorham, Deborah. *The Victorian Girl and the Feminine Ideal.* London: Croom Helm, 1982.

Gorsky, Susan R. "Old Maids and New Women." *Journal of Popular Culture* 7 (1973): 68–85.

Grand, Sarah. *The Heavenly Twins.* New York: Cassell, 1893.

Greenblatt, Stephen. "Fiction and Friction." In *Reconstructing Individualism*, ed. Thomas C. Heller, Monton Sosna, and David E. Wellbery, 30–52. Stanford, Calif.: Stanford University Press, 1986.

Gregory, Isabella Augusta (Persse), Lady. *Lady Gregory's Journals 1916–1930*, ed. Lennox Robinson. New York: Macmillan, 1947.

Grosskurth, Phyllis. *Havelock Ellis: A Biography.* New York: New York University Press, 1985.

Grundy, Sidney. *The New Woman.* London: Chiswick, 1894.

Gubar, Susan. "Blessings in Disguise: Cross-Dressing as Re-Dressing for Female Modernists." *Massachusetts Review* 22 (1981): 477–508.

Hamilton, Cicely. *A Pageant of Great Women.* London: The Suffrage Shop, 1920.

Hardy, Thomas. *Jude the Obscure.* 1895. Reprint. Harmondsworth: Penguin, 1986.

Hartley, C. Gasquoine [Mrs. Walter M. Gallichan]. *The Truth About Woman.* New York: Dodd, Mead, 1914.

Heilbrun, Carolyn G. *Toward a Recognition of Androgyny.* New York: Alfred A. Knopf, 1973.

Henderson, Archibald. *George Bernard Shaw: Man of the Century.* New York: Appleton Century Crofts, 1956.

Herr, Cheryl. *Joyce's Anatomy of Culture.* Urbana: University of Illinois Press, 1986.

Hickok, Kathleen. *Representations of Women: Nineteenth-Century British Women's Poetry.* Westport, Conn.: Greenwood, 1984.

Hill, Holly. *Playing Joan: Actresses on the Challenge of Shaw's Saint Joan.* New York: Theatre Communications Group, 1987.

Holledge, Julie. *Innocent Flowers: Women in the Edwardian Theatre.* London: Virago, 1981.

Holroyd, Michael. "George Bernard Shaw: Women and the Body Politic." *Critical Inquiry* 6 (Autumn 1979): 17–32.

———. *The Search For Love.* Vol. 1 of *Bernard Shaw.* New York: Random House, 1988.

Huysmans, J. K. *Against the Grain* (1884). Trans. John Howard. New York: Lieber and Lewis, 1922.

Hwang, David Henry. *M. Butterfly.* New York: New American Library, 1988.

Jones, Howard Mumford. "Shaw as a Victorian." *Victorian Studies* 1 (Dec. 1957): 165–72.

Jordan, Ellen. "The Christening of the New Woman: May 1894." *Victorian Newsletter* 63 (1983): 19–21.

Kidd, Beatrice Ethel. "The Superwoman." *Englishwoman's Review*, 15 Jan. 1904, 67–70.

Kimbrough, Robert. "Androgyny Seen through Shakespeare's Disguise." *Shakespeare Quarterly* 33 (1982): 17–33.

Le Mesurier, Mrs. *The Socialist Woman's Guide to Intelligence: A Reply to Mr. Shaw*. London: Ernest Benn, 1929.

Lindblad, Ishrat. *Creative Evolution and Shaw's Dramatic Art*. Uppsala, Sweden: Uppsala University Press, 1971.

Linton, E. Lynn. "The Partisans of the Wild Women." *Nineteenth Century* 31 (Jan.–June 1892): 455–64.

———. "The Wild Women." *Nineteenth Century* 30 (July 1891): 79–88.

———. "The Wild Women as Social Insurgents." *Nineteenth Century* 30 (Oct. 1891): 596–605.

Lorichs, Sonja. *The Unwomanly Woman in Bernard Shaw's Drama and Her Social and Political Background*. Uppsala, Sweden: Uppsala University Press, 1973.

Low, Sidney. "The Species of the Female." *Standard* (London), 23 October 1911, 13.

Mander, Raymond, and Joe Mitchenson. *Pantomime: A Story in Pictures*. New York: Taplinger, 1973.

McCarthy, Lillah. *Myself and My Friends*. New York: E. P. Dutton, 1933.

McDowell, Frederick P. W. "Shaw's Abrasive View of Edwardian Civilization in *Misalliance*." *Shaw Review* 23 (1980): 63–76.

Meisel, Martin. *Shaw and the Nineteenth Century Theater* 1963. Reprint. New York: Limelight Editions, 1984.

Meredith, George. *Lord Ormont and His Aminta: A Novel*. London: Chapman and Hall, 1894.

Millet, Kate. "The Debate over Women: Ruskin vs. Mill." In *Suffer and Be Still: Women in the Victorian Age*, ed. Martha Vicinus, 121–39. Bloomington: Indiana University Press, 1972.

Morgan, Margery M. *The Shavian Playground: An Exploration of the Art of George Bernard Shaw*. London: Methuen, 1972.

Munich, Adrienne. "Notorious Signs, Feminist Criticism and Literary Tradition." In *Making a Difference: Feminist Literary Criticism*, ed. Gayle Greene and Coppélia Kahn, 238–59. London: Methuen, 1985.

Neff, Wanda Fraiken. *Victorian Working Women: An Historical and Literary Study of Women in British Industries and Professions 1832–1850*. London: George Allen and Unwin, 1929.

Nethercot, Arthur H. *Men and Supermen: The Shavian Portrait Gallery*. 2d ed. New York: Benjamin Blom, 1966.

Newton, Esther. "The Mythic Mannish Lesbian: Radclyffe Hall and the New Woman." In *The Lesbian Issue: Essays From "SIGNS,"* ed. Estelle B. Freedman et al., 7–25. Chicago: University of Chicago Press, 1985.

Noel, Thomas. "Major Barbara and Her Male Generals." *Shaw Review* 22 (1979): 135–41.

Park, Clara Claiborne. "As We Like It: How a Girl Can Be Smart and Still Popular." In *The Woman's Part: Feminist Criticism of Shakespeare*, ed. Carolyn

Ruth Swift Lenz, Gayle Greene, and Carol Thomas Neely, 100–116. Urbana: University of Illinois Press, 1980.

Pascal, Gabriel, producer. *Pygmalion.* London: Loew's Inc., 1938.

Peters, Margot. *Bernard Shaw and the Actresses.* Garden City, N.Y.: Doubleday, 1980.

Peters, Sally. "Shaw's Double Dethroned: *The Dark Lady of the Sonnets, Cymbeline Refinished,* and *Shakes Versus Shav.*" *Shaw* 7 (1987): 301–16.

Plato. "Symposium." In vol. 5 of *The Loeb Classical Library: Plato,* trans. W. R. M. Lamb, 73–245. London: William Heinemann, 1925.

Quigley, Austin E. "Stereotype and Prototype: Character in the Plays of Caryl Churchill." In *Feminine Focus: The New Women Playwrights,* ed. Enoch Brater, 25–52. New York: Oxford University Press, 1989.

Rhondda, Margaret Haig (Thomas) Mackworth, Viscountess. "Shaw's Women." *Time and Tide,* 7 Mar.–11 Apr. 1930, 300–301, 331–34, 364–66, 395–96, 436–38, 468–70.

Robertson, John Mackinnon. "Mr. Shaw and 'The Maid.'" In *"Saint Joan" Fifty Years After,* ed. Stanley Weintraub, 86–91. Baton Rouge: Louisiana State University Press, 1973.

Robins, Elizabeth. *Ancilla's Share.* 2d ed. London: Hutchinson, 1924.

Rosset, B. C. *Shaw of Dublin: The Formative Years.* University Park: Pennsylvania State University Press, 1964.

Rover, Constance. *The Punch Book of Women's Rights.* Cranbury, N.J.: A. S. Barnes, 1971.

Schuler, Catherine. "Bernard Shaw and Bertolt Brecht: A Comparative Study Utilizing Methods of Feminist Criticism." Ph.D. diss, Florida State University, 1984.

Schmidt, J. E. *Medical Discoveries: Who and When.* Springfield, Ill.: Charles C. Thomas, 1959.

Schreiner, Olive. "The Woman Question." In *An Olive Schreiner Reader: Writings on Women and South Africa,* ed. Carol Barash, 63–100. London: Pandora, 1987.

Schwenger, Peter. "The Masculine Mode." In *Speaking of Gender,* ed. Elaine Showalter, 101–12. New York: Routledge, 1989.

Searle, William. *The Saint and The Skeptics: Joan of Arc in the Work of Mark Twain, Anatole France, and Bernard Shaw.* Detroit: Wayne State University Press, 1976.

Sedgwick, Eve Kosofsky. *Between Men: English Literature and Male Homosocial Desire.* New York: Columbia University Press, 1985.

Senelick, Laurence. "The Evolution of the Male Impersonator on the Nineteenth-Century Popular Stage." *Essays in Theatre* 1 (1982): 29–44.

Shaw, George Bernard. *The Adventures of the Black Girl in Her Search for God.* New York: Dodd, Mead, 1933.

———. *Agitations: Letters to the Press 1875–1950.* Ed. Dan H. Laurence and James Rambeau. New York: Frederick Ungar, 1985.

———. *Annajanska, the Bolshevik Empress: A Revolutionary Romancelet* (1919). In Shaw, *Selected One Act Plays,* 125–44.

———. *Arms and the Man: An Anti-romantic Comedy* (1898). In Shaw, *Plays Pleasant*, 17–89.

———. *Back to Methuselah: A Metabiological Pentateuch* (1921). Harmondsworth: Penguin, 1977.

———. "Blaming the Bard." In Shaw, *Dramatic Opinions and Essays*, 2:51–60. New York: Brentano's, 1906

———. *The Bodley Head Bernard Shaw: Collected Plays with Their Prefaces*. Ed. Dan H. Laurence. 7 vols. London: Max Reinhardt, The Bodley Head, 1970–74.

———. *Caesar and Cleopatra: A History* (1900). Baltimore: Penguin, 1974.

———. *Cashel Byron's Profession* (1886). London: Penguin, 1979.

———. *Candida: A Pleasant Play* (1898). New York: Penguin, 1984.

———. *Collected Letters*. Ed. Dan H. Laurence. 4 vols. London: Max Reinhardt, 1965–88.

———. *The Collected Works of Bernard Shaw: Ayot St. Laurence Edition*. 30 vols. New York: William H. Wise, 1930–32.

———. *Cymbeline Refinished: A Variation on Shakespear's Ending*. In Shaw, "*Geneva*," "*Cymbeline Refinished*," *and "Good King Charles*," 131–50.

———. *The Doctor's Dilemma: A Tragedy* (1911). New York: Penguin, 1980.

———. *Dramatic Opinions and Essays*. Ed. James Huneker. New York: Brentano's, 1906.

———. *Fanny's First Play: An Easy Play For a Little Theatre* (1914). In Shaw, "*The Shewing Up of Blanco Posnet*" *and "Fanny's First Play*," 105–82. Harmondsworth: Penguin, 1987.

———. *Farfetched Fables*. In Shaw, *The Bodley Head Bernard Shaw*, 7:377–466.

———. "*Geneva*," "*Cymbeline Refinished*," *and "Good King Charles*." London: Constable, 1946.

———. *Getting Married: A Disquisitory Play* (1911). In Shaw, "*Getting Married*" *and "Press Cuttings*," 7–222.

———. "*Getting Married*" *and "Press Cuttings*." Harmondsworth: Penguin, 1986.

———. *Great Catherine (Whom Glory Still Adores)* (1915). In Shaw, *Selected One Act Plays*, 265–311.

———. *Heartbreak House: A Fantasia in the Russian Manner on English Themes* (1919). New York: Penguin, 1977.

———. *Immaturity*. Vol. 1 of Shaw, *Collected Works*.

———. "*In Good King Charles Golden Days*": *A True History That Never Happened*. In Shaw, "*Geneva*," "*Cymbeline Refinished*," *and "Good King Charles*," 152–234.

———. Introduction to *The Theatrical "World" of 1894* by William Archer, xi–xxx. London: Walter Scott, 1895.

———. *The Irrational Knot*. 1885–87. Vol. 2 of Shaw, *Collected Works*.

———. *Love Among the Artists* (1900). Vol. 3 of Shaw, *Collected Works*.

———. *Major Barbara* (1907). Harmondsworth: Penguin, 1982.

———. *Major Critical Essays*. Intro. Michael Holroyd. Harmondsworth: Penguin, 1986.

———. *Man and Superman: A Comedy and a Philosophy* (1903). Middlesex: Penguin, 1983.

———. *The Man of Destiny: A Fictitious Paragraph of History* (1898). In Shaw, *Plays Pleasant*, 161–208.

———. *The Millionairess* (1936). Baltimore: Penguin, 1961.

———. *Misalliance* (1914). In *"Misalliance" and "The Fascinating Foundling,"* by Bernard Shaw, 7–205. Harmondsworth: Penguin, 1984.

———. *Mrs Warren's Profession: A Facsimile of the Holograph Manuscript*. Intro. Margot Peters. New York: Garland, 1981.

———. *Mrs Warren's Profession: A Play* (1898). In Shaw, *Plays Unpleasant*, 179–286.

———. *The Music Cure*. In *Ten Short Plays*, by Bernard Shaw, 153–68. New York: Dodd, Mead, 1960.

———. *My Dear Dorothea: A Practical System of Moral Education for Females Embodied in a Letter to a Young Person of That Sex*. London: Phoenix, 1956.

———. *Pen Portraits and Reviews*. Vol. 29 of Shaw, *Collected Works*.

———. *The Perfect Wagnerite* (1898). In Shaw, *Major Critical Essays*, 177–307.

———. *The Philanderer: A Facsimile of the Holograph Manuscript*. Intro. Julius Novick. New York: Garland, 1981.

———. *The Philanderer: A Topical Comedy* (1898). In Shaw, *Plays Unpleasant*, 97–178.

———. *Platform and Pulpit*. Ed. Dan H. Laurence. New York: Hill and Wang, 1961.

———. *Plays Pleasant* (1898). London: Penguin, 1988.

———. *Plays Unpleasant* (1898). Harmondsworth: Penguin, 1983.

———. *The Portable Bernard Shaw*. Ed. Stanley Weintraub. New York: Viking, 1977.

———. Preface to *Salt and His Circle*, by Stephen Winsten, 9–15. London: Hutchinson, 1951.

———. *Press Cuttings: A Topical Sketch Compiled From the Editorial and Correspondence Columns of the Daily Papers During the Women's War of 1909* (1909). In Shaw, *"Getting Married" and "Press Cuttings,"* 223–69.

———. *Pygmalion: A Romance in Five Acts* (1913). New York: Penguin, 1982.

———. *The Quintessence of Ibsenism* (1891). In Shaw, *Major Critical Essays*, 23–176.

———. *Saint Joan: A Chronicle Play in Six Scenes and an Epilogue* (1924). New York: Penguin, 1977.

———. *Selected One Act Plays*. Harmondsworth: Penguin, 1984.

———. *The Simpleton of the Unexpected Isles* (1936). In Shaw, *The Bodley Head Bernard Shaw*, 6:741–846.

———. *Sixteen Self-Sketches*. New York: Dodd, Mead, 1949.

———. *Too True to Be Good* (1934). In Shaw, *The Bodley Head Bernard Shaw*, 395–534.

———. *An Unfinished Novel*. Ed. Stanley Weintraub. London: Constable, 1958.

———. *An Unsocial Socialist* (1884). Vol. 5 of Shaw, *Collected Works*.

———. *Village Wooing: A Comediettina for Two Voices* (1934). In Shaw, *Selected One Act Plays*, 145–74.

———. *Widowers' Houses: A Play* (1898). In Shaw, *Plays Unpleasant*, 29–96.

———. "Woman as I Have Seen Her." *New York American*, 14 Nov. 1920, sec.2, p.12; 21 Nov. 1920, sec.2, p. 5.

———. "Woman—Man in Petticoats" (1927). In Shaw, *Platform and Pulpit*, 172–78.

———. "Woman Since 1860 as a Wise Man Sees Her." *McCall's* 47 (1920): 10–11, 27.

———. *You Never Can Tell: A Comedy in Four Acts* (1898). In Shaw, *Plays Pleasant*, 209–316.

———, trans. *Jitta's Atonement*. By Siegfried Trebitsch. 1926. In Shaw, *The Bodley Head Bernard Shaw*, 5:717–808.

———, ed. *Fabianism and the Empire: A Manifesto by the Fabian Society.* London: Grant Richards, 1900.

Shaw, Mary. "My 'Immoral' Play: The Story of the First American Production of 'Mrs. Warren's Profession.'" *McClure's* 38 (1912): 684–94.

Sheldon, F. "Various Aspects of the Woman Question." *Atlantic Monthly* 108 (Oct. 1866): 425–34.

Showalter, Elaine. "Introduction: The Rise of Gender." In *Speaking of Gender*, ed. Elaine Showalter, 1–13. New York: Routledge, 1989.

———. *A Literature of Their Own: British Women Novelists from Brontë to Lessing.* Princeton: Princeton University Press, 1977.

———. *Sexual Anarchy: Gender and Culture at the Fin de Siècle.* New York: Viking, 1990.

———, ed. *Speaking of Gender.* New York: Routledge, 1989.

Silver, Arnold. *Bernard Shaw: The Darker Side.* Stanford: Stanford University Press, 1982.

Simmonds, Reginald Claud. *The Institute of Actuaries 1848–1948: An Account of the Institute of Actuaries During Its First One Hundred Years.* Cambridge: Cambridge University Press, 1948.

Smith, Warren Sylvester. "The Adventures of Shaw, the Nun, and the Black Girl." *Shaw* 1 (1981): 205–22.

Stead, W. T. "The Journal of Marie Bashkirtseff." *Review of Reviews* 1 (1890): 539–49.

Stedman, Thomas Lathrop. *Stedman's Medical Dictionary.* 25th ed. Baltimore: Williams and Wilkins, 1990.

Stimpson, Catharine R. "The Androgyne and the Homosexual." *Women's Studies* 2 (1974): 237–48.

St. John, Christopher, ed. *Ellen Terry and Bernard Shaw: A Correspondence.* New York: G. P. Putnam's Sons, 1932.

Stubbs, Patricia. *Women and Fiction: Feminism and the Novel 1880–1920.* Sussex: Harvester, 1979.

Stutfield, Hugh E. M. "The Psychology of Feminism." *Blackwood's Edinburgh Magazine* 161 (Jan. 1897): 104–17.

"The Subjection of Women." *Edinburgh Review* 266 (1869): 291–306.

"Super-Man and Sub-Woman." *Saturday Review*, 25 Apr. 1925, 433–34.

Tittle, Walter. "Mr. Bernard Shaw Talks About St. Joan." In *"Saint Joan" Fifty*

Years After, ed. Stanley Weintraub, 8–14. Baton Rouge: Louisiana State University Press, 1973.

Valency, Maurice. *The Cart and the Trumpet: The Plays of George Bernard Shaw.* New York: Oxford University Press, 1973.

Wall, Vincent. *Bernard Shaw: Pygmalion to Many Players.* Ann Arbor: University of Michigan Press, 1973.

Watson, Barbara Bellow. "The New Woman and the New Comedy." In *Fabian Feminist,* ed. Rodelle Weintraub, 114–29. University Park: Pennsylvania State University Press.

———. "Sainthood for Millionaires: *Major Barbara.*" *Modern Drama* 11 (1968): 227–44.

———. *A Shavian Guide to the Intelligent Woman.* 1964. Reprint. New York: Norton, 1972.

Watson, Jean. "Coleridge's Androgynous Ideal." *Prose Studies* 6 (1983): 36–56.

Webb, Beatrice. *The Diary of Beatrice Webb.* Ed. Norman and Jeanne MacKenzie. 4 vols. Cambridge: Harvard University Press, 1982–85.

Webb, Sidney and Beatrice. *The Letters of Sidney and Beatrice Webb.* Ed. Norman MacKenzie. 3 vols. Cambridge: Cambridge University Press, 1978.

Weintraub, Rodelle. "The Irish Lady in Shaw's Plays." *Shaw Review* 23 (1980): 77–89.

———. "Johnny's Dream: *Misalliance.*" *Shaw* 7 (1987): 171–86.

———, ed. *Fabian Feminist: Bernard Shaw and Woman.* University Park: Pennsylvania State University Press, 1977.

Weintraub, Stanley. "G. B. S. Borrows From Sarah Grand: *The Heavenly Twins* and *You Never Can Tell.*" *Modern Drama* 14 (1971): 288–97.

———, ed. *"Saint Joan" Fifty Years After.* Baton Rouge: Louisiana State University Press, 1973.

Weissman, Philip. *Creativity in the Theater: A Psychoanalytic Study.* New York: Basic Books, 1965.

West, Rebecca. "Contesting Mr. Shaw's Will: An Analysis of G. B. S.'s Final Word on Women and Socialism." *Bookman* 67 (1928): 513–20.

Winsten, Stephen. "Editorial Note." In Shaw, *My Dear Dorothea,* 53–55.

Wisenthal, J. L. *Shaw's Sense of History.* Oxford: Clarendon, 1988.

Woolf, Virginia. *A Room of One's Own.* 1929. Reprint. New York: Harcourt Brace Jovanovich, 1957.

Additional Works Consulted

Adam, Ruth. *What Shaw Really Said.* New York: Schocken, 1966.

Adams, Elsie B. "Bernard Shaw's Pre-Raphaelite Drama." *PMLA* 81 (1966): 428–38.

———. "Feminism and Female Stereotypes in Shaw." *Shaw Review* 17 (1974): 17–22.

Allen, Grant. "The Girl of the Future." *Universal Review* 7 (1890): 49–64.

Barr, Alan P. "Diabolonian Pundit: G. B. S. as Critic." *Shaw Review* 11 (1968): 11–23.

Bauer, Carol, and Lawrence Ritt, eds. *Free and Ennobled: Source Readings in the Development of Victorian Feminism.* Oxford: Pergamon, 1979.

Bax, Clifford, ed. *Florence Farr, Bernard Shaw, W. B. Yeats: Letters.* New York: Dodd, Mead, 1942.

Beers, Henry A. "The English Drama of To-Day." *North American Review* 180 (1905): 746–57.

Bentley, Joseph. "Tanner's Decision to Marry in *Man and Superman.*" *Shaw Review* 11 (1968): 26–28.

Britain, Ian. "A Transplanted Doll's House: Ibsenism, Feminism, and Socialism in Late-Victorian and Edwardian England." In *Transformations in Modern European Drama,* ed. Ian Donaldson, 14–54. Atlantic Highlands, N.J.: Humanities Press, 1983.

Brown, Ivor. "Saint Joan and Saint Henrik." *Saturday Review,* 5 Apr. 1924, 349–50.

———. *Shaw in His Time.* London: Thomas Nelson and Sons, 1965.

Brown, Nathaniel. "The 'Double Soul': Virginia Woolf, Shelley, and Androgyny." *Keats-Shelley Journal* 33 (1984): 182–204.

Bunyan, John. *The Pilgrim's Progress.* 1678. Reprint. New York: American Tract Society, n.d.

Burstyn, Joan N. *Victorian Education and the Ideal of Womanhood.* London: Croom Helm, 1980.

Cather, Willa Sibert. "Plays of Real Life." *McClure's* 40 (1913): 63–72.

Chappelow, Allan. *Shaw "The Chucker Out": A Biographical Exposition and Critique.* London: George Allen and Unwin, 1969.

———, ed. *Shaw the Villager and Human Being: A Biographical Symposium.* New York: Macmillan, 1962.

Chesterton, Gilbert K. *George Bernard Shaw.* New York: John Lane, 1910.

Ciolkowska, Muriel. "Les Journaux." *Mercure de France* 96 (1912): 169–70.

Cowper, Katie. "The Decline of Reserve Among Women." *Nineteenth Century* 27 (1890): 65–71.

Cruse, Amy. "The New Woman." In her *The Victorians and Their Reading,* 337–63. 1935. Reprint. Boston: Houghton Mifflin, 1962.

"C. V. D." "Fools of God and Doctors of the Church." *Century Magazine* 108 (1924): 718–20.

Dent, Alan, ed. *Bernard Shaw and Mrs. Patrick Campbell: Their Correspondence.* New York: Alfred A. Knopf, 1952.

Dietrich, Richard F. "Deconstruction as Devil's Advocacy: A Shavian Alternative." *Modern Drama* 29 (1986): 431–51.

"Dramaticus." "The Play: Press Cuttings." *Graphic,* 24 July 1909, 126.

DuCann, C. G. L. *The Loves of George Bernard Shaw.* New York: Funk and Wagnall's, 1963.

Duffin, Henry Charles. *The Quintessence of Bernard Shaw.* London: George Allen and Unwin, 1920.

Dukore, Bernard F. *Bernard Shaw, Director.* London: George Allen and Unwin, 1971.

———. "Shaw's Doomsday." *Educational Theatre Journal* 19 (1967): 61–71.

Gaskell, Catherine Milnes. "Women of To-Day." *Nineteenth Century* 26 (1889): 776–84.

Gill, Stephen. *Political Convictions of G. B. Shaw.* Cornwall, Ontario: Vesta, 1980.

"The Girl of the Period." *Saturday Review,* 14 March 1868, 339–40.

Gregory, Isabella Augusta (Persse), Lady. *Our Irish Theatre: A Chapter of Autobiography.* New York: Oxford University Press, 1972.

Hackett, Francis. "The Post-Victorians." *Bookman* 71 (1930): 20–26.

Hand and Brain: A Symposium of Essays on Socialism by William Morris, Grant Allen, George Bernard Shaw, Henry S. Salt, Alfred Russel Wallace, and Edward Carpenter. Aurora, N.Y.: The Roycroft Shop, 1898.

Harris, Frank. *Bernard Shaw: An Unauthorized Biography Based on First Hand Information.* New York: Simon and Schuster, 1931.

Henderson, Archibald. "Bernard Shaw on Women and Children." *Golden Book Magazine* 9 (1929): 75–77.

———. "The Duel of Sex." *Dial,* 16 July 1904, 33–34.

Holroyd, Michael, ed. *The Genius of Shaw: A Symposium.* London: Hodder and Stoughton, 1979.

———. *The Pursuit of Power.* Vol. 2 of *Bernard Shaw.* New York: Random House, 1989.

Hyde, Mary, ed. *Bernard Shaw and Alfred Douglas: A Correspondence.* New Haven and New York: Ticknor and Fields, 1982.

Hynes, Samuel. *The Edwardian Turn of Mind.* 1968. Princeton: Princeton University Press, 1975.

"The Intelligent Woman and G. B. S." *Spectator,* 2 June 1928, 837–38.

Irvine, William. *The Universe of G. B. S.* New York: McGraw-Hill, 1949.

Johnson, Josephine. *Florence Farr: Bernard Shaw's "New Woman."* Totowa, N.J.: Rowman and Littlefield, 1975.

Kent, Christopher. "Image and Reality: The Actress and Society." In *A Widening Sphere,* ed. Martha Vicinus, 94–116. Bloomington: Indiana University Press, 1977.

Khanna, Savitri. "Shaw's Image of Woman." *Shavian* 4 (1973): 253–59.

Knepper, B. G. "Shaw Rewriting Shaw: A Fragment." *Shaw Review* 12 (1969): 104–10.

Knight, G. Wilson. *The Golden Labyrinth: A Study of British Drama.* London: Phoenix House, 1962.

Krafft-Ebing, Richard von. *Psychopathia Sexualis* (1886). Trans. Harry E. Wedeck. New York: G. P. Putnam's Sons, 1965.

Laity, Cassandra. "W. B. Yeats and Florence Farr: The Influence of the 'New Woman' Actress on Yeats's Changing Images of Women." *Modern Drama* 28 (1985): 620–37.

Laurence, Dan H., ed. *Bernard Shaw: A Bibliography.* 2 vols. Oxford: Clarendon, 1983.

Leary, Daniel J. "Dialectical Action in *Major Barbara.*" *Shaw Review* 12 (1969): 46–58.

Lenz, Carolyn Ruth Swift, Gayle Greene, and Carol Thomas Neely, eds. *The*

Woman's Part: Feminist Criticism of Shakespeare. Urbana: University of Illinois Press, 1980.

Liechti, Robert. "Male Impersonation on the Stage: A Brief Survey of Its Past." *Call Boy,* Dec. 1968, 16–19.

Lindblad, Ishrat. "'Household of Joseph': An Early Perspective on Shaw's Dramaturgy." *Shaw Review* 17 (1974): 124–38.

Malet, Lucas. "The Threatened Re-Subjection of Women." *Fortnightly Review* 83 (1905): 806–19.

Matlaw, Myron. "Will Higgins Marry Eliza?" *Shavian* 12 (1958): 14–19.

Maude, Cyril. *The Haymarket Theatre: Some Records and Reminiscences.* London: Grant Richards, 1903.

May, Keith M. *Ibsen and Shaw.* New York: St. Martin's, 1985.

Mayer, David. *Harlequin in His Element.* Cambridge, Mass.: Harvard University Press, 1969.

———. "The Sexuality of Pantomime." *Theatre Quarterly* 4 (1974): 55–64.

Mill, John Stuart. *The Subjection of Women.* 1869. Reprint. Cambridge, Mass.: MIT Press, 1970.

Murphy, Karleen Middleton. "'All the Lovely Sex': Blake and the Woman Question." *Io* 29 (1982): 272–75.

Nathan, George Jean. "Mr. Shaw and the Ogre." *American Mercury* 17 (1929): 371–72.

Nethercot, Arthur H. "Bernard Shaw, Mathematical Mystic." *Shaw Review* 12 (1969): 2–26.

———. "G. B. S. and Annie Besant." *Shaw Bulletin* 1 (1955): 1–14.

Novy, Marianne. *Love's Argument: Gender Relations in Shakespeare.* Chapel Hill: University of North Carolina Press, 1984.

———. "Shakespeare's Female Characters as Actors and Audience." In *The Woman's Part,* ed. Carolyn Ruth Swift Lenz, Gayle Greene, and Carol Thomas Neely, 256–70. Urbana: University of Illinois Press, 1980.

"S. O." "'Heartbreak House' and—an Actress." *English Review* 33 (1921): 426–28.

O'Donnell, Norbert F. "On the 'Unpleasantness' of *Pygmalion.*" *Shaw Bulletin* 1 (1955): 7–10.

Orme, Michael. *J. T. Grein: The Story of a Pioneer 1862–1935.* London: John Murray, 1936.

Palmer, John. "Life and the Theatre." *Saturday Review,* 27 June 1914, 826–27.

"Past and Present Heroines of Fiction." *Saturday Review,* 28 July 1883, 107–8.

Patterson, Ada. "Bernard Shaw as Seen by an American Actress." *Theatre* 19 (1914): 234–36.

"'Pygmalion' as a Pronouncing Dictionary: Mr. Shaw's Latest Jest." *Graphic,* 18 Apr. 1914, 684.

"J. R." "Cashel Byron's Profession." *Our Corner* 7 (1886): 301–5.

Regan, Arthur E. "The Fantastic Reality of Bernard Shaw: A Look at *Augustus* and *Too True.*" *Shaw Review* 11 (1968): 2–10.

Riviere, Joan. "Womanliness as a Masquerade." *International Journal of Psycho-Analysis* 10 (1929): 303–13.

Robins, Elizabeth. *Both Sides of the Curtain*. London: William Heinemann, 1940.

———. "Woman's War: A Defense of Militant Suffrage." *McClure's* 40 (1913): 41–52.

Romanes, George J. "Mental Differences Between Men and Women." *Nineteenth Century* 21 (1887): 654–72.

Russell, Frances Theresa. "Complicated Bernard Shaw." *University of California Chronicle* 32 (1930): 468–90.

Salmon, Eric, ed. *Granville-Barker and his Correspondents: A Selection of Letters by Him and to Him*. Detroit: Wayne State University Press, 1986.

Scanlop, Leone. "The New Woman in the Literature of 1883–1909." *University of Michigan Papers in Women's Studies* 2 (1976): 133–59.

Shainess, Natalie, M.D. *Sweet Suffering: Woman as Victim*. Indianapolis: Bobbs-Merrill, 1984.

Shakespeare, William. *The Riverside Shakespeare*. Ed. G. Blakemore Evans. Boston: Houghton Mifflin, 1974.

Shaw, George Bernard. *Advice to a Young Critic*. New York: Crown, 1955.

———. "Bernard Shaw on American Women." *Cosmopolitan* 43 (1907): 557–61.

———. *Bernard Shaw's Letters to Granville Barker*. Ed. C. B. Purdom. New York: Theatre Arts, 1957.

———. "The Case for Equality." In *Shavian Tract No. 6*. London: The Shaw Society, 1958.

———. "Christmas, Communism, and Panto." *Era*, 28 Dec. 1934, 1.

———. "Grimaldi is Dead: Why Not Bury Him?" *World Film News* 2 (1938): 23.

———. *London Music in 1888–89*. London: Constable, 1937.

———. "The Menace of the Leisured Woman." 1927. In Shaw, *Platform and Pulpit*, 168–71. (See Works Cited.)

———. *Our Theatres in the 'Nineties*. Vols. 23–25 of Shaw, *Collected Works*. (See Works Cited.)

———. *Practical Politics: Twentieth-Century Views on Politics and Economics*. Ed. Lloyd J. Hubenka. Lincoln: University of Nebraska Press, 1976.

———. Preface to *Three Plays by Brieux*, vii–liv. New York: Brentano's, 1913.

———. *Shaw: An Autobiography*. Ed. Stanley Weintraub. 2 vols. New York: Weybright and Talley, 1970.

———. *Shaw on Dickens*. Ed. Dan H. Laurence and Martin Quinn. New York: Frederick Ungar, 1985.

———. "Sir Almroth Wright's Polemic." *New Statesman*, 18 Oct. 1913, 45–47.

———. "Why All Women Are Peculiarly Fitted to Be Good Voters." *New York American*, 21 Apr. 1907, sec. 3, p. 2.

———. "Women in Politics." *Liverpool Echo*, 2 Mar. 1948, 4.

———. "Women in Politics." *Leader Magazine*, 25 Nov. 1944, 5–6.

———, ed. *Fabianism and the Empire: A Manifesto by the Fabian Society*. London: Grant Richards, 1900.

Singer, June. *Androgyny: Toward a New Theory of Sexuality*. Garden City, N.Y.: Anchor/Doubleday, 1976.

Smith, Warren Sylvester. *Bishop of Everywhere: Bernard Shaw and the Life Force.* University Park: Pennsylvania State University Press, 1982.

Spong, Hilda. "Working With Pinero, Barrie and Shaw." *Theatre* 32 (1920): 32, 34.

Stedman, Jane W. "From Dame to Woman: W. S. Gilbert and Theatrical Transvestism." In *Suffer and Be Still*, ed. Martha Vicinus, 20–37. Bloomington: Indiana University Press, 1972.

Terry, Ellen. "From Lewis Carroll to Bernard Shaw." *McClure's* 31 (1908): 565–76.

———. *The Story of My Life.* 1908. Reprint. New York: Schocken, 1982.

Thompson, Marjorie. "*Rise Up Woman!*" *Shavian* 5 (1975): 9–10.

Turco, Alfred, Jr. *Shaw's Moral Vision: The Self and Salvation.* Ithaca, N.Y.: Cornell University Press, 1976.

———, ed. *Shaw: The Neglected Plays.* Spec. issue of *Shaw* 7 (1987).

Tyson, Brian. *The Story of Shaw's "Saint Joan."* Kingston and Montreal: McGill-Queen's University Press, 1982.

"The Utopia of G. B. S." *Saturday Review*, 9 July 1921, 43–44.

Valency, Maurice. *The Flower and the Castle: An Introduction to Modern Drama.* New York: Schocken, 1982.

Vicinus, Martha, ed. *Suffer and Be Still: Women in the Victorian Age.* Bloomington: Indiana University Press, 1972.

———, ed. *A Widening Sphere: Changing Roles of Victorian Women.* Bloomington: Indiana University Press, 1977.

Voltaire (François-Marie Arouet). *Candide* (1759). Trans. Lowell Bair. Toronto: Bantam, 1984.

Wearing, J. P., ed. *G. B. Shaw: An Annotated Bibliography of Writings About Him.* 3 vols. DeKalb: Northern Illinois University Press, 1986–88.

Weintraub, Stanley. *Private Shaw and Public Shaw: A Dual Portrait of Lawrence of Arabia and G. B. S.* New York: George Braziller, 1963.

———. *The Unexpected Shaw: Biographical Approaches to G. B. S. and His Work.* New York: Frederick Ungar, 1982.

West, Rebecca. *The Young Rebecca: Writings of Rebecca West 1911–1917.* Ed. Jane Marcus. New York: Viking, 1982.

Whitman, Robert F. *Shaw and the Play of Ideas.* Ithaca, N.Y.: Cornell University Press, 1977.

Wisenthal, J. L. *The Marriage of Contraries: Bernard Shaw's Middle Plays.* Cambridge, Mass.: Harvard University Press, 1974.

"Women and Morality." *English Review* 14 (1913): 624–36.

Yorks, Samuel A. *The Evolution of Bernard Shaw.* Washington, D.C.: University Press of America, 1981.

Index

Shaw, Bernard (*continued*)
75–79; intellectual development of, in
the late nineteenth century, viii; and
the Life Force, 23, 44, 50, 90, 93, 179–
80, 185, 193, 208–9, 211, 224, 242, 247,
253; as a novelist, 19–22; pseudonym
of, "Amelia Mackintosh," 126–27; as a
Victorian, viii, 4; on the "womanly
woman," 4–5, 47–49, 54, 58, 91–94,
114, 141, 144, 253
Shaw, Bernard, characters in plays of: A,
125–26; Acis, 151; Annajanska, 110–14,
132, 134; Baker, Julius (Gunner), 135,
198, 211; Balsquith, Prime Minister,
121–23; Barnabas, Franklyn, 150;
Basham, Mrs, 104–5; Baudricourt, Captain Robert de, 142; The Black Girl, 172–
80, 255; Blenderbland, Adrian, 189,
191; Bluebeard, 252; Bohun, 46;
Bridgenorth, General, 131, 246; Britomart, Lady, 162, 187, 218–20, 223;
Bumpas, Aurora, 41; Burgess, 25, 27,
31; Byron, Cashel, 20, 189; Caesar, 59,
167, 202, 214–18, 226, 256; Cairns, Letitia, 19–20, 248; Candida, 25–28, 30–31,
87, 101, 144, 222, 247; Carew, Lydia, 20,
167, 189; Catherine the Great, 107–10,
112, 132, 251; The Chaplain, 143, 145–
46; Charles (the Dauphin), 143, 148,
252; Charles II (king of England), 104–
6; Charmian, 216–17; Charteris,
Leonard, 51–57, 59–61, 249; Clandon,
Dolly, 41–42, 44, 119–20; Clandon, Gloria, 35–37, 41–47, 59–60, 62, 103, 199,
215, 219, 248; Clandon, Mrs Lanfrey,
5, 17, 36, 42–47, 51–52, 120, 199, 246,
249; Clandon, Philip, 41–42, 44, 119–
20; Cleopatra, 202, 213–18, 224, 226,
257; Cokane, 185; Connolly, Susanna,
19–20; Crampton, 45–47, 103, 120; Craven, Daniel, 51–55, 57, 61; Craven,
Julia, 47, 50–53, 55–56, 59–61, 101, 184,
249; Craven, Sylvia, 50, 54–57, 62, 86,
122, 184, 225, 249; Crofts, Sir George,
36–37, 39; Cusins, Adolphus, 221–23,
257; Cuthbertson, Joe, 52–55, 57, 61–
62, 184; Cymbeline, 102–3; di Parerga,
Epifania, 188–93; The Doctor, 187, 191–
93; The Domestic Minister, 150, 253;
Doolittle, Alfred, 230, 249; Doolittle,

Eliza, 162, 167, 202, 214, 224–39, 249,
251, 256; Dorothea, 165–67, 171, 227,
232; Dubedat, Louis, 128; Dunn, Ellie,
196, 198–202, 225, 256; Dunn, Mazzini,
201; Dunois, 147–48; Edstaston, Captain, 107; Emmy, 104; Eynsford Hill,
Clara, 232–33, 257; Eynsford Hill,
Freddy, 224, 232, 239; Fitzambey, Lord
Reginald, 128–31; Fitzfassenden, Alastair, 189; Fox, George, 105–6; Ftatateeta, 214, 216–18; Gardner, Frank,
35–37, 39–40, 128, 195, 250; Garnett,
Proserpine, 25–32, 57, 62, 247; Grantham, Lesbia, 130–31, 136, 246, 251,
255; Guiderius, 103; Guinness, Nurse,
199–200; Gwynn, Nell, 104–6, 132; He-
Ancient, 151–53, 201; The Hermaphrodite, 254; Higgins, Henry, 162, 167,
187–88, 191, 202, 214, 224, 226–39, 249,
254, 256–57; Higgins, Mrs, 228, 231,
234, 256; Hill, Jenny, 251; Hushabye,
Hector, 200, 256; Hushabye, Hesione,
199; Iachimo, 101; Imogen, 101–3; The
Inquisitor, 143, 145–46; Iras, 216–17;
Jack, Owen, 167; La Hire, 252; Lickcheese, 186; Lilith, 149–50, 152, 178–79,
207, 253; Louka, 247; Lubin, 150; Mangan, Boss, 198–201; Marchbanks, 27–
28, 30–31, 87, 101, 128, 222; Mill, Lexy,
25, 27, 29–32; The Minister of Health,
253–54; Mitchener, Lord, 121–22;
Morell, James, 25–27, 29–31, 87, 101,
222; Napoleon, 114–18, 251; O'Dowda,
Count, 182–83, 255; O'Dowda, Fanny,
182–85, 187; Paramore, Dr, 55, 57, 60–
61; The Patient, 224–25; Pearce, Mrs,
230, 233–39, 256; Percival, Joey, 133–
34, 197, 201; Petkoff, Raina, 41, 248;
Pickering, Colonel, 228, 230–32, 238–
39, 249; Pisanio, 103; Posthumus, 101–
3; Pothinus, 214; Poulengey, Monsieur
de, 142, 252; Praed, 35–38, 128, 195;
Ptolomy, 214, 256; Pygmalion, 225;
Ramsden, Roebuck, 204; Robinson, Octavius, 158, 207, 249; Russell, Harriet,
19–20; Saint Joan, 10, 132, 136–48, 168,
193, 246, 252–53; Sartorius, 33, 169,
185–88, 202; Sartorius, Blanche, 50,
169, 185–88, 195, 201–2, 216, 238, 255–
56; She-Ancient, 151–53, 201; Shotover,